The Making of Canadian Food Aid Policy

Since the implementation of the Colombo Plan in the early 1950s, food aid has been an important and highly visible component of the Canadian development assistance program. Until the early 1970s, the Canadian food aid program was little more than a loosely connected collection of disparate programs designed to meet a host of sometimes conflicting objectives. However, in the wake of the world food crisis of 1974–75, there were a growing number of groups who began to question the developmental effectiveness of food aid. In response, the Canadian government undertook an extensive review and assessment of its food aid program. This resulted in a series of new policy initiatives designed to change both the substance of food aid programs and the manner in which they were administered. These changes marked a watershed in the history of the Canadian food aid program by setting out fundamental policy themes that have been consolidated and refined in the 1980s and early 1990s.

This book examines the evolution of the Canadian food aid program during this critical period of policy reform. Focusing on the rationale of the food aid program, the nature of the planning and programming process, the selection of delivery channels, the make-up of the food aid commodity basket, and the nature of donor-recipient relations, Charlton provides a number of useful insights into the overall objectives and priorities of Canadian foreign policy in the Third World. In the final chapter, the author examines the politics of policy reform in the Canadian food aid program and what these can tell us about the impact of domestic economic interests, Canadian political culture, bureaucratic politics, and the global food aid regime on the evolution of Canadian aid policies.

MARK W. CHARLTON is an associate professor of Political Science at Trinity Western University.

The Making of Canadian Food Aid Policy

MARK W. CHARLTON

McGill-Queen's University Press
Montreal & Kingston • London • Buffalo

© McGill-Queen's University Press 1992
ISBN 0-7735-0937-2 (cloth)
ISBN 0-7735-0938-0 (paper)

Legal deposit fourth quarter 1992
Bibliothèque nationale du Québec

Printed in Canada on acid-free paper

This book has been published with the help of a grant
from the Social Science Federation of Canada, using
funds provided by the Social Sciences and Humanities
Research Council of Canada. Funding has also been
assisted by a grant from the J.B. Smallman and
Spencer Memorial Fund, University of Western
Ontario. Publication has also been supported by the
Canada Council through its block grant program.

Canadian Cataloguing in Publication Data

Charlton, Mark William, 1948–
    The making of Canadian food aid policy
    Includes index.
    ISBN 0-7735-0937-2 (bound) –
    ISBN 0-7735-0938-0 (pbk.)
    1. Food relief, Canadian – Developing countries.
    I. Title.
    HV696.F6C43 1992   363.8'83'097124   C92-090384-3

Typeset in Palatino 10/12 by
Caractéra production graphique inc., Quebec City.

For Lucille, Christopher, Daniel, and David

Contents

Tables

Acknowledgments

During the course of the research on this book many people have helped me, and to all of them I am most grateful. Theodore Cohn and Harry Qualman first stimulated my interest in studying food aid policy. The comments and suggestions of Theodore Cohn, Cranford Pratt, and Paul Barker have also been very helpful.

Because a great deal of the research for this study was based on interviews, I am especially indebted to those civil servants who gave many hours of their time. A guarantee of anonymity prevents me from citing them by name, but in every case they were fully co-operative in granting me their time (more than once in many cases) and in answering my questions with candour. Special mention should be made of the staff of the Food Aid Coordination and Evaluation Centre (CIDA), who provided me with a wealth of data on Canadian food aid and assisted in arranging a number of interviews. Girve Fretz, MP, also assisted me in a number of ways during my frequent visits to Ottawa.

I would also like to thank the Social Science Federation of Canada for a publication grant under its Aid to Scholarly Publications Programme. The author also acknowledges the assistance of the J.B. Smallman Publication Fund, Faculty of Social Science, the University of Western Ontario. In addition, I would like to express my gratitude to Philip Cercone, executive director at McGill-Queen's University Press and Joan McGilvray, coordinating editor, for their assistance in transforming the manuscript into final book form.

Permission to reprint material of my own that appeared previously has been granted by the Canadian Institute of International Affairs to use an updated and revised version of "The food aid conundrum and Canadian aid strategy: the issue of donor control," *International Journal* 42, no. 3 (Summer 1987). Permission has also been granted by the *Canadian Journal of Development Studies* to use an expanded version of "The management of Canada's bilateral food aid: an organizational perspective," *Canadian Journal of Development Studies* 7, no. 1 (1986).

Finally, I must acknowledge a special debt to my family. Christopher and Daniel have been patient with sacrifices of their time, and Lucille has provided useful comments, criticisms, and encouragements at each stage of the project.

Abbreviations

LIFT   Lower Inventory For Tomorrow
LDCS   less developed countries
LLDCS   least developed countries
MCC   Mennonite Central Committee
MOU   Memorandum of Understanding
MSA   most seriously affected (countries)
NATO   North Atlantic Treaty Organisation
NFU   National Farmers Union
NGO   Non-Governmental Organisation
ODA   Overseas Development Assistance
OECD   Organisation of Economic Cooperation and Development
OPEC   Organisation of Petroleum Exporting Countries
PDS   Public Distribution System
SMP   skim milk powder
TBS   Treasury Board Secretariat
UMR   usual marketing requirement
UN   United Nations
UNICEF   United Nations Children's Fund
UNRWA   United Nations Relief and Works Agency for Palestinian Refugees in the Near East
USAID   United States Agency for International Development
VADA   Voluntary Agricultural Development Aid
WFC   World Food Council
WFP   World Food Program

The Making of Canadian Food Aid Policy

Introduction:
The Food Aid Conundrum
and Canadian Aid Strategy

Few types of developmental assistance elicit as much emotion and criticism as food aid. As recent events in Ethiopia and Sudan have shown, aid agencies are frequently under intense public pressure to undertake highly visible food relief operations. When successful, such operations can enhance the image of an aid agency and strengthen public support for development assistance in general.

However, food aid programs can also draw attention to the weaknesses and shortcomings of foreign aid and generate media "horror stories" that undermine the public confidence in the donor aid programs. Indeed, in the past four decades since food aid programs were first established, the volume of literature highly critical of food aid has grown remarkably. By now most of the shortcomings of food aid are familiar: food aid discourages local agricultural production; it creates a taste for expensive imported foods; it enables governments to forestall necessary agricultural policy reforms; and it fosters a dependency that makes recipient governments vulnerable to political manipulation.[1]

During the past four decades, Canada has come to play an important role in the global food aid system. Since its first shipment of wheat to India in 1951 Canada has provided over 22.5 million tonnes of Canadian agricultural commodities to Third World countries. Canadian officials like to point out that Canada is the largest per capita donor of food aid, and that it has regularly been the second largest contributor to the United Nations/Food and Agriculture Organisation (UN/FAO) World Food Program (WFP). But, as an important food aid donor, Canada has not been immune to the frequent criticisms levelled at food aid generally. Indeed, during the seventies and early eighties the Canadian food aid program was beset by what may well be called "a crisis of confidence." Such diverse agencies as the Science Council of Canada[2] and the Canadian Council on International Co-operation[3] called for the abolition of Canadian food aid except in the case of genuine emergencies, and similar critiques have come from both sides of the political spectrum. Robert Carty and Virginia Smith concluded that "food aid is the most dramatic failure among our aid programs."[4] The Citizens for Foreign Aid Reform called food aid "a prescription for disaster."[5] Others, such as the North-South Institute,[6] Theodore Cohn,[7] and David Hopper,[8] argued for significant changes in the food aid program.

Despite these shortcomings, or perhaps because of them, the demand for food aid continues to grow. Recent projections suggest that the demand for food imports will continue to expand significantly, especially in sub-Saharan Africa.[9] This need is growing at a time when many countries are less able to finance such increases through commercial imports. Stagnating exports, falling commodity prices, high energy import bills, and heavy debt repayment loads have combined to reduce the foreign exchange available to pay for commercial food imports. Thus, many countries will be forced to rely increasingly on aid to meet food needs. As a major food-exporting country, Canada is under pressure from recipient countries, international food agencies, and other donor agencies to continue to shoulder its fair share of the global food aid burden. A recent document of the Canadian International Development Agency (CIDA) notes: "There will be continuing international pressure on Canada, a major food exporter, to continue and expand its food aid programme."[10]

In this context, Canada, like other donors, faces what has been described as an "impossible conundrum."[11] If donors continue to provide food aid as they have in the past, they may only perpetuate policies that lead to increased food dependency. Yet the complete abolition of food aid programs is not a viable option. As the response to the famines in Ethiopia and Sudan demonstrates, citizens of Canada and other donor countries expect their governments to respond generously to highly publicized needs. Even the most ardent critics of food aid stop short of calling for total abolition, recognizing that there are cases of genuine humanitarian need. What, then, is the solution to this conundrum?

During the past decade and a half, Canadian officials have struggled with an answer to this question. Re-examination of Canadian food aid policy took place in the wake of the "world food crisis" of the early 1970s. Prior to that time, the Canadian government had never formulated a clearly stated food aid policy that was accepted on an interdepartmental basis. Instead, Canadian food aid policy had developed and evolved largely on an ad hoc basis, depending on changing political and economic forces. However, critical global food shortages and the resulting politicization of the food issue led to greater scrutiny and criticism of Canadian food aid than had ever occurred before. In response to the kinds of criticism cited above, Canadian officials have made a serious effort in the last decade to re-examine Canadian food aid policies and define a more coherent policy for the 1980s and beyond. For the first time, a comprehensive interdepartmental statement of food aid policy has been agreed upon. Subsequently, several reviews of the food aid program have been undertaken, with resultant changes made to both the rationale and the operation of the Canadian food aid program.

These efforts represent a significant rethinking of the ground rules under which the Canadian food aid program has traditionally operated. This book examines the effort to reform Canadian food aid policy and the resultant impact on the evolution of both the strategy used to allocate the food aid and the administrative mechanisms in which this is carried out. By examining the evolution of Canadian food aid policy I hope to gain greater insight into the various forces which shape not only food aid policy but the making of Canadian development assistance policy in general. Before doing this, it is useful to define the basic framework in which I will analyse the Canadian food aid program.

To begin, it is important to note that this study focuses only on one specific aspect of the Canadian development assistance program– food aid. As defined by D. A. Fitzgerald in a Food and Agriculture Organization (FAO) study, food aid includes: "(a) agricultural commodities, usually but not invariably in surplus, furnished as aid to receiving countries and (b) monetary resources that may be used only for (i) the purchase, processing, packaging, and transportation of such commodities, and (ii) costs of administration."[12]

These commodities may be provided as an outright grant to the recipient or as a loan on concessionary terms. According to this definition of food aid, commodities that are purchased at prevailing commercial prices and with the receiving country's foreign exchange are classified as commercial exchanges and not as food aid. In focusing on food aid, this study looks specifically at the provision of agricultural commodities as aid. I will not discuss, for example, other types of financial and technical assistance designed to increase food production within recipient countries but which do not involve the exchange of commodities.

My analysis will focus primarily on the strategy used to allocate Canadian food aid and the administrative mechanisms through which this is carried out. Aid strategy is a term generally used to refer to the "characteristic modes of action employed by the donors in their distribution of economic assistance to LDC's [less developed countries]."[13] It is these "modes of action" that are important in determining the essential nature of the aid relationship which exists between donor and recipient governments. The nature of this strategy is important in defining the role of the donor aid agency, particularly as it relates to the amount of control the donor will attempt to exercise over its aid program and ultimately over the recipient.[14]

As Andrzej Krassowski argues, all of the important "technical aspects of an aid policy are dependent on the type of aid strategy chosen."[15] Therefore, the delineation of a particular strategy will answer such key questions as (i) how specific aid projects are identified and developed, (ii) what types of aid programs and mechanisms are used for the distribution of aid, (iii) what targets are selected for receiving the aid, and (iv) what sequences and steps are established to link objectives to outcomes in the aid program.

The pursuit of a specific type of aid strategy in turn demands of the aid agency a particular set of diagnostic and analytical skills and administrative resources. As George Cunningham has aptly put it, the selection of an aid strategy is closely related to both operational decisions (e.g., administrative mechanisms, programming processes, etc.) and substantive issues (e.g., type of aid, terms and conditional, quantity, etc.).[16] It thus becomes evident that an aid strategy is intimately linked to both the structure of the donor agency and its management arrangements.

In reviewing the literature on aid strategies, it is possible to identify several aspects of what I will call the "management structure" of the donor that significantly effect an aid strategy.[17] These features can be summed up in three essential questions: (i) How are the donor's administrative structures organized to plan and implement the aid allocations? (ii) What type of planning process exists to determine the size, content, and target of aid allocations? (iii) To what extent does the donor attempt to establish control over the ultimate disposition and impact of its aid funds?

The first element is the organization of the food aid decision-making process. The objectives of Canadian food aid cannot be achieved without the existence of an appropriate program structure. The way in which this decision-making structure is organized has two important implications for our study. First, the organizational design determines the capabilities of the food aid program in key areas such as planning and analysis, data collection and evaluation, and program implementation. Second, the organizational structure determines the particular perspectives and interests which are introduced into the allocation process and the weights and priorities that are assigned to them.

In relating organization to aid strategy, several key questions arise. What type of personnel is involved in the aid decision-making process and where in the organizational structure are they located? Is the organizational structure through which the decisions are made highly centralized with clearly defined roles or is it decentralized with involvement of different participants on an ad hoc basis? Is there consistency or conflict in objectives and interests pursued by the various actors in the process?

Planning is the second significant element in the donor management structure to be studied. Several key features can be identified here which are important to an aid strategy. What roles do the donor and recipient play in the planning process? Does one play a larger role in initiating the aid process? Are decisions regarding allocations made according to specific criteria determined by the donor or are they made largely in response to recipients' requests? What is the scope of the discussions and negotiations between the recipient and the donor? What time horizon does the donor use in planning its allocations and making its commitments? In the context of this study, I will attempt to answer these questions by looking at two different aspects of the food aid planning: (i) the selection of bilateral recipients and the determination of their allocations, and (ii) the selection of food commodities to be included in the aid program.

The third significant aspect of the donor management structure analysed is control features. These features relate primarily to the extent to which the donor seeks to establish control over the uses and ultimate impact of its aid funds. Here the central questions to be answered are, what is the scope of the donor's efforts to establish control over aid uses? Is the use of aid funds monitored by the donor? What kinds of conditions and terms are placed on the aid? Does the donor make explicit certain performance criteria which the recipient is expected to meet in using the aid funds? What efforts are made by the donor to influence or exercise some leverage over the recipient? I will attempt to answer these questions by examining the instruments that Canadian policy makers have had at their disposal for establishing control over their food aid and how they have been used.

Examining how CIDA has answered these questions allows us to see the type of aid strategy that Canada has pursued, and, in particular, the extent to which reforms made to the food aid program during the past decade have represented a shift in the Canadian aid strategy as it pertains to food aid.

From the literature on foreign aid, it is possible to put together a number of classifications of aid strategies. The typologies can in most cases be placed on a continuum running from a reactive, passive donor aid strategy on one end to an activist, interventionist strategy at the other. [18] Although these two categories may be ideal types, with no single donor exactly fitting all characteristics at a given time, the characteristics of each strategy can be outlined as shown in Table 1. A passive strategy is generally reactive in nature, with the donor playing a minimal role in the aid relationship. In organizational terms, the donor's administrative structure may be decentralized and loosely co-ordinated, with a low level of specialization of tasks and distribution of decision-making responsibilities often taking place in an ad hoc fashion. Aid is made available in response to requests from recipients. Administratively, the donor is content with a loosely structured aid mechanism which does not involve complicated planning, surveillance, or evaluation. The donor has no explicitly stated guidelines of eligibility criteria, has little interest in the end uses of the aid, and limits aid negotiations to routine administrative issues. Such an aid strategy is generally responsive and "hands-off" in its approach to the aid relationship with recipients.

At the other end of the continuum is the activist strategy of aid-giving. An activist strategy is essentially characterized by a more interventionist role on the part of the donor. In this strategy, the donor determines not only the total amount of aid, its distribution, and its terms but also attempts to play a direct role in formulating development plans at both the macro and micro levels within the recipient country. Eligibility criteria are explicitly stated and may be tailored to meet the needs of specific recipients. Aid allocations may be more concentrated to maximize impact, and the donor may carry out planning and commitment of its aid allocations on a multi-year basis, perhaps in the context of a mutually agreed-upon development plan. Control measures, such as monitoring, conditions on the use of the aid, and performance criteria, are used to ensure that donor objectives are being met. Administration of the aid program is more complex, with a large organization for programming the aid, overseeing its uses, and evaluating its impact. Roles may be more specialized, with a greater percentage of the staff operating within the recipient country itself. While most donors can be placed

Table 1
Typical features for two types of aid strategies

Donor Structure	Passive	Active
ORGANISATIONAL		
1 Nature and location of personnel	small number, generally headquarters-based	large number, specialised; high percentage in the field
2 Degree of co-ordination	ad hoc, dispersed	highly coordinated
3 Degree of division of labour	dispersed, low specialisation	highly specialised
PLANNING		
1 Aid initiation-response	recipient initiates; donor responds	donor initiates; recipient responds
2 Allocations	ad hoc, reactive and unplanned	integrated into overall aid program planning
3 Scope of discussions	narrow, relating only to specific request	broad, encompassing recipient's non-aid policies
4 Eligibility criteria	unstated or globally applied	clearly stated, but modified to each recipient's needs
5 Degree of concentration	widely dispersed	concentrated to maximise impact
6 Length of commitment	short-term, one year agreements	longer term, multi-year agreements
7 Evaluation	absent or minimal	fairly extensive impact study
CONTROL		
1 Scope	ensuring probity of transfers	ensuring probity and efficiency
2 Monitoring	minimal	extensive
3 Conditions and terms	broad guidelines applicable to all recipients	specific requirements designed for each recipient
4 Performance criteria	not emphasised	emphasised
5 Efforts at leverage	minimal or indirect through rewards	direct through persuasion and punishment

somewhere on the continuum between these two types, the United States Agency for International Development (USAID) is often cited as the most developed example of the activist strategy of aid-giving.[19]

The variables identified in Table I provide a useful framework for identifying the type of aid strategy that Canadian policy makers have pursued. They also provide a useful perspective from which to analyse attempts to reform the Canadian food aid program in the late 1970s and 1980s. By examining the changes that have been made to the organizational, planning, and control aspects of the food aid program, we can determine the extent and nature of any shifts in the Canadian food aid strategy resulting from these policy reviews. After examining the evolution of the food aid program, I show how the forces that shape Canadian policy can be better understood if the findings of this study are placed in the context of the general literature on the determinants of Canadian aid policy.

APPROACHES TO EXPLAINING CANADIAN DEVELOPMENT ASSISTANCE POLICY

In recent years there has been a steady proliferation of studies of Canadian development assistance policies.[20] This literature represents a wide diversity of approaches, although in many cases the theoretical assumptions of the authors are only implicitly stated. Much of this literature is essentially evaluative and prescriptive in nature. Virtually every author has identified significant discrepancies between the conceptualization (the rhetoric) and the actualization (the reality) of Canadian aid policies, and a major preoccupation in this literature has been to explain why there is such an obvious gap between stated policy intentions and actual outcomes. As Kim Nossal notes, the predominant question posed by every analyst is, "what accounts for a Canadian development policy that is by all accounts so limited, and so wanting in terms of achieving development objectives for the South?"[21]

In order to address this question most writers have drawn attention to the multiplicity of aid goals, their potential conflicts, and the struggle over which goals should receive priority. Nossal argues that this approach, which he labels the "mixed motives model," is the "usual method" for studying Canadian aid policy.[22] This model contends that Canadian aid policies can be explained by a trinity of interests: humanitarian, economic, and politico-strategic. The assumption is that if there is a gap between stated policy and its outcomes it must be because one set of objectives has come to predominate over the others, usually to the detriment of humanitarian values. The writing of S.G. Triantis on Canadian development assistance typifies this approach. Triantis identifies the various motives underlying the Canadian aid program and then proceeds to eliminate each one until he has demonstrated that strategic foreign policy interests tend to dominate other interests in the aid program, in part because the Canadian public is only weakly committed to humanitarian values.[23]

In constructing an explanation of Canadian aid policy, scholars have taken two divergent approaches to the mixed motives model. Most have adopted a society-centred approach on which the explanation for Canadian development assistance policy is found within the realm of domestic politics, where social forces or political groups struggle for influence over the aid program. Society-centred approaches actually come in two basic variants: the pluralist and the dominant class.

The pluralist version explains aid policy as the outcome of a struggle among various affected groups who compete for influence over particular policy decisions. Specific outcomes reflect the varying ability of certain groups to organize and give their interests prominence in the policy process. According to the pluralist view, the Canadian public is, to a large extent, motivated by humanitarian concerns and is generally supportive of Canadian aid programs. However, because of ambiguities or contradictions in development goals, non-developmental goals sometimes come to predominate. For example, Theodore Cohn, in a study of Canadian food aid, has argued that priority "is often given to Canadian economic interests in surplus utilization, value added benefits from processing, and trade expansion,"[24] while at the same time there is "a persistent tendency to downgrade LDC interests."[25] Pluralists argue that recipient interests are often downplayed not out of malevolence but because recipients are outside the domestic political arena of the donor and therefore lack an effective political voice. As a result, the particular aid strategy that emerges is explained largely in terms of the interests and capabilities of particular interest groups or coalitions within the donor's society. Aid strategies can thus be changed, especially towards more developmentally oriented goals, only to the extent that the donor agency administering the aid program can be insulated from the demands of domestic interest groups.

The dominant class perspective is more pessimistic in tone and assumes that aid policy is primarily a reflection of the preferences of the dominant class in society. Thus, according to Cranford Pratt, Canadian aid policies demonstrate a persistent "bias to business" because they are designed to serve, first and foremost, the interests of the Canadian corporate community.[26] Because aid policies are believed to be deeply rooted in the class structure of society, advocates of the dominant class perspective are much more pessimistic about the possibilities of reform. Carty and Smith argue that the food aid program is so deeply rooted in the self-interest of the capitalist class that it would be better to abolish the program altogether, with the exception of some emergency relief operations.[27] Linda Freeman contends that the dominant class that shapes Canadian aid policies is really the American corporate elite that resides South of the border; she sees little hope of reforming Canadian aid policies until Canada has transformed its dependent economic relationship with the United States.[28]

Despite these obvious differences, on both these perspectives the state is seen as an essentially passive actor. Pluralists view state institutions primarily as an arena where group competition is fought out. The state organization's only role is as a disinterested referee for competing groups. For the dominant class theorist, the state is largely the instrument of the dominant class, the business elite. In both cases, the primary function of state institutions is to provide aid policies that satisfy the demands of the most successful domestic players.

Recently there has been new interest in the role of the state in foreign policy studies, particularly in the area of foreign economic policy. Responding to what is seen as the limited explanatory value of both traditional pluralist and neo-Marxist approaches, there has been renewed interest in treating state institutions as an important variable in explaining foreign policy. Within the literature on Canadian aid policy, Nossal exemplifies a more state-centred approach to the mixed motives model. He argues that, unlike society-centred perspectives which focus on the interests of donors and recipients, his statist approach concentrates on "the organization which effects the transfer of resources between them – the state."[29] The nature and type of aid policy pursued in Canada can thus best be explained by a new trinity of motives: prestige, organizational maintenance, and limitation of real expenditures. A widely dispersed aid program brings prestige to the foreign policy elite who interact with other state officials outside of Canada. A capital intensive, project-oriented, tied-aid program serves the interests of Canadian aid officials in organizational maintenance. The limited size of Canadian Overseas Development Assistance (ODA) and the high level of tied aid is explained by the desire of state officials to limit the real costs of an aid program to the Canadian economy. This latter interest, which stems from the "intra-state conflict over resources and the relative power of the foreign affairs bureaucracy" is what places a brake on the "unbounded growth" of what, from Nossal's perspective, would be a totally self-serving development assistance policy.[30]

In shifting our focus to the interests of the aid organization itself Nossal makes a useful contribution, reminding us of the importance of looking into the "black box" of policy making to gain a fuller understanding how an aid strategy emerges. In this regard, Nossal is referring to John White, who argued a decade and a half ago that "the makings of an aid policy lie in the hands of those who actually administer it."[31]

However, I would not go as far as Nossal in arguing that his statist perspective is an alternative heuristic model that should completely replace the orthodox "mixed motives" model for explaining aid policy. Instead, the approach adopted in this book has stronger affinities with what Peter Evans has labelled as a "politicized state-centric approach to policy formation."[32] Evans notes that this approach is "politicized" in the sense that it takes into account "the way in which interest-based constituent demands drive policy, operating on policy formation through the struggles among different segments of the state apparatus."[33] Thus, while I do not accept the position of dominant class theorists that the organizational process is simply a reproduction of the power configurations and basic contradictions in society, I do not ignore the existence of powerful domestic political and social forces. What I am interested in asking, in the context of Canadian food aid policy, is how these social forces are transmitted and mediated within the "black box" of government, particularly in the process of formulating and implementing aid strategy.

Evans notes that his approach is "state-centric" in that it acknowledges "the independent role of the state apparatus in initiating, directing, and constraining policy responses to economic problems."[34] As James March and Johan Olsen argue, "political institutions are more than simple mirrors of social forces ... they are also collections of standard operating procedures and structures that define and defend interests. They are political actors in their own right."[35] As a result, institutional structures determine which particular perspectives are introduced into the policy process and what weights and priorities are assigned to them. As Peter Hall contends, "organization does more than transmit the preferences of particular groups, it combines and ultimately alters them."[36] Similarly, Stephen Cohen has noted that organizational structures do not "erase the dynamics of bureaucratic politics" but "can control or distort" these dynamics.[37] Thus, while giving attention to the various interests shaping the food aid program, I am also interested in gaining some insight into how the institutional characteristics of the state can influence the policy process, particularly the ability of state officials to formulate and implement a Canadian aid strategy.

ORGANIZATION

Chapter 1 introduces the reader to the subject of Canadian food aid by placing the program in the context of both Canada's foreign agricultural policy and Canadian foreign policy, especially as it relates to the field of development assistance. Following an overview of the historical development of the food aid program, chapter 1 concludes with an examination of the size and importance of the Canadian contribution, the role of food aid in the Canadian economy, the form in which Canadian food aid is given, and an analysis of who receives the aid.

Chapter 2 explores in more detail the various objectives that Canadian policy makers see food aid as meeting. Particular attention is given to the ways in which Canadian officials have used food aid to address three broad areas of policy concern: (1) domestic agricultural and commercial policy, (2) general foreign policy, and (3) humanitarian and development policy. Examples are given of the uses of food aid in each of these areas to demonstrate their relative importance to the food aid program.

Chapter 3 begins with an examination of the strategic planning aspect of the Canadian food aid program, which determines the overall volume of food aid as well as the balance between the alternative channels and mechanisms through which Canadian food aid is distributed. It shows how changing priorities within the Canadian government and bureaucratic constraints within CIDA have influenced the relative emphasis given to each channel.

Our attention in chapter 4 shifts to the issue of commodity selection. In approaching this subject I first examine the domestic economic interests that have a stake in the composition of Canada's food aid basket. This is followed by an analysis of the process by which commodities are selected. Several case studies are used to show that, as a result of the intrusion of domestic economic interests, CIDA's planning priorities in commodity selection have been frequently overruled. This is followed by a discussion of CIDA's efforts to establish greater control over the selection process, and the resistance of other government departments to these measures.

Chapter 5 focuses on an analysis of the process by which Canadian bilateral food aid allocations are actually planned. Due to the multiple objectives of Canadian food aid, competing interests have frequently led to a diffusion of responsibility, a lack of co-ordination, and a fragmented, ad hoc approach to food aid programming. Even in cases where CIDA officials have direct responsibility for food aid decision making, their decisions have frequently been shaped by policy constraints outside their control. Much of CIDA's preoccupation with reform of the institutional and planning aspect of the food aid program have been attempts by the agency to gain greater control over uncertain elements in its domestic planning environment.

Chapter 6 focuses on the nature of Canada's relationship with recipient countries. The chapter begins with a discussion of the importance of the issue of donor control in the aid-giving process. I then discuss why a "hands off" approach to food aid control has typified the Canadian aid program in the past. This is followed by a look at recent efforts to shift the Canadian food aid strategy towards a much more activist approach on the part of the donor, and the implications of this for the administration of the aid program.

The final chapter seeks to place the findings of this study within the context of the broader literature on the determinants of Canadian aid policy. In particular, I look at five possible determinants of Canadian food aid policy: (i) domestic economic interests; (ii) foreign policy considerations; (iii) the Canadian public philosophy; (iv) bureaucratic interests; and (v) the global food aid regime. I conclude with a discussion of possible future directions for Canadian food policy.

THE DATA

Information for this study comes from a number of sources, including published and unpublished government documents. Research on Canadian food aid quickly reveals a relative paucity of published material on many aspects of the food aid decision-making process. Consequently, in carrying out this study I have relied on interviews with government officials who were or are directly involved in the food aid program. Since September 1978, when I first became interested in food aid, I have held a series of confidential interviews with officials from various government departments in Ottawa and with members of the non-governmental development community. A subsequent series of interviews were conducted to chart the evolution of Canadian food aid policy throughout the 1980s. The interviews were unstructured and each was tailored to the position of the respondents. Some respondents have been interviewed more than once. No attempt was made to draw a representative sample, since that would have been impractical for this type of study. In order to maintain the reliability of information emanating from these interviews, a deliberate effort was made to confirm important details and observations by using two (or in many cases several) interviewees. These techniques enabled me to overcome, to a significant degree, some of the constraints imposed by the relative paucity of published material on the management aspects of Canada's food aid strategy and on some of the policy developments of the past decade.

Readers will note that my main interest is in explaining how a donor's aid strategy is formulated and changes over time. Thus this study focuses primarily on the donor side of the relationship. Consequently, I have not attempted to carry out an independent evaluation or audit of the impact of the food aid program based on field observations within recipient countries.

1 The Canadian Food Aid Program: An Overview

In order to understand clearly the evolution of Canadian food aid policy in the 1970s and 1980s, it is necessary to have some insight into the history of the program and the policy priorities that have shaped it. These priorities have emerged from the dual role that food aid has played as both an extension of Canada's domestic agricultural policies and an instrument of foreign policy. The tensions inherent in this dual role have been a principal driving force behind the nature of Canada's food aid program.

THE ORIGINS OF A SURPLUS DISPOSAL PROGRAM

Any analysis of Canadian food aid must necessarily begin with a discussion of Canada's status as a grain exporting nation. During the 1950s and 1960s the international wheat economy was dominated by two exporting countries, Canada and the United States. Together the two countries controlled from 60 to 70 per cent of the world's wheat exports.[1] Despite their predominant position, both countries were beset with troublesome agricultural problems, aggravated by mounting domestic agricultural surpluses. As a result, both governments undertook measures to assist their ailing agricultural economies, although each pursued significantly different courses of action.[2]

In the United States, the government initiated a broad range of policies, including direct price support to farmers, supply management programs, and income supplement payments. But, most significantly, the United States government tackled the problem of growing wheat surpluses by undertaking a massive aid program to generate greater external demand for American grain. In the period immediately following World War II, the US sent fully 29 per cent of its Marshall Plan aid to Europe in the form of food, feed, and fertilizers. From 1950 to 1953, shipments of food were sent to Yugoslavia, Pakistan, and other countries under the Mutual Security Act and in 1954 the American government formally institutionalized its food aid program with the passage of the Agricultural Trade and Development Assistance Act, commonly known as PL 480. The act included a number of commercial objectives: the development of new markets for American agricultural products, the disposal of surplus stocks, the promotion of US foreign policy, and the encouragement of recipient economic development. The new program grew rapidly. Within the first three years of the program, US $2.8 billion worth of American farm products were shipped abroad at concessional rates, and over half of all American farm exports were soon being shipped under such subsidies.[3]

During this period the Canadian government also sought ways to come to terms with its declining agricultural sector and the mounting surplus problem. The excess of export supplies over effective world demand was of particular concern to Canadians. The absorptive capacity of the Canadian domestic grain markets was comparatively smaller than that of the United States, making the export of grain more critical. The economies of the Prairie provinces were highly dependent on large grain sales. At the same time, the grain market played a significantly larger role in Canada's national economy and balance-of-payments situation than in those of the United States.[4]

In approaching the problem, Canadian policy makers pursued a more modest course than the Americans. Production controls and export subsidies were too expensive. Consequently, the Canadian government sought to stabilize world market prices at a reasonable level and provide assistance in the marketing, storage, and transportation of grain. The Canadian Wheat Board, created in 1935 and given a monopoly on the marketing of Prairie grain in 1943, served as the government's principal mechanism for facilitating exports and providing assistance to Canadian farmers.[5]

However, as the smaller of the two major exporting powers, Canada found itself in a vulnerable position. As a result of its smaller resource base, the Canadian government was not in a position to undertake the same massive surplus disposal which was being pursued south of the border. Although the size of wheat stocks held by Canada were comparable to those held in the United States, they placed a significantly higher burden on the Canadian economy.[6] Thus American policies that could indirectly lead to an increase in Canadian surplus stocks were viewed as a serious threat to the Canadian economy. Because the United States was the largest grain exporting country, the Canadian share of world wheat markets was constantly threatened by the large American export assistance programs.

Due to this precarious export position, Canadian policy makers were already predisposed to the idea of using food aid as an escape valve for Canada's surplus problem. The opportunity for such a program first arose in 1951 when Canada agreed to join the Colombo Plan, designed to assist in the development of Commonwealth Asian countries. On 21 February 1951, Lester Pearson announced the government's intention to ask Parliament for $25 million for aid to India. Immediately after this announcement, the government opened discussions with India to determine whether it would accept part of that aid in the form of Canadian wheat.[7] These discussions led to the first shipment of Canadian food aid, a $10 million allocation of wheat to India. By the following year, talks were opened with Pakistan and Ceylon to determine their interest in accepting Canadian wheat as aid.

While the launching of the Colombo Plan provided Canadian officials with a convenient mechanism for dealing with their domestic agricultural concerns, it was also clear that the program had distinctly political objectives. The countries of South Asia were considered to be weak and vulnerable to subversive movements. By targetting the Colombo Plan to the newly independent Commonwealth nations in Asia, officials believed that it would be instrumental in preventing the spread of communism in this important region. If economic development were promoted, many of the frustrations that could lead these countries toward the Communist Bloc would be alleviated.[8] The Liberal minister for External Affairs, Lester Pearson, defended Canada's participation in the plan by noting that "if Southeast Asia and South Asia are not to be conquered by Communism, we of the free democratic world must demonstrate that it is we and not the Russians who stand for national liberation and economic and social progress."[9] Opposition Conservative leader John Diefenbaker took a similar line, noting that "fifty million dollars a year ... would be cheap insurance for Canada to halt communism in Asia."[10]

For many Canadian officials at the time the provision of food was seen as an important element in this anti-Communist strategy. Prime Minister St Laurent noted the connection between peace and food in a speech before the Canadian Federation of Agriculture: "I doubt if we can ever hope for the secure peace in the world which we all want so much as long as great numbers of people are barely able to eke out an existence ... It has been ably stated that never before has the close relationship between food and peace, food and justice, and food and happiness been so widely accepted."[11]

When the first allocation of food aid to India appeared to be delayed, an opposition member of Parliament was quick to point out the strategic importance of such food aid deliveries; failure to deliver food, it was argued, would soon drive India closer to the Soviet Union and China. The consequences would be, the member of Parliament warned, that "we would never get India back because it is hardly likely that you would accept a former friend who had refused you food when you were starving."[12]

As part of Canada's contribution to the Colombo Plan, the food aid program was narrowly focused on only three countries – India, Pakistan, and Ceylon. Like Canada's overall foreign aid orientation at the time, food aid remained entirely an Asian operation. It also continued to be seen as essentially a temporary measure. As a result, allocations were approved only on a year-to-year basis. These shipments were either funded out of the Colombo Plan monies or were voted by Parliament on an ad hoc basis in the case of emergency shipments requiring additional monies.

Canadian food aid during this period consisted entirely of bulk shipments of commodities which were sent directly to recipient governments. As part of the aid agreement signed with Colombo Plan participants, the recipient government would then sell the food to its own population on the open market. Revenues from these sales would then be deposited in local currency in a separate account known as a counterpart fund. This fund was to be used to finance the local cost of development projects mutually agreed on by Canada and the recipient government.

Since there were serious questions as to whether food for immediate consumption could be called developmental, the counterpart fund became the primary mechanism for establishing its legitimacy as development assistance. In 1965, the auditor general examined Canadian aid disbursements to determine if they in fact fulfilled the purpose for which Parliament had authorised them. In focusing on Vote 114, which states that the funds were to "assist in the economic development of such countries," the auditor general argued that only if counterpart funds were established and clearly designated for use in development projects could the allocations be considered as aid. Lacking such procedures the exchanges would be viewed as commercial purchases of wheat.[13]

From the beginning Canadian administrators expressed their own reservations about whether food aid should legitimately play a role in Canada's foreign aid program. This is best illustrated in the testimony of the chief administrator of Canada's aid program before the Standing Committee on External Affairs and Defence in 1955. Arguing that people would be without enough food if long-term development were not promoted, he noted that "we are anxious ... not to dissipate our funds in relief measures."[14] A year later he also noted that the value of Canadian wheat was questionable since the recipient populations are "rice-eaters who would not know what to do with wheat if we sent it."[15] Despite such reservations, concessional transfers of wheat accounted for close to 10 per cent of total Canadian wheat exports by the late 1950s.

AN EXPANDED SURPLUS DISPOSAL PROGRAM

Although food aid shipments soon became a regular feature of Canadian foreign policy, the program remained relatively modest in size during most of the 1950s. In the final year of the St Laurent government food aid amounted to only a $645,000 shipment of flour to Ceylon and represented about 1.9 per cent of the total bilateral aid budget for that year.[16] This could hardly be compared to the US $1.5 billion of foodstuffs provided by the United States under PL 480 in 1957.

This situation changed dramatically when John Diefenbaker's Conservative government was voted into power in 1957 on a tide of Western resentment over alleged neglect of Western agriculture by the Liberals. In the Throne Speech opening the new session of Parliament, the government served notice that "every possible effort is now being made and will continue to be made to seek new markets for agricultural products as well as to regain those that have been lost."[17]

The Canadian food aid program was seen as one way of fulfilling the government's pledge to expand exports. By 8 January 1958, the minister of Trade and Commerce was able to announce that $10 million of Canadian wheat had been pledged to India, Pakistan, and Ceylon, and that additional amounts were already being discussed. The minister noted somewhat apologetically that "the totals could not be as large as we might have wished ... because the funds had already been largely committed for urgent purposes of national development."[18]

More food aid was soon negotiated, resulting in an allocation of $26 million in 1958/59. Thus in two years food aid mushroomed from a meagre 1.9 per cent of Canadian foreign aid to fully 46.6 per cent. The rapid rise in food aid disbursements led to a search for new outlets. Burma, Indonesia, Nepal, Vietnam, and Palestinian refugees in the Middle East were added to the list of recipients. Diefenbaker noted that such offers of additional aid in the form of wheat had "served a useful purpose in our wheat program."[19]

Not content with these expanded outlets for Canadian surpluses, Diefenbaker began discussing other alternatives. In 1958, he began promoting the idea, presented to him by the Canadian Federation of Agriculture (CFA), of the establishment of an international food bank under the auspices of the Food and Agriculture Organization (FAO). While Diefenbaker endorsed the concept of an international food bank, he suggested that it be established through the North Atlantic Treaty Organisation (NATO). The main purpose of this, Diefenbaker noted, would be to "remove the overhanging surpluses that today have a detrimental effect on agriculture in general."[20]

Although Canadian policy makers were quickly learning how useful this surplus disposal mechanism could be, they still shared with other exporting nations a growing concern about the impact that such dumping practices could have on commercial markets. In 1953 the FAO had directed its Committee on Commodity Problems to study the surplus disposal issue. This resulted in the establishment of the Consultative Subcommittee on Surplus Disposal (CSD) in 1954 as a forum to deal with these issues. In addition a set of guidelines known as the Principles of Surplus Disposal, were established to guide the subcommittee in its work.[21] Canada played an active and prominent role in the Committee on Commodity Problems, in the subcommittee, and in the various International Wheat Agreements which began in 1949 and were designed to provide for more orderly marketing of agricultural products.

In the late 1950s, the aggressive export practices employed by the United States continued to annoy Canadian farmers. They complained that from 1955 to 1957 Canadian exports of wheat declined by 48 million bushels while American exports grew by 100 million bushels. In 1959 a study of the surplus problem noted that "responsible Canadians regard U.S. export programs as both unfair competition and a serious threat to Canada's ability to export wheat on a normal commercial basis."[22] Canada thus protested vigorously against American disposal practices such as export subsidies, sales for local currencies, barter deals, and tied sales, which were all common features of the PL 480 program. Through such protests Canadian officials were able to constrain some US disposal practices. For example, the curtailment of both the US barter program and the use of "tied UMR's" (usual marketing requirements) has been attributed to pressure from Canada.[23]

By the 1960s Canadian officials had both established food aid as a significant factor in Canada's foreign agricultural policy and helped to shape international regulations that would protect Canadian commercial interests from the worst abuses of surplus disposal. However, changing market conditions in the early sixties led to a brief lull in the growth of the food aid program. Faced with a period of tighter grain markets, the Conservative government made all of its austerity cut-backs for bilateral assistance in the area of food aid. This diminished role for food aid was continued by the new Liberal government in 1963/1964. Food aid as a share of bilateral assistance fell dramatically, from 23.1 per cent in 1961/62 to 8.7 per cent and 6.8 per cent for 1962/63 and 1963/64 respectively.[24]

Despite this lull in the growth of the Canadian food aid program, a major development in food aid policy took place in 1963 with the establishment of the UN/FAO sponsored World Food Program (WFP) on an experimental basis. Prior to the fall of his government John Diefenbaker had given enthusiastic support to the idea as a potential new outlet for Canadian farm products. Later he noted that "it was not difficult to reconcile the objectives of my proposal for a World Food Bank with the protection of commercial interests."[25] The Conservative External Affairs minister noted that such a program "would facilitate the disposal of certain goods presently in storage."[26]

As a result, when the WFP was established in 1963 Canada joined the agency as the fourth largest donor among sixty-seven initial donor countries. With its emphasis on the utilization of foodstuffs as an input into such developmentally oriented schemes as food-for-work projects, Canadian support for the WFP, while clearly in its own interest, also marked the beginning of some concern about the developmental impact of food aid. Canadian contributions to the WFP doubled from $4.2 million in 1966/67 to $8.7 million in 1969/70, or about 18 per cent of the total Canadian food aid. Beginning with the WFP's second pledging period in 1966–68 Canada regularly ranked second among donor countries, pledging nearly 15 per cent of the agency's cash and commodities.[27]

Canadian participation in the WFP received the strong endorsement of Canadian farm groups. In 1964 the Canadian Federation of Agriculture called on the Federal Cabinet for a "greatly expanded" contribution.[28] Three years later the National Farmers Union suggested that Canada should "substantially increase its contributions to the World Food Programme up to the objective of 1% of national income."[29] (This would have meant a huge increase in the food aid program since Canada's total ODA in 1967 represented only 0.3% of GNP!)

A second significant development during the 1960s was the establishment of food aid as a legitimate activity in its own right. This occurred for the first time in 1964/65 when a separate food aid subvote was included in the Main Estimates, under vote 35.[30] This subvote, which was under the administration of the External Aid Office, consolidated the World Food Program, the United Nations Relief and Works Agency for Palestinian Refugees in the Near East (UNRWA), and the relevant parts of the Colombo Plan into a distinct and separate food aid program, recognizing such aid as a legitimate form of development assistance. Identification of food aid as a separate activity in spending authorizations continued when the Canadian International Development Agency (CIDA) was established in 1968.

It is significant to note that the establishment of a separate food aid vote in the Appropriation Act effectively removed the legal basis of counterpart funds. This mechanism was no longer necessary to legitimize the developmental element of the food transfers. Nevertheless the use of counterpart funds continued as a part of the food aid policy, although they were now treated as an internal matter by aid administrators and were no longer reviewed by Parliament or cabinet.

Although the early sixties saw a leveling-off of overall Canadian food aid, concern over the impact of grain surpluses re-emerged as an issue in the mid and late 1960s. A number of factors contributed to a changing market situation that threatened Canadian exports. Many Third World countries experienced a series of successful harvests. Grain producers outside North America, such as Australia, Argentina, the USSR, and France, witnessed important increases in their grain output. Changes in American food aid and farm support programs after 1964 led to a more aggressive move toward market expansion by the United States. In 1965, for example, the United States began undercutting Canadian export prices even though they had previously cooperated in setting wheat prices. Finally, technological developments in the baking industry which permitted the greater use of soft wheat led to an erosion of demand in traditional markets for Canadian hard wheat.[31]

The threat that these changing circumstances posed for Canadian grain exports meant that current surplus situations continued to have a significant impact on the development of Canadian food aid policy. Changes in annual allocations can be clearly traced to immediate market circumstances. In July 1963 Minister for Trade and Commerce Mitchell Sharp announced in Parliament that "the government has decided that the time has come to move forward on another front which should prove of both short run and long run advantage to western wheat producers."[32] Sharp then proceeded to say that the government would undertake a renewed food aid program that would soon grow to a target of $40 million. Two days later he noted: "It is important when we undertake this program that it should result in a genuine increase in the disposal of Canadian wheat and flour."[33]

However, the rapid expansion of the food aid program was postponed within a few months when large sales of wheat to the Soviet Union temporarily relieved the surplus pressures.[34] Despite this delay, the Canadian food aid program grew dramatically during the mid-1960s. From 1963/64 to 1964/65, the program increased nearly five-fold, from $4 million to $19 million. The following year it increased almost another 100 per cent to $35 million.

In 1966, Maurice Strong became director of the External Aid Office. With the aim of developing new directions and carrying out reforms in the aid programs, Canada's foreign aid jumped from $208 million to $309 million in a single year. At the same time food aid increased dramatically. This resulted primarily from the convergence of two important factors: the continued accumulation of Canadian surpluses and two successive poor monsoons which threatened famine for the Indian sub-continent. In one year Canadian food aid tripled, passing the $100 million mark for the first time in 1966/67 and accounting for fully 40.5 per cent of total Canadian ODA. Thus within a decade the Canadian food aid program had grown from its meagre allocation of $640,000 in 1956/57 into an important instrument of the federal government.

The growth of food aid as a component of Canadian aid policy was taking place at a time when Canadian foreign policy towards the Third World in general was broadening in perspective. Policy makers were becoming increasingly interested in Africa. As a result, Canadian aid programs expanded beyond Ghana to include almost all of Commonwealth Africa as those countries became independent. Because of the federal government's concern with Quebec's nationalistic aspirations, a number of major aid projects were undertaken in francophone Africa following recommendations made by the Chevrier Commission in 1968.[35]

This broadening of interest by Canadian policy makers is clearly reflected in the expansion of the food aid program beyond Asia into Africa. By 1968/70, the list of food aid recipients included sixteen countries. In 1966/67 Algeria, Ghana, Morocco, and Senegal became the first non-Asian recipients of Canadian food aid. Tunisia and Tanzania were added in 1967/68, with Niger and Nigeria becoming recipients a year later. Thus during the 1960s the Canadian food aid program not only became increasingly aware of its potential beyond mere surplus disposal, it also grew in size and complexity. At its highest point in the decade, during the famines in India, food aid had grown to fully 57 per cent of the entire Canadian aid program. As a result, in the latter part of the 1960s food aid constituted one of the most important contact points that Canadian policy makers had with the Third World.

A PERIOD OF TURBULENCE AND CRISIS

Following the election of the Trudeau government in 1968, the field of development assistance became an area of international affairs where the new government was determined to distinguish itself. Peter Dobell notes that policy makers saw the aid field "as providing a new role where, with the weakening of u.s. will, Canada can set an example internationally and at the same time implement a policy which cannot be criticized as being a pale reflection of the Americans."[36]

The increased attention paid by the Trudeau government to the Third World, especially in the area of aid, led to a rapid transformation of Canadian aid policies. In 1968 the External Aid Office was replaced by CIDA. Under the leadership of Maurice Strong and, beginning in 1969, Paul Gérin-Lajoie, the program grew rapidly. From 1969/70 to 1976/77 the Canadian aid budget tripled, from $339 million to $963 million. At the same time the geographical disbursement of Canadian aid was broadened as increased amounts were channeled towards francophone Africa. As well, Trudeau's concern with the neglect of Canadian-Latin American relations led to the establishment of new aid programs in that region.[37]

The entire orientation and administration of Canadian aid underwent review. In 1970 the government included a booklet on international development in its review of Canadian foreign policy. The document focused attention not only on the need to increase the size of Canadian official development assistance but also on the steps necessary to improve its quality. Reduction of tied aid, increased multilateral aid, and greater emphasis on non-governmental organizations (NGO's) were among the document's many conclusions.[38] The 1970 foreign policy review noted that "food aid must be provided with discretion since large amounts of food ... can depress agricultural prices ... and discourage investment and expansion in the agricultural sector."[39] Nevertheless the review pledged that Canada would "continue to provide substantial quantities of food aid as ... conditions require."[40]

However, it was changes in the international economic environment, particularly in the United States, that again shaped Canadian food aid policy in the early seventies. After a decade of expansion and consolidation, the Canadian food aid program in the 1970s was marked by a period of turbulence and uncertainty in the areas of both agricultural and food aid policy. This change began in 1969 with the installation of the Nixon administration in Washington. The appointment of Earl Butz as secretary of Agriculture signaled a shift in American agricultural policy toward a "free market" approach. The United States began offering wheat sales at prices below those which had been agreed on in the 1967 International Grains Agreement (IGA), effectively undermining it. Aided by a devalued dollar, US agricultural exports doubled between 1971 and 1973. Domestic wheat reserves fell dramatically, from 209 million bushels in 1972 to 18.9 million bushels in 1973. Programs to divert US farm land from production were ended.[41] At the same time the success of the European Economic Community's Common Agricultural Policy (CAP) led to growing surpluses that the European Economic Community (EEC) increasingly tried to export outside the community through an aggressive export subsidy program.

Canada's foreign agricultural and food aid policy was not immune to the dramatic changes that were taking place in the international environment. As a result of the aggressive export policies of the Nixon administration, Canadian export sales suffered and Canadian carry-over stocks of wheat increased rapidly from 11.4 million metric tons in 1966 to 27.4 million metric tons in 1970.[42] In response Canadian officials undertook several policy initiatives. In 1970 the Lower Inventory For Tomorrow (LIFT) program was established to reduce wheat acreage. This marked the first time that the Canadian government had established such a large production control program. Studies have estimated that it led to a decrease in expected wheat acreage in 1970 from 22 million acres to 12 million acres.[43]

In 1971 the Canadian Grain Marketing Committee reported that the federal government had undertaken two additional measures to assist grain exports. One was an expanded food aid program, which increased Canadian food aid in 1970/71 to $104.2 million or 1,163.5 million metric tonnes, the largest amount to date. The second was a series of sales to developing countries such as Algeria, Brazil, and Syria, these sales were negotiated under special subsidized credit terms in hopes of maintaining Canada's position in these markets.[44]

At the same time that US agricultural policy was shifting toward aggressive export expansion, a complex set of circumstances led to a rapid increase in world demand for grains. The Soviet Union, Asia, and Africa all experienced poor grain harvests. The Peruvian anchovy fishery suffered a sudden unexpected slump. Many of the major industrialized countries, such as the Soviet Union and Japan, responded by making major food and food grain purchases, particularly in the United States.[45]

Third World countries looking for expanded food supplies faced a very difficult situation. The competition for grain supplies had caused wheat prices to nearly triple in three years. In addition, the quadrupling of OPEC oil prices made the purchase of petroleum-based products such as fertilizers and pesticides prohibitively expensive. Increased inflation and reduced availability of food aid because of high commercial export demand created a very restricted food supply situation for many Third World countries. The "world food crisis" soon emerged as a major issue on the international political agenda.

As world wheat prices began to rise rapidly in 1972 and world markets became tight, Canadian officials preferred to give commercial customers first priority. Total Canadian food aid decreased by 23.4 per cent between 1970/71 and 1971/72. Although the program soon recovered to reach new highs in dollar value in response to the growing world demand for concessional transfers, from 1970/71 to 1974/75, Canadian wheat aid actually dropped in volume by 55.3 per cent to the smallest volume of food aid shipped in a decade.[46] The preference for commercial sales at a time of high food prices is reflected in the fact that while agricultural exports to LDC's in dollar value increased by 48 per cent, from $724 million to $1.4 billion between 1973 and 1974, food aid's share of this total declined from 12 per cent to only 9 per cent.[47]

The decline in Canadian wheat aid was halted only when the federal government, under pressure from opposition parties and Canadian NGO's, committed itself at the World Food Conference in Rome in 1974 to supply one million tons of grains every year for the following three years. In implementing this pledge the Canadian food aid program grew to its largest level to date, shipping over $240 million of foodstuffs to the Third World in 1976/77, a 40 per cent increase in the actual volume of food aid.

Although Canadian officials did eventually respond to the "world food crisis," expanding total food aid levels to new highs, the politicization of the food security issue on a global level had led to a growing debate within Canada about the appropriateness of food aid in a development program. Media coverage of the "food crisis" of 1974–75 not only stimulated public attention about global food issues but also focused attention on many cases where food aid was not reaching the starving populations, as the public may have believed. Numerous press stories were published which reported the loss of millions of tons of grain in India due to rodents and poor storage facilities.[48] Other stories reported cases of corruption and mismanagement of food aid, with elite groups such as the military and civil service receiving the bulk of the food instead of the poorest populations.[49] This led some opposition critics, such as Conservative MP Douglas Roche, to ask increasingly pointed questions about who was receiving Canadian food aid and why it was not being made clearer that the food was being sold rather than given away by the recipient government.[50] The president of CIDA, Paul Gérin-Lajoie, attempted to deal with the growing criticism by making a highly publicized trip to Bangladesh to review the handling of Canadian food aid. In his subsequent report Gérin-Lajoie appeared to confirm the worst fears of his critics. "Despite some recent improvements," the CIDA president found that "the rural landless ... get an extremely meagre share of rationed food, while the system takes care of the urban areas, and within the rural areas, gives priority to the army, teachers, and public servants."[51]

At the same time CIDA itself was coming under considerable criticism for mismanagement of its programs. The aid program as a whole had grown dramatically since 1968. By 1972, the annual CIDA budget had surpassed the one billion dollar mark for the first time. The size of the budget alone attracted critical attention about the way in which the funds were being spent. In 1975 cases of mismanagement of CIDA funds and criticisms of the flamboyant style of Gérin-Lajoie were subjects of frequent press reports.[52] The auditor general added his voice to the debate by citing several examples of poor management of the aid program. He singled out the food aid program in particular as being poorly coordinated and administered.[53]

Within this context, Canadian officials began to review Canadian practice in food aid giving for the first time and to suggest new directions for the program. The first review effort was an internal study carried out by the Task Force on Food and Renewable Resources in 1975. The mandate of the task force was essentially to review CIDA's performance in the renewable resources sector and to suggest ways in which the agency could make a more effective contribution. However, the task force also noted that until significant expansion in Third World agriculture occurred, CIDA would find it necessary to continue giving large amounts of food aid.[54] Thus the task force devoted seventeen of its forty-six recommendations to food aid. Some of these recommendations were subsequently included in CIDA's *Strategy for International Development Cooperation 1975–80*, where they were subject to a broader public debate.[55]

These two CIDA documents constituted an important step in the agency's attempt to define a food aid strategy for the seventies. A central theme of both documents is that the increase of domestic agricultural production within Third World countries should be the central objective of CIDA's assistance policies. Food aid is thus conceived of as being a transitional measure to be employed only until such production increases occur. Implicit in this view is the argument that food aid should be complementary, and not detrimental, to a recipient government's agricultural development strategies. Both documents suggest ways in which the Canadian food aid program could be modified to more readily accommodate the interest of LDC recipients. Reform of Canada's food aid strategy was seen as fundamental to the achievement of humanitarian and developmental objectives.

The next important phase in the process of formulating a food aid strategy in the seventies occurred in 1976. In August of that year the deputy minister of the Treasury Board requested that Gérin-Lajoie carry out an overall review and evaluation of food aid as a form of development assistance. The immediate justification for such an evaluation was the need to develop a basis for planning of food allocations when the Rome pledge expired after the 1977/78 allocation.

The joint Treasury Board–CIDA study represented the first serious attempt in the history of the Canadian food aid program to evaluate the overall effectiveness of the program in meeting its stated objectives. The study attempted to measure the impact of the transfers in terms of their efficiency as a resource transfer, their allocative and distributional impact on the recipient, and their impact on Canada's economy. Although the study tried to be comprehensive, it covered primarily food aid allocations for the budget years of 1975/76 and 1976/77. The report's conclusions were largely negative. In examining the Canadian emergency response to the Sahelian famine the study concluded that there were "serious problems in the programming, budgeting, procurement, delivery and distribution of bilateral emergency food aid."[56] In many cases it found that the food had arrived too late or was an over-reaction, "providing too much food aid too late."[57] In addition it concluded that the commodities sent to the Sahel frequently "do not appear to have been suitable to the diets of the population groups most affected."[58]

The report was equally condemnatory of CIDA's approach to bilateral food aid in non-emergency situations. Here the study focused on Canada's allocations to five countries during 1975/76 and 1976/77, which collectively accounted for nearly 75 per cent of Canada's total bilateral food aid budget. It found that in three out of the five countries studied the recipient probably would not have maintained the same level of imports if food aid had not been available. It went on to conclude that "in all five countries examined, food aid appears to accommodate policies discouraging domestic production in both the

short and long term."[59] The Treasury Board study was equally pessimistic about the distributional impact of food aid. "Bilateral program food aid," it concluded, "does not reach the poorest segments
of the population of recipient countries."[60] Only in one country, Sri
Lanka, did the study find that "poorest people gain reasonable access
to food aid through the public distribution system."[61]

The Treasury Board study then went on to look at the effectiveness
of channelling food aid through the WFP. Again its sample was small,
representing only 20 out of 218 projects available on the WFP terminal
reports. Although the study concluded that most of the projects did
not appear to have a negative impact on local agricultural production,
it found nevertheless that "only three of the twenty development
projects examined substantially achieved their purposes."[62] It then
went on to conclude that "WFP projects have less nutritional impact,
provide less incentive to worker participation, and ... involve lower
levels of labour productivity than might at first be expected."[63] Given
such negative conclusions it is not surprising that the government
never made the Treasury Board study public.

Because the Treasury Board study raised serious questions about
the overall effectiveness of the Canadian food aid program and
seemed to confirm the arguments of CIDA's critics, CIDA began an in-
house review of the program in May 1977. It was decided to broaden
participation in the review in order to gain as wide as possible
acceptance of the food aid policy guidelines on an interdepartmental
basis. In September 1977 an Interdepartmental Working Group on
Food Aid Policy was established. It was composed of representatives
from CIDA, the Departments of Agriculture, External Affairs, Finance,
Industry, Trade, and Commerce, the Grains Marketing Office, the
Privy Council, and the Treasury Board secretariat. The working group
met twenty-four times in an effort to come to an agreement on a
document entitled *Food Aid Policy Recommendations*. These recommendations were submitted to the Interdepartmental Committee on Economic Relations with Developing Countries for review in June 1978.
With only a few small changes, the document was given final
approval and became the basis for subsequent Canadian food aid
policy. The preparation of the *Food Aid Policy Recommendations* is of
particular importance to the development of the Canadian food aid
program since it represents the first effort to formally articulate a
comprehensive and coherent policy on a broad interdepartmental
basis.

One of the most important contributions of the working group
was its effort to establish an order of priority among the numerous
objectives that Canadian food aid could serve. In its final

recommendations the working group concluded that humanitarian concerns must be the "main rationale" for Canadian food aid. From this, the committee established the following general principles to guide food aid decision making. First, food aid should address primarily the nutritional needs of the poorer segments of recipient country populations. Second, it should have a social developmental impact that extends beyond its immediate consumption. Third, it should be programmed to meet primarily the "food gap" rather that the overall resource gap. Fourth, the food aid should be complementary to the recipient country's agricultural strategy. The report then went on to outline a number of ways in which these objectives could be implemented through the food aid program.[64]

The *Food Aid Policy Recommendations* was a significant stage in the development of Canadian food aid policy. It affirmed the concept of food as a transitional measure, complementary to the recipient's own agricultural development needs. The recommendations also called for a more rationalized, systematic approach to planning that would integrate the many diverse elements of the food aid program into a coherent and comprehensive allocation strategy.

At the same time the 1978 food aid recommendations sought to accommodate non-developmental objectives in the program. While priority was assigned to humanitarian and developmental objectives, the document also noted that food aid should both take account of Canada's economic interests, through surplus disposal on one hand and increased value added to agricultural commodities on the other, and be consistent with the goals and objectives of Canada's foreign policy and development assistance efforts.[65] The interest of all of the participants in the working group were thus covered to some extent. This attempt to accommodate a broad spectrum of objectives in the food aid policy had a significant impact on the outcome of the group's deliberations. As subsequent chapters will show, a number of CIDA's own recommendations for improving the developmental impact of food aid failed to gain interdepartmental approval. The tensions inherent in the Canadian food aid program, stemming from the pursuit of multiple potentially conflicting objectives, continued to place a significant constraint on any efforts to move towards a more developmental approach to food aid giving. This tension was reflected in the number of new products included in the food aid program during the seventies. Although there were no longer pressures to move large grain surpluses, new products, such as skim milk powder, canned beef, canola oil, and powdered eggs, were added to the food aid basket as a direct result of domestic political pressures.[66]

Despite the continuing tension between commercial and developmental objectives, CIDA did take an important step with the creation of the Food Aid Co-ordination and Evaluation Centre (FACE) in 1978. The centre was given the broad mandate "to improve the efficiency and effectiveness of Canadian food aid."[67] In order to do this the new centre was given authority to "be involved in policy and financial management issues for all of CIDA's food aid program."[68] After an initial start-up period, the staff was more than doubled and the centre rapidly established itself as a participant in nearly every aspect of food aid decision-making. This marked the first time in the history of the food aid program that a bureaucratic unit had existed specifically to deal with food aid issues on a regular on-going basis.

The decade of the seventies thus represented a period of new initiatives and reforms to the food aid program. For the first time steps were taken to place food aid on a much firmer institutional basis within the framework of Canada's overall aid program. These changes to the food aid program were largely stimulated by the turbulent "crisis" atmosphere in the early seventies. By the end of the decade stability in world food prices was restored and concern about global food shortages had largely receded from the public mind. Thus when CIDA made cuts in proposed spending as a part of the Liberal government's newly announced austerity measures in 1978 the food aid program bore the brunt of the cuts. This was especially true of the bilateral food aid program, which was reduced by 38.9 per cent between 1977/78 and 1979/80.[69] By 1980/81 the volume of Canadian food aid had sunk to its lowest level since 1965.

MAKING FOOD AID RESPECTABLE

Although the 1970s marked the beginning of efforts by Canadian officials to formulate a more coherent food aid policy, considerable scepticism remained regarding the developmental utility of food aid in the Canadian aid program. Indeed, the Canadian food aid program was beset by a growing crisis of confidence. Such diverse agencies as the Science Council of Canada[70] and the Canadian Council on International Co-operation[71] called for the abolition of Canadian food aid except in the case of genuine emergencies. These critics suggested that by providing cheap food Canadian food aid discouraged local agricultural production, created a taste for expensive imported foods, and enabled recipient governments to postpone necessary agricultural reforms. Similar critiques came from both sides of the political spectrum. Writing from a radical perspective, Robert Carty and Virginia Smith concluded that "food aid is the most dramatic failure among our aid programs."[72] The Citizens for Foreign Aid Reform, an ultra-conservative organization, argued that the Canadian food aid program is "a prescription for disaster and must be rejected as a foreign aid option."[73] Others, such as the North-South Institute[74] and Professor Theodore Cohn",[75] while rejecting the "abolitionist" argument, called for significant changes in the food aid program if it were to be continued. David Hopper, a World Bank vice-president and former director of the International Development Research Centre, urged the Canadian government to "tie our food aid with some pretty strong strings."[76]

As public criticism of food aid continued, these views were given a public forum with the convening of the Parliamentary Task Force on North-South Relations in 1980. Although the task force examined the whole range of issues regarding relations between developed and developing countries, one of the five policy chapters in the final report dealt exclusively with food aid and agricultural assistance. Some members of the committee, such as Conservative MP Douglas Roche, and New Democrat MP Father Robert Ogle, were long-standing critics of food aid. These committee members in particular pushed witnesses hard on the issue of food aid and its effectiveness. They were especially concerned about the role of Canada's bilateral program food aid and the extent to which the poorer population groups were benefitting. Even the director of FACE was forced to admit that food aid distribution tended to be biased in favour of urban populations and that the poorest population groups frequently did not have access to Canadian food aid.[77] Another CIDA official observed under questioning that "there are only a few circumstances in the world where food aid makes good sense."[78]

Despite such damning testimony, even on the part of CIDA's own officials, the committee stopped short of recommending the elimination of the food aid program, or even a significant reduction in its budget. Instead it recommended that more emphasis be placed on the provision of project food aid through multilateral agencies such as the World Food Program. In addition, it proposed that more food aid funds should be untied for the purchase of commodities in Third World countries for shipment to food deficit neighbours. In cases where bilateral food aid was still being given, it was suggested that the aid should be given only if it was linked to "a detailed and well-integrated food production plan" and that aid agreements should specify a decline and termination of food aid with accompanying increases in assistance to food production.[79]

Despite the negative view of food aid voiced by the Parliamentary Committee on North-South Relations in 1980, the trend in the 1980s has been towards an increasingly larger food aid program. From

1980/81 to 1984/85, the budget of the Canadian food aid program increased by 110 per cent, primarily through an expansion of bilateral food aid. During this period bilateral food aid expanded by 193 per cent, causing the share of multilateral food aid to fall to 32.4 per cent of the program in 1984/85, its lowest share of the program in a decade.

The renewed growth of the Canadian food aid program is in part a reflection of the changing international grain markets, which have witnessed an increasingly aggressive export war in the 1980s. Competitive patterns of subsidized over-production and export have resulted in a global grain surplus and a resultant drop in prices. The downward spiral of falling prices and decreasing income have led both the United States and the European Economic Community to undertake more aggressive "export enhancement" programs. Thus by 1985 it was estimated that American export credits and food aid totalled US $7 billion, while comparable European Community programs approached US $1 billion annually.[80] As a result Canadian grain exports have been threatened as the Europeans and Americans have undercut Canadian sales in some of its traditional markets. Although Canadian officials have tried to avoid an all-out trade war, they have attempted to cope with the problem by offering subsidized sales to some of their traditional Third World buyers such as Algeria, Syria, and Saudi Arabia. In the context of this market situation there are strong domestic pressures to maintain an expanding food aid program in order not to lose still further markets.[81]

However, it is not only domestic economic pressures that have encouraged expansion of the food aid program in the 1980s. This growth in the food aid program occurred at the same time that CIDA began channelling increased amounts of food aid to Africa. Even during the Sahelian famines of the early seventies, Africa never accounted for more than 19 per cent of the total Canadian food aid. However, the amount of bilateral food aid directed to Africa increased from 17.4 per cent in 1980/81 to 44.4 per cent in 1984/85. As a result, Africa's share of the Canadian bilateral program more than doubled within a period of four years.[82]

This shift in the geographical focus of the Canadian food aid program can be attributed in part to specific famine conditions in certain countries. Although some twenty countries were reported by the FAO to be experiencing serious food shortages in the early 1980s, most public attention during this period was focused on Ethiopia. Following the broadcast of a BBC documentary in October 1984 on the emerging famine conditions in Ethiopia, there was unprecedented interest and involvement in mobilizing relief for Ethiopia.

Individuals and groups across Canada organized events to raise funds for African relief. A reported one-third of the total Canadian population personally contributed to Ethiopian famine projects. On a global level, popular events such as the Live Aid rock concert received an enthusiastic response.

In Canada, the government responded by establishing a $65 million Special Fund for Africa for relief and rehabilitation projects, $15 million of which was set aside to match donations from individual Canadians. In a novel move, the Canadian government appointed a former Conservative cabinet minister, David McDonald, to act as Canadian Emergency Coordinator for the African Famine. He was given a broad mandate not only to assess and monitor famine conditions in Africa but also to act as a "facilitator" for public involvement at home. MacDonald combined overseas missions to assess African food needs with the organization of events such as the African Round Tables to stimulate discussion in Canada on solutions to Africa's food problems.[83] While Canadian efforts included medical aid and rehabilitation assistance, a significant share was, of course, food aid. Canada's total shipment of food aid to Ethiopia, through all channels, grew from $16.3 million in 1983/84 to $52.7 million in 1985/86, the largest amount of food aid ever allocated to an African country in a single year.[84]

As dramatic as the events in Ethiopia were, the famine was not the only reason that Canadian food aid allocations have shifted toward the African continent during the past decade. The deteriorating economic climate in the region as a whole has also been an important factor. There has been a steady decline of per capita food aid production and consumption in Africa, accompanied by continued high rates of population growth. As a result Africa is the only region in the world where per capita food production has declined for the past two decades. This declining production, accompanied by dietary changes, especially in urban areas, has led to significant increases of food imports; Africa's food imports have doubled in recent years. This growing level of food imports to Africa is occurring at a time when these countries are least able to finance such increases on a commercial basis. Stagnating exports, falling commodity prices, high energy import bills, and heavy debt repayment loads have all combined to reduce the foreign exchange available to pay for commercial food imports.[85] As a result African states have increasingly turned to food aid to finance their food import needs. Program food aid which can be dispersed relatively quickly is once again seen by donors as an inexpensive way of providing balance-of-payments and general budgetary support to financially strapped recipient governments. In the 1980s Canada, like other donors, found itself transferring increased amounts of food aid toward the African continent. From the donor's point of view, however, this type of long-term food aid poses a difficult dilemma. Given the growing domestic criticism of food aid, CIDA was concerned about ways to continue to supply food aid without perpetuating its negative effects and creating new horror stories about aid mismanagement. This issue has become the principal preoccupation of Canadian policy makers in the 1980s.

CIDA's response to this dilemma was outlined by its president, Margaret Catley-Carlson, in an address to the Committee on Food Aid Policies and Programmes of the WFP in October 1985. Catley-Carlson began by noting that funding for aid is increasingly limited and that, despite global grain surpluses, recipient countries should not take an increasing supply of food aid for granted. Instead she stated that "food aid is a scarce resource and we must manage it accordingly." [86] CIDA's president went on to argue that "we will have to demonstrate convincingly that it is a good 'investment' in future agricultural productivity, a development transfer which is at least as efficient and effective as competing claims for scarce resources."[87] She then warned recipient countries that "unless we can demonstrate that our food aid is not a disincentive to local farmers, that it supports and complements agricultural development activities, that it is doing something to prevent recurring emergencies, that it assists and encourages recipient governments to invest in their rural areas and maintain a policy framework which will stimulate productivity ... unless we can prove all these points, we will not be able to maintain public and parliamentary support for a substantial Canadian food aid programme."[88]

What is significant for Canada's food aid strategy is that this emphasis on the need to demonstrate food aid effectiveness at home has been accompanied by an effort by CIDA to link food aid with policy dialogue and policy conditionality. The basis for this policy was outlined in a corporate evaluation of the food aid program carried out in 1984. Overall, this evaluation presents a much more positive portrait of the Canadian food aid program than the Treasury Board evaluation. Based on a review of thirteen country evaluations carried out by CIDA, the report contends that Canadian food aid represents an additional resource for development, that it substitutes for commercial imports, and that it does not appear to act as a disincentive for local food production. In addition it argues that, given the conditions existing in recipient countries, the delivery and distribution of Canadian food aid generally occurred in a timely and effective fashion. The report found that, contrary to most public criticism, there was an emerging consensus that food aid is indeed a useful developmental resource.[89]

Although the corporate evaluation goes on to make some recommendations regarding the management and administration aspects of the program, its most significant contribution appears to be its articulation of a rationale for long term "developmental" food aid that has since been restated in a number of CIDA documents. Developmental food aid can serve two rationales. First, it can be used in support of continued balanced growth in cases where the recipient country is already pursuing macro-economic and agricultural policies that are consistent with increased food production. In this case Canadian food aid "can free scarce foreign exchange for additional investment in agriculture, reduce upward pressure on domestic food prices, and smooth adjustments in the agricultural sector."[90] Second, food aid can be used as part of a structural adjustment program. This occurs in cases where the recipient has not adopted economic and developmental policies that the donor believes to be sound. In this context food aid is seen as a resource which can be used to influence changes in the recipient's domestic agricultural policies. Recent CIDA documents have identified several ways in which food aid can contribute to this process: (i) food aid, especially if offered on a multi-year basis, can provide a recipient government with assured external support while reforms are being carried out; (ii) the sale of food aid can generate revenues to be used to finance producer incentive schemes agreed to during the dialogue process; (iii) negotiation over counterpart funds can provide CIDA with some measure of control to insure that investments are directed toward the agricultural sector and are not being misdirected, and; (iv) the foreign exchange saved can be used to import the necessary inputs needed to expand agricultural development projects.[91] In addressing the Committee on Food Aid Policies in Rome, the president of CIDA informed recipients that this latter rationale would be given greater priority, making it clear that future food aid flow would depend on whether recipient countries were willing to engage in policy dialogue with Canada and undertake structural policy adjustment reform programs deemed to be necessary by the donor community.[92]

Despite CIDA's efforts to present a more carefully articulated rationale for long term food aid and to defuse criticism of short term emergency relief efforts, there continues to be strong resistance to the food aid program among many parliamentarians who do not appear to share the "emerging consensus" defined by CIDA. This is reflected in the treatment given to food aid by the parliamentary committee mandated by the Conservative government of Brian

Mulroney to carry out a full-scale review of the Canadian foreign aid program. This study, tabled in 1987 under the title *For Whose Benefit?*, is perhaps the most comprehensive review of aid policy ever carried out by a parliamentary committee. Nevertheless the committee devoted only a 1½ pages of its 140 pages to the topic of food aid. Like the report of the Committee on North-South Relations in 1980 the Winegard report, as it is called, suggested greater untying of food aid purchases and more use of project food aid. But, more important, it went on to note that "given the mixed record of food aid, it is a channel that should be handled with greater care and used more sparingly than in the past."[93] To ensure this the committee recommended that a ceiling be put on the amount of food aid given by Canada by limiting non-emergency food aid to no more than 10 per cent of the total ODA budget. Since at the time food aid made up 16 per cent of the Canadian ODA budget, this represented a significant cut in the food aid budget.

In spite of the efforts by the Winegard committee to place a ceiling on Canadian food aid levels, actual food aid levels continued to be governed by shifts in the international economic environment and Canadian domestic political concerns. The Winegard committee's recommendations came at a time when the Canadian government was increasingly preoccupied with a growing domestic farm crisis. It had already been forced to provide Canadian farmers with a $1 billion special assistance support to cushion their 30 per cent drop in farming income during the second half of 1986. In the same month that the Winegard committee released its report three western premiers called on the federal government to buy up surplus grain for use in the food aid program. Although CIDA officials quickly announced their opposition to the use of more wheat aid as a method for dealing with Canadian surpluses, the timing was not good for placing a ceiling on the growth of the food aid budget.[94] Thus, while the Conservative government took a positive approach to the Winegard report in accepting, in full or in part, 111 of its 115 recommendations, the recommendation for a limit on the food aid program was one of only four recommendations that it rejected outright. Instead the government indicated that it planned to continue increasing food aid at a rate of 5 per cent annually, noting that "it considers the use of food aid an effective and flexible instrument for helping developing countries face emergency situations or major balance of payments deficits."[95]

Despite this commitment food aid soon faced cuts, but not because of the Winegard committee's call for a ceiling on food aid. Following the 1988 election the Mulroney government turned its attention to issues relating to fiscal management and deficit reduction. In April 1989 the government announced a 12 per cent cut in CIDA's budget for 1989/90, with a total of $1.8 billion to be cut from the aid budget over the next five years. Significantly, the government announced that $66 million of these cuts would come from the food aid program, while an additional $67 million would come from CIDA administrative expenditures. As in the austerity cuts of a decade earlier, food aid was seen as an easy area to target.[96]

Christopher Stevens has noted that food aid has developed a special politics and psychology of its own. Because food aid has been widely criticized and yet remains a highly visible and symbolic element in aid programs, donors are anxious to emphasize its positive benefits. As a result, Stevens notes, "not only do donors make quite unwarranted claims for the impact of food aid ... but they link it to every passing development fad and fancy ... The object is to make food aid respectable."[97] There is little doubt that in the 1980s CIDA has been concerned about improving the management of its food aid program and communicating more effectively what it sees as the positive aspects of food aid. Yet CIDA has still not succeeded in making food aid completely respectable among its domestic constituents. The recommendation of the Winegard report for a significant cut in the food aid program reflected the continuing scepticism of many Canadians about food aid's legitimate role in a development assistance program.

THE CANADIAN FOOD AID PROGRAM IN PERSPECTIVE

This chapter has outlined briefly the evolution of the Canadian food aid program from a surplus disposal mechanism to a multi-faceted policy instrument shaped by domestic agricultural and foreign policy and development assistance priorities. Before examining more fully how the dynamic interaction of these factors has shaped particular aspects of the food aid program, it is important to understand the dimensions and component elements of the Canadian food aid program. In particular, it is useful to examine the size and importance of the food aid program, the form in which the aid is given, and finally how recipient countries are determined.

Since 1951 the Canadian government has spent more than $4.3 billion on food aid allocations. Table 2 provides an indication of the value and volume of Canadian farm products shipped as aid during this period. The vagaries of Canadian surpluses and world food demand are clearly reflected in the sharp fluctuations in yearly allocations. Some anomalies are also clearly evident. For example, Table 2 shows that while the food aid budget grew in value by 97.5 per cent between 1971/72 and 1974/75, the actual volume of food aid provided to recipients was 30.3 per cent lower. Canadian food aid has always been budgeted for in terms of dollars, not volume. As a result, the volume of food aid actually delivered is dependent on the price of food commodities at a particular time. Thus the volume of food aid declines as world prices rise. For example, in 1975/76 it took 126.2 per cent more money to provide 11.2 per cent less food aid than in 1970/71.[98]

Canadian officials have frequently stressed the importance of Canadian food aid by noting that Canada is the largest per capita food aid donor in the world.[99] However, a number of other indicators can help us to put the importance of Canadian food aid into proper perspective. On a global scale, Canadian food aid in fact represents a relatively small share of the total effort. Although accurate data is difficult to find, it is estimated that annual global shipments of food aid in the 1980s averaged over US $2.5 billion worth of commodities. A major portion of this was provided by members of the Development Assistance Committee (DAC) of the Organization of Economic Cooperation and Development (OECD). Table 3 shows Canada's participation in this transfer of food resources. The United States has historically dominated these transfers, with other donors playing only a relatively small role. For example, in 1963 the United States contributed fully 94 per cent of the total DAC food aid while Canada, the second largest donor, contributed only 4 per cent.[100] As a result of pressure from the United States to participate in "burden sharing," and the emergence of the EEC as a major agricultural surplus producer, the American share of global food aid has declined to about 55 per cent of the total. In 1981 the United States accounted for only 43 per cent of the global total, its lowest share since food aid programs begin in earnest in the fifties. However, as the EEC became increasingly aggressive in using subsidies to challenge US commercial grain markets, the US share of total food aid returned to just over the 50 per cent level. From 1973 to 1984 Canada accounted for an annual average of 8.9 per cent of the total DAC food aid. In six of these twelve years Canada ranked as the second largest bilateral donor, after the United States.

However, as the food aid program of EEC member countries has grown, Canada's share of DAC food aid has slipped in some years. For example, following the austerity cuts in 1979/80 and 1980/81 Canada accounted for only 5.5 per cent of the total DAC food aid. As a result Canada ranked only as the sixth largest donor, after the United States (43 per cent), Japan (11.8 per cent), West Germany (9.4 per cent),

Table 2
Canadian food aid disbursements, 1951/52 – 1990/91

Fiscal Year	Volume Q(MTN)	Value C$(000,000)	Food Aid as % of total ODA
1951/52	114.1	10.0	37.5
1952/53	115.5	10.0	35.2
1953/54	67.4	5.7	17.4
1954/55	9.9	0.8	2.7
1955/56	34.2	2.2	5.6
1956/57	14.9	0.6	1.3
1957/58	271.9	17.9	36.2
1958/59	405.9	26.0	47.0
1959/60	193.1	12.6	16.6
1960/61	184.9	12.5	17.6
1961/62	165.3	12.5	24.5
1962/63	47.5	4.0	8.7
1963/64	44.3	4.0	6.8
1964/65	249.9	19.1	23.0
1965/66	390.8	35.5	38.2
1966/67	1098.3	100.4	57.0
1967/68	742.5	70.3	44.8
1968/69	750.1	66.0	40.5
1969/70	763.8	73.4	30.0
1970/71	1163.5	104.2	29.8
1971/72	941.1	79.8	20.0
1972/73	801.4	112.4	21.1
1973/74	712.0	115.7	19.4
1974/75	665.2	174.5	23.3
1975/76	1033.1	222.6	24.5
1976/77	1102.8	240.1	26.3
1977/78	971.5	230.4	21.9
1978/79	711.8	191.2	16.4
1979/80	558.4	187.7	15.0
1980/81	521.5	183.4	14.0
1981/82	568.2	235.7	15.1
1982/83	777.6	273.2	16.4
1983/84	900.0	332.5	18.0
1984/85	948.8	385.5	18.4
1985/86	850.4	347.8	15.9
1986/87	1334.8	402.7	15.9
1987/88	1533.3	436.7	16.6
1988/89	1055.4	431.5	14.7
1989/90	865.2	371.6	13.1
1990/91	1049.4	382.3	12.3

Source: CIDA, Food Aid Centre, "Bilateral Food Aid Program as of 30 June 1978"; "1990/91: Food Aid Program Annual Report"; and CIDA, *Annual Reports*, various years.

United Kingdom (6.0 per cent), and France (5.7 per cent) (see Table 3).

Another way to assess the importance of Canadian food aid is to examine its role in Canada's own aid and trade policies. As a share of Canada's official development assistance, food aid has played an important but highly variable role. It has gone from a low of 6.8 per cent of Canada ODA in 1963/64 to a high of 57 per cent in 1966/67. As the Canadian aid program continued to grow during the 1970s and 1980s, the relative importance of food aid declined. Since the 1980s food aid has never made up more than 18 per cent of Canada's total ODA budget (see Table 2). However, the Canadian aid program continues to include a larger percentage of food aid than the programs of other countries, with the exception of the United States. For example, during the past decade the share of food aid disbursements in the overall ODA of all DAC members has generally stood at 10 per cent or less (see Table 4).

Another measure of the importance of Canada's food aid is its contribution to the Canadian economy. In terms of overall Canadian food production and agricultural trade, food aid plays a relatively insignificant role. Without subtracting transportation costs and the income accruing to processors, gross food aid expenditures in 1986 represented only 1.6 per cent of net farm incomes in that year. In 1983/84 Canada's food aid budget of $332 million represented only 11.9 per cent of the total agri-food expenditures by federal government agencies. Even if one considers the role of food aid in Canada's total agricultural trade, food aid plays a surprisingly small role. As Table 5 shows, food aid has rarely accounted for more than 5 per cent of Canada's total agricultural exports. When budgets cuts were made in the food aid program in the late 1970s, food aid as a share of Canada's agricultural exports declined to a low point of 1.9 per cent in 1980/81. Table 5 also reveals that Canada's food transfers to developing countries remain an essentially commercial operation. Only twice since 1969 has food aid constituted 20 per cent of Canada's agricultural exports to developing countries. This table readily demonstrates that when food prices were high and supplies were scarce in the early 1970s Canada tended to honour its commercial commitments first; thus food aid as a share of agricultural exports to developing countries actually reached its lowest point in 1974 during the "world food crisis." The share of food aid in agricultural exports to LDC's has doubled since 1980/81, reflecting the increasing difficulty that many recipients have in importing their food needs on a commercial basis, as well as the re-emergence of surplus difficulties in several Canadian commodities.

Table 3
Percentage share of major donors in total DAC food aid, various years

Donor	1974	1976	1978	1980	1981	1982	1983	1984	1985
Australia	4.9	2.0	2.0	2.4	3.5	4.1	4.1	4.0	1.7
Canada	9.1	10.5	11.0	6.3	5.5	8.6	8.4	10.6	8.6
France	6.9	2.8	3.8	4.6	5.7	5.7	3.8	5.0	4.1
German Fed. Rep.	9.4	5.0	8.0	8.1	9.4	9.1	6.6	8.5	6.6
Japan	4.9	0.5	11.1	10.0	11.8	5.7	5.7	0.4	0.9
United Kingdom	2.8	1.9	3.9	4.5	6.0	6.0	3.9	4.8	4.5
United States	47.8	67.3	54.6	49.9	43.0	45.0	53.5	52.0	50.6
Other DAC donors	14.1	10.0	15.6	14.2	15.1	15.8	14.0	14.7	23.0

Source: FAO, Food Aid Bulletin, various years.

Table 4
Share of net food aid disbursements in the official development assistance of selected DAC member countries (in percentages), 1978–87

Countries	1978	1979	1980	1981	1982	1983	1984	1985	1986	1987
Australia	6.9	12.8	9.6	15.9	11.5	13.5	15.1	6.8	11.2	9.6
Canada	21.2	14.8	15.4	13.6	17.9	14.9	19.2	16.1	15.5	15.9
France	2.9	2.4	3.0	4.0	3.5	2.5	3.9	3.2	2.4	1.6
German Fed. Rep.	7.0	5.1	6.0	8.7	7.2	5.3	9.0	6.9	5.9	5.2
Japan	1.0	4.2	7.8	10.9	4.6	3.8	1.0	0.7	1.2	1.4
United Kingdom	5.5	4.0	6.3	8.1	8.2	6.2	9.9	9.0	5.6	6.3
United States	19.7	27.8	18.3	21.8	13.8	16.7	17.7	19.8	15.9	16.9
Total for all DAC countries	10.2	10.0	9.6	11.5	8.9	9.1	10.4	10.6	8.0	6.9

Source: FAO, Food Aid Bulletin, various years.

Although food aid has played a relatively small role in Canada's overall agricultural trade with LDC's, Table 6 shows that when individual commodities are examined food aid has differing significance as an export opportunity. In the case of wheat, pulses, and maize, food aid represents only a small portion of overall Canadian exports. However, for wheat flour, skim milk, and canned herring and sardines food aid is a very significant outlet for Canadian production. The importance of food aid as an export outlet for Canadian commodities often varies significantly from year to year depending on current Canadian production levels and overseas demand. For example, although food aid in canola oil accounted for only 15.6 per cent of Canadian exports in 1984/85, it accounted for fully 87 per cent of Canadian canola exports in 1976/77.

Table 5
Food aid as a share of Canada's agricultural trade, 1969–87

Year	Food aid as a percentage of total agricultural exports	Food aid as a percentage of total agricultural exports to LDC's
1969	5.2	21.7
1970	4.0	15.3
1971	3.2	11.4
1972	2.9	11.7
1973	2.9	12.9
1974	3.2	8.8
1975	4.4	14.5
1976	4.2	18.1
1977	4.0	13.0
1978	3.3	10.3
1979	2.5	10.1
1980	2.5	11.6
1981	1.9	12.5
1982	2.4	14.9
1983	3.4	17.0
1984	3.2	15.5
1985	3.7	18.6
1986	3.9	20.4
1987	4.1	18.0

Source: Agriculture Canada, Canada's Trade in Agricultural Products, 1978, 1979 and 1980 (Ottawa: 1981), Table 38, and Agriculture Canada, Canada's Trade in Agricultural Products, 1985, 1986, and 1987 (Ottawa: 1987), Table 38. International Programs Branch, Agriculture Canada.

Another aspect of the food aid program which is of interest concerns the commodity composition of the Canadian food aid basket. Since the establishment of the program a total of more than 20 food products have been included in the food aid basket. But, like other donors, Canada has traditionally contributed primarily grains in its food aid program. During the first two decades of operation wheat and wheat flour made up about 90 per cent of the total. Since the early 1970s wheat and wheat flour have constituted about 75 per cent of the total value of the Canadian food aid basket. Commodities other than wheat and wheat flour have generally entered the food aid basket in times of surpluses. Some products, such as canned meat or powdered eggs, have been given only on a short term basis to deal with a domestic over-supply crisis in Canada. Other products, such as skim milk powder (SMP), canola oil, and fish, have become permanent features of the aid program. However, their volume and

Table 6
Selected Canadian food aid commodities as a share of domestic production and exports, 1984/85

Commodity	Production	Exports	Food Aid	Food aid as percentage of production	Food aid as percentage of exports
Wheat	21 million t.	18 million t.	714,000 t.	3.4	3.9
Wheat Flour	1.8 million t.	314,000 t.	138,000 t.	7.6	43.9
Maize	7 million t.	554,000 t.	11,000 t.	0.15	1.9
Canola Oil	514,000 t.	237,000 t.	37,000 t.	7.1	15.6
Skim Milk Powder	113,000 t.	63,000 t.	16,000 t.	14.0	25.3
Pulses	194,000 t.	142,000 t.	16,000 t.	8.2	11.2
Canned Herring/Sardines	9,840 t.[1]	6,676 t.[1]	1,336 t.[2]	13.5	20.0

Source: CIDA, Food Aid: A Programming Manual (Hull: mimeographed March 1986).
Notes: [1] 1982
       [2] 1982/83

share of the food aid basket have tended to fluctuate widely from year to year depending on the availability of surpluses and the current state of Canada's export markets (see Table 7).

A number of different channels have been used to disburse Canadian food aid. As Table 8 shows, direct government-to-government transfers of food aid to bilateral recipients have historically made up the largest share of the program. Before the founding of the World Food Program in 1961 all Canadian food aid was transferred bilaterally. Until 1975 bilateral food aid still made up 80 to 90 per cent of the program. After this date the share of bilateral food aid dropped until 1978/79 when, for the first time, it was exceeded by multilateral contributions. Since 1981/82 just over a half of Canadian food aid has been channelled as bilateral assistance. In recent years 20 to 25 per cent of the global food aid has been moved through multilateral channels.[101] Thus a much larger share of Canada's food aid is multilateralized than is the case for most donors.

Canada has directed its multilateral food aid through several organizations, including the WFP, the International Emergency Food Reserve (IEFR), operated by the WFP, the United Nations Relief and

Table 7
Commodity composition of Canadian food aid (values in millions of Canadian dollars), 1972–91.

Fiscal Year	Wheat	Wheat flour	Dried Skim Milk	Fish	Oil	Other
1972/73	57.0	10.3	8.2	1.9	2.4	3.0
1973/74	82.8	9.1	5.7	.7	9.3	5.1
1974/75	97.2	12.1	12.9	.6	14.9	11.5
1975/76	150.5	24.8	10.5	3.2	24.4	8.8
1976/77	114.0	14.7	14.0	1.0	31.9	2.8
1977/78	93.0	43.6	18.6	2.7	36.6	3.9
1978/79	84.0	55.7	13.1	7.5	15.0	5.9
1979/80	96.7	34.0	8.7	6.0	25.6	4.1
1980/81	97.6	31.6	10.1	5.8	10.3	13.5
1981/82	122.5	35.5	12.7	17.3	14.0	6.7
1982/83	157.6	38.6	16.6	9.6	24.1	7.1
1983/84	171.8	49.1	19.1	20.8	33.2	38.2
1984/85	156.9	51.1	17.4	30.2	33.7	21.8
1985/86	127.9	57.2	18.3	29.3	35.0	14.6
1986/87	162.6	46.8	20.0	27.4	62.0	10.5
1987/88	199.5	48.1	11.3	33.2	33.0	26.2
1988/89	182.5	45.5	13.1	37.0	35.9	26.6
1989/90	162.8	33.3	17.9	29.2	21.3	22.4
1990/91	162.5	32.1	18.2	30.2	19.0	24.6

Source: CIDA, Food Aid Centre

Works Agency for Palestinian Refugees (UNRWA), the United Nations Children's Fund (UNICEF), and the International Committee of the Red Cross. However, more than 95 per cent of Canada's multilateral food aid is provided through the WFP. Canada has consistently ranked as the second-largest donor to the WFP, accounting for about 20 per cent of the program's total resources. Although the WFP has frequently not received much publicity, it has emerged as the second largest source of development funds after the World Bank. In 1985/86 it provided food and related assistance valued at US $1.35 billion. Although the WFP was created as a mechanism to allow food aid to be used as a resource in long-term development projects, there have been increased demands for a multilateral mechanism to handle emergency food aid allocations. As a result the IEFR was created in 1976 to facilitate a faster international response to emergencies. Administered by the WFP, the IEFR distributes free food directly to vulnerable population groups affected by food shortages.

    Canadian food aid has also been distributed through several channels referred to as "special programs." The first program of this type was the non-governmental (NGO) SMP program established in 1976

Table 8
Channels of Canadian food aid (in millions of Canadian dollars), 1970–91

		Multilateral		Bilateral		NGO's	
Year	Total Food Aid Value	Value	Percentage of total	Value	Percentage of total	Value	Percentage of total
1970/71	104.2	17.0	16.3	87.1	83.4	–	–
1971/72	79.8	15.6	19.5	64.2	80.8	–	–
1972/73	112.4	16.4	14.5	96.0	85.4	–	–
1973/74	115.7	20.9	18.0	94.8	81.9	–	–
1974/75	174.5	16.1	9.2	158.4	90.7	–	–
1975/76	222.6	105.5	47.4	117.1	52.6	–	–
1976/77	240.1	89.1	37.1	151.0	62.9	–	–
1977/78	230.4	91.3	39.6	139.1	60.4	2.1	0.9
1978/79	194.5	98.0	50.5	93.1	47.9	3.3	1.7
1979/80	187.7	97.8	52.1	85.7	45.7	4.1	2.2
1980/81	183.4	106.8	58.2	73.1	39.9	3.5	1.9
1981/82	235.7	113.4	48.1	118.3	50.2	4.0	1.7
1982/83	273.2	122.0	44.4	141.4	51.8	9.7	3.6
1983/84	332.5	146.3	43.9	175.8	52.9	10.3	3.2
1984/85	385.5	149.6	38.8	214.4	55.6	21.4	5.6
1985/86	347.8	150.3	43.2	163.1	46.9	34.3	9.9
1986/87	402.7	166.3	41.2	210.9	52.3	25.4	6.3
1987/88	436.6	172.7	39.5	237.8	54.4	26.1	5.9
1988/89	431.5	188.4	43.6	217.9	50.4	23.9	5.5
1989/90	371.6	173.6	46.7	174.5	47.0	23.5	6.3
1990/91	382.3	182.1	47.6	176.8	46.2	23.4	6.1

Source: CIDA, Annual Reports, various years.

on a trial basis. Under this program Canadian NGO's can request milk powder for use in their overseas development projects. CIDA pays for the cost of the milk powder, while the NGO picks up the cost of the transportation and distribution. This milk is used mostly in mother and child health projects and in programs directed to vulnerable population groups.

A second outlet for NGO food aid has been the Canadian Food-grains Bank (CFB). Originally established by the Mennonite Central Committee, the CFB is now a consortium of church and voluntary development agencies. It gathers contributions from members, largely farmers who generally contribute food commodities rather than cash. Initially the program focused on western Canada, where farmers contributed grain. More recently the CFB has become more active in Ontario, where it receives contributions of pulses and corn. CIDA funded the value of CFB fund raising on a 3:1 basis until 1985/86, when it established a funding level of $16 million.

One other channel, although quite small, has been the Voluntary Agricultural Development Aid (VADA) program established in 1975. This program is operated jointly with the provinces. For the food aid aspect of the program, VADA will pay the shipping costs of food commodities donated by provincial governments, Canadian NGO's, and private corporations or individuals.[102]

Since their inception in the mid-1970s, the special programs have remained a relatively minor component of the overall food aid budget generally, constituting less than 10 per cent of the total. Of particular significance, however, has been the growth of this channel in recent years. In 1980/81 NGO's accounted for only $3.5 million or 1.9 per cent of the food aid budget. By 1985/86 special programs had grown by over 900 per cent to $34.4 million or 9.9 per cent of the total. This can be attributed both to the rapid growth of the Canadian Food-grains Bank and to the fact that CIDA has decided to channel a large share of its emergency food aid to Ethiopia through NGO's. In 1985/86 CIDA directed $23.4 million of its food aid to Ethiopia through Canadian NGO's, as compared to only $12.4 sent through government-to-government channels. Despite the recent growth in the amount of food aid funnelled through Canadian NGO's, they still play a small role compared to NGO's in the United States. For example, in 1981 two US voluntary agencies, Cooperative for American Relief Everywhere (CARE) and Catholic Relief Services (CRS), alone were responsible for distributing 52 per cent of the US Title II food aid.[103]

Another important aspect of the food aid program is the terms under which aid is given. Nearly all of Canadian food aid has been given in the form of grants which do not require repayment by the recipients. All of Canada's multilateral food aid is in grant form. Similarly, all of Canadian bilateral food aid has been given as grants with the exception of a bilateral food aid loan to Jamaica.[104] This contrasts sharply with the practice of the United States where in 1985 99 per cent of bilateral transactions reported to the FAO were in the form of credit sales.[105]

Table 9 shows a breakdown of Canadian bilateral food aid according to the terms of the transaction as reported to the FAO's sub-committee on surplus disposal. Although most Canadian food aid has been given on a grant basis, it is not exactly the "free gift" directly to starving populations that the public usually perceives it to be. Instead, prior to 1984 more than 80 per cent of Canada's food aid was provided to the recipient government, which then resold the food aid to its population.[106] Since 1984 the share of food aid intended for direct distribution to consumers has increased as Canada has shipped larger amounts of food aid to African countries experiencing food emergencies.

Table 9
Share of Canadian bilateral food aid transfers[a] by type[b] of transaction, 1974–86

Type	1971	1974	1977	1980	1983	1984	1985	1986
1	–	1.5	2.7	12.5	14.2	51.5	60.9	40.2
2	87.5	98.5	97.3	81.9	85.5	48.5	39.1	59.8
10	–	–	–	5.6	–	–	–	–
11	12.5	–	–	–	–	–	–	–

Source: FAO, *Food Aid Bulletin*, various years.

Notes: [a] As reported to the FAO Sub-Committee on Surplus Disposal

[b] As in the catalogue of transactions listed in FAO Council Resolution 1153

The types of transactions are:

1 Gifts or donations for distribution directly to consumers.

2 Gifts or donations for distribution by means of sale on open market of importing country.

10 Sales on credit with interest rate, period of repayment or other terms that do not conform to those prevailing on the world market.

11 Sales in which funds for purchase of commodities are obtained under a loan from the exporting country tied to the purchase of those commodities.

Because CIDA traditionally has not identified emergency food aid as a separate and distinct category, it is difficult to measure exactly the role that emergency food shipments have played historically in the Canadian food aid program. The best guess of CIDA officials themselves was that only about 10 per cent of Canada's bilateral food aid was really targetted for direct famine relief in the 1970s.[107] In the 1980s, as CIDA has redirected more of its food aid toward Africa, a larger share of Canadian food aid has been targetted towards famine relief. According to a recent CIDA estimate 27 per cent of its total food aid between 1983/84 and 1988/89 took the form of emergency assistance. By 1990/91 this figure had reached fully 37 per cent of total Canadian food aid.[108]

Finally, which countries receive Canadian food aid? In principle, any country deemed by the Canadian cabinet to be eligible for Canadian development assistance is able to receive Canadian food aid. In practice, in general the Canadian food aid program has been much more concentrated than the bilateral aid program. Since 1980 a total of 125 countries have received government-to-government assistance from Canada. In contrast, during the same period only 34 countries received shipments of government-to-government Canadian food aid.

Tables 10 and 11 show the major recipients of bilateral food aid and their geographical distribution. During the first three decades of the program four Asian countries, India, Bangladesh, Sri Lanka, and Pakistan, accounted for fully 75 per cent of the $1.6 billion that Canada gave as bilateral food aid. Between 1981/82 and 1986/87 these

Table 10
Distribution of Canadian food aid by region, 1975–91

Year	Percentage share of total bilateral food aid		
	Asia	Africa	Americas
1975/76	85.1	13.0	1.8
1976/77	78.8	19.3	1.8
1977/78	66.3	18.9	9.2
1978/79	72.9	15.4	13.7
1979/80	75.6	17.4	8.3
1980/81	39.8	38.4	3.4
1981/82	42.0	42.8	15.0
1982/83	67.4	32.5	–
1983/84	59.9	26.7	14.0
1984/85	47.5	44.4	7.9
1985/86	51.5	37.8	10.2
1986/87	57.0	30.0	12.7
1987/88	44.3	47.8	9.1
1988/89	39.5	46.8	13.5
1989/90	36.1	51.4	12.0
1990/91	33.9	50.3	15.7

Source: CIDA, *Annual Reports*, Various years.

four Asian countries continued to receive, on average, 54 per cent of all bilateral food aid. Since its independence in 1971 Bangladesh has been the largest single recipient of Canadian food aid, accounting for 30 per cent or more of the total bilateral budget each year.

Since 1980/81 there has been a significant shift in Canadian bilateral food aid towards the African continent. In 1980/81, for the first time, Asian countries received less than half of Canadian bilateral food shipments. Although there have been some fluctuations due to changing conditions from year to year, by 1989/90 Africa accounted for 51.4 per cent of total bilateral food aid. This mirrors a global trend by both bilateral and multilateral donors to channel increased amounts of food aid to the African continent in response to growing need there. Unlike Canadian food aid to Asia, aid to Africa tends to be more widely disbursed. For example, in 1989/90 thirteen African countries received food aid, with the largest recipient, Mozambique, receiving only about half the amount of food aid shipped to Bangladesh. Even during the height of the African famine in 1984/85, four non-African countries (Bangladesh, India, Sri Lanka, and Jamaica) received more bilateral food aid than Ethiopia. Nevertheless, as Table 10 shows, there has been a shift in geographical priorities as the number of African countries which are recipients of large amounts

Table 11
Major recipients of Canadian bilateral food aid, 1975–91

1975/76		1980/81		1985/86		1990/91	
India	51.5	Bangladesh	39.3	Bangladesh	49.67	Bangladesh	45.7
Bangladesh	27.9	Senegal	6.8	Jamaica	16.78	Mozambique	17.7
Pakistan	17.5	Ethiopia	3.9	Pakistan	13.93	Ethiopia	16.8
Tanzania	5.8	India	2.9	India	13.13	Jamaica	14.7
Sri Lanka	3.9	Tanzania	2.9	Ethiopia	12.45	Pakistan	13.9
Ghana	3.7	Somalia	2.8	Sudan	11.95	Sudan	10.9
Mali	2.	Mozambique	2.6	Sri Lanka	7.80	Ghana	6.9
Niger	2.7	Zaïre	2.4	Ghana	5.05	Angola	5.9
Vietnam	2.5	Jamaica	2.4	Mauritania	4.78	Peru	5.9
Haiti	0.9	Zimbabwe	2.4	Niger	4.39	Rwanda	5.1
Percentage of total	98		94		85		81
Total no. of recipients	12		14		21		22

Source: CIDA, *Annual Report*, various years.

of Canadian food aid grows. Looking more specifically at these recent bilateral food aid allocations, two trends can be noted. First, in response to domestic demands that food aid be more "hunger-responsive," larger amounts of food aid are being directed towards countries experiencing serious food shortages, especially where this has been exacerbated by domestic conflict. Thus, during the past five years increased amounts of food aid have been channelled to countries such as Ethiopia, Sudan, and Mozambique. The effect of these emergencies on the distribution pattern of Canadian food aid is reflected in the fact that in the mid-1980s only 20 per cent of Canadian food aid was directed towards what were then designated as category II and III countries. By 1989/90 fully 38 per cent of Canada's bilateral food aid was being channelled to "non-core" countries.[109]

Second, increased amounts of food aid are being channelled to countries facing severe economic crises or involved in structural adjustment programs, with food aid seen as a means of increasing the flow of resources to these countries. This explains the inclusion of a growing number of countries that historically have not been regular recipients of Canadian food aid (such as Ghana, Zambia, Egypt, Bolivia, and Peru), or have not received Canadian food aid for some time (such as Tunisia, Morocco). In each of these cases Canadian food aid is seen as contributing to a broader process of policy dialogue with the recipient government within the context of a structural adjustment program. In 1989/90 23.5 per cent of Canada's

Table 12
Canadian aid and food aid disbursements to LLDCS (government-to-government), 1972–90

Fiscal Year	Percentage of total Canadian ODA to LLDCS	Percentage of total Canadian food aid to LLDCS
1972/73	31	38
1973/74	30	52
1974/75	38	57
1975/76	27	33
1976/77	24	26
1977/78	34	48
1978/79	31	58
1979/80	35	54
1980/81	34	71
1981/82	32	59
1982/83	36	66
1983/84	37	61
1984/85	32	50
1985/86	34	58
1986/87	36	45
1987/88	35	42
1988/89	37	42
1989/90	40	58

Source: Calculated from CIDA, *Annual Reports*, various years.

bilateral food aid was channelled to countries categorized as middle-income countries. Some of these countries, such as Peru, Jamaica, and Tunisia, are not even classified as food deficit countries by the United Nations. Thus, while a larger amount of food aid appears to be shipped as emergency assistance to countries facing severe food shortages, a growing amount of Canadian food aid is being allocated to countries as a form of stabilization aid to assist them in coping with broader economic crises or as support for structural adjustment programs.

On a number of occasions Canadian officials have voiced a commitment to concentrating Canadian development assistance on the poorest countries. One means of measuring this commitment is to examine the role that the "least developed countries," as categorised by the United Nations, have played as recipients of Canadian food aid. Table 12 demonstrates that, in fact, LLDC's have accounted for a significant share of Canada's bilateral food aid in most years. Canadian officials have generally been more successful in directing a larger share of food aid to LLDC's than they have with other forms of Canadian ODA. This is partly because some of the poorest recipients have experienced serious recurring food crises, but also because it is easier to give bulk shipments of food aid to many of the poorest recipients than it is to plan and administer other types of development assistance.

CONCLUSIONS

From this overview it is evident that the Canadian food aid program has grown in size and complexity since its foundation in 1951. Although established as only a temporary measure, it has since become a permanent and highly visible aspect of Canada's relations with the Third World. The growth of the Canadian food aid program has been closely related to changing economic and political circumstances within Canada. At the same time the program's purposes have become more numerous and complex.

As the program has grown in size and complexity, so too has the controversy surrounding its appropriate role in Canadian development assistance. Criticism of the Canadian food aid program appeared to reach its peak in the late 1970s and early 1980s, when a growing number of critics called for significant changes if not outright abolition of the program. Even the government's own internal reviews raised serious questions about the effectiveness of the program.

Despite the growing "crisis of confidence" concerning food aid in the 1970s, the program has remained an important element in CIDA's overall aid-giving effort. As a result of increased public attention to food issues in the 1970s, Canadian food aid policies and programs underwent a period of substantial change and reform. This resulted in a number of new policy initiatives designed to change both the substance of Canadian food aid programs and the manner in which they are administered. These changes mark a watershed in the history of Canadian food aid, which has been followed by a period of consolidation and restructuring as many of the policy themes introduced after the World Food Crisis were elaborated and refined in the 1980s and early 1990s. In the following chapters, I will examine these changes in much greater detail as I analyse the various forces that have shaped these policy reforms.

2 The Multiple Objectives of Canadian Food Aid

A significant feature of Canadian food aid policy is its multiple objectives. Since food aid represents a highly visible aspect of Canada's relationship with the Third World, it has become an important policy instrument in this relationship. As such, it has come to serve and reflect a broad spectrum of Canadian interests in LDC's. Because of this, the Canadian food aid program in any particular country may be designed to serve a variety of objectives simultaneously. These objectives cover three broad areas of policy concerns: domestic agricultural and commercial policy, general foreign policy, and humanitarian and development policy. Within each of these policy areas a number of more specific sub-objectives can be readily identified. The allocation of food commodities may be simply one of several policy instruments that Canada has employed in its relationship with a particular country.

Each of these policy concerns has been promoted by various governmental and societal actors. The relative priority given each objective has fluctuated over time, depending on changing political and economic forces. As a result the decision-making process for Canadian food aid transactions is an arena in which many interests converge and compete. Since the organizational structures, food aid practices, and conditions applied by donors are often a reflection of the compromises made between competing objectives, a study of the various objectives pursued by policy makers provides an important basis for understanding how the Canadian food aid strategy has evolved.

This chapter presents an overview of the various objectives that Canadian policy makers see food aid as fulfilling. The intent is to provide the reader with a sense of the range of situations in which food aid has been used as an instrument of Canadian policy. In subsequent chapters we will see how the promotion of particular objectives by various governmental and societal actors has shaped Canadian aid policy and how the organisational environment in which the food aid program is implemented facilitates and constrains the achievement of particular objectives.

DOMESTIC AGRICULTURAL AND COMMERCIAL OBJECTIVES

Given its position as an important food-producing and exporting nation, it is not surprising that Canada's food aid objectives are closely intertwined with its agricultural policy. The Task Force on the Orientation of Canadian Agriculture has noted that food aid assists agricultural goals by providing a fairer and more stable level of support to Canadian producers.[1] As CIDA's *Annual Aid Review 1978* pointed out, food aid can provide support to the Canadian economy in two ways: through surplus disposal and through increased value added to agricultural commodities.[2]

Surplus disposal is perhaps the most commonly identified commercial objective of Canadian food aid, especially among the critics of the program. The reduction of excess inventories of agricultural products through aid programs can benefit the Canadian economy in two ways. First, surplus disposal reduces the costs entailed in the storage and handling of excess stocks. Second, it reduces the depressive effect that large surpluses have on the markets of agricultural products. Disposal thus helps both to stabilise domestic prices and to provide a larger return to Canadian producers.

The advantages of such disposal programs have frequently been cited by Canadian officials. Eugene Whelan, in announcing CIDA's agreement to purchase 75 million pounds of skim milk powder in 1976, argued that the purchase "will mean that dairy farmers will not have to handle storage, financing costs, holding charges, etc., for the product."[3]

The priority assigned to this objective, however, is highly variable, depending to a large extent on changing market conditions. During some periods, such as the late sixties, surplus disposal was a primary objective of Canadian wheat aid. During the boom years of the seventies, however, Canada could export all of its wheat on commercial terms. As a result, during this period surplus utilization of food aid shifted to other products, such as skim milk powder, dried eggs, canned meat, and fish.

The second economic benefit provided is the value derived from the processing of food aid commodities. By shipping flour instead of wheat, or canola oil instead of raw canola seed, further economic benefits can be provided for the Canadian economy. Such processing of food aid commodities enables Canadian processors to maintain higher levels of production and capacity utilization. Flour, semolina, canola oil, milk powder, and fish are examples of products which provide such value-added benefits. This objective has been particularly attractive in the case of flour and canola because of the persistently low levels of capacity utilization in both flour-milling and oilseed crushing facilities.[4]

It is difficult to estimate the exact benefit derived from the reduction in excess inventories or the processing of food aid commodities. However, in 1978 the Treasury Board estimated that between 1975 and 1977 canola oil and skim milk powder provided a savings in inventory financing of 8 per cent and 18 per cent respectively of the total value of shipments during this period.[5] The same study found that flour, semolina, and fish provided value-added benefits of 20 per cent, 13 per cent, and 100 per cent of the total food aid shipments during this period. The Treasury Board estimated the total domestic economic benefit derived from food aid during this three year period to be about $20 million per year.[6] This estimate may be lower than in many years, since the study covered a period when Canada was selling all of its available wheat. In more recent years, as fish has come to play an important role in the aid program, CIDA estimates that its purchases of fish products keep the equivalent of two fish-processing plants open in the Maritimes.

Although surplus disposal and value-added benefits have been given the most mention in CIDA policy statements, Canadian officials have clearly pursued additional commercial objectives. Primary among these are market development and market maintenance. The distinction between what constitutes simple commodity dumping, as a temporary pressure-release mechanism, and purposeful market development is frequently a fine one. While the Canadian Wheat Board identifies the aid program as one of several policy instruments used to promote exports, wheat aid does not appear to have been used aggressively as a marketing tool to develop new markets for Canadian wheat sales.[7] It is true that some of the early recipients of Canadian wheat aid, such as Algeria, Burma, Indonesia, Tunisia, Morocco, were later "graduated" from the status of food aid recipient to that of full paying customer, but these countries make up only a small portion of Canada's wheat market. In many of these cases wheat aid appears to have served the purpose of keeping a foothold in some markets that were under threat by Canada's competitors.

The clearest illustration of this use of food aid was the granting of reduced terms of credit to Algeria, Brazil, Egypt, Pakistan, Peru, the Philippines, and Syria in the early 1970s. Otto Lang, the minister responsible for the Canadian Wheat Board, announced that this program had resulted in "substantial Canadian sales" in markets where no sales had been achieved in the previous few years.[8] Industry, Trade and Commerce reported that the combination of food aid and expanded credit facilities had been successful in assisting "in maintaining Canada's share of the world grain market."[9]

Although food aid has often been used to protect markets, Canadian officials have frequently voiced the belief that Canadian food aid helps to develop new markets by familiarizing recipients with the quality of Canadian products and introducing a taste for Canadian wheat or other products. Canadian officials have pointed to certain market-development success stories whenever they wish to justify the food aid program to domestic agricultural audiences. Foremost among these successes is the case of canola (rapeseed) exports.

Canola is a great success story in Canadian agricultural science. It played a relatively small role in the Canadian agricultural economy until the late 1960s, when Canada's share of the world wheat market began to decline. At that time the federal government began to encourage the development of canola production as part of its crop diversification program. Canadian scientists worked to improve the breeds of canola, and particularly to reduce the plants erucic acid content which limited its use in human food products. The development of improved strains of canola led to a rapid growth in the domestic production of canola, and within a short period of time Canada emerged as the world's largest exporter of canola. However, the growth of domestic production levels soon outstripped the growth of export markets. As a result increased quantities of canola oil were included in the aid program as one means to familiarize overseas customers with the Canadian product. In some years food aid has accounted for a very large share of the canola oil export market, making up fully 87 per cent of exports in 1976/77. A large share of the canola aid was shipped to Bangladesh and India, which are seen as potential long-term commercial markets. In particular, a CIDA official explained that Canada's large shipments of canola aid to India, as part of the India Oilseeds Project, have not only helped to "establish a national vegetable oil capacity but also a familiarity with Canadian canola in a very large and important market."[10] The same CIDA official went on to cite an emergency food aid shipment of canola oil to Peru as an example of market development when Canadian officials were able to use the opportunity "to have the vegetable oil tariff schedule changed to allow shipments of Canadian canola, thus potentially opening a new market ... [that] ... has previously been restricted to USA soya."[11]

The use of food aid to develop markets has not been limited only to agricultural products. In the early 1980s Fisheries and Oceans developed a strategy to expand and diversify overseas markets for Canadian fish, especially in the Third World, and to protect existing markets in countries such as Jamaica, which was experiencing economic difficulties. As a result Canadian fish aid has increased rapidly in recent years, climbing from $5.9 million in 1980/81 to a high of $37.0 million in 1988/89.[12]

In some cases food aid may not be used so much to protect threatened markets as to make up for lost ones. An example of this is cited by the director of the CIDA's Food Aid Centre, who notes that CIDA worked closely with the Canadian National Millers' Association to reverse the decline in wheat flour aid after Canada lost its important share of the Cuban flour market.[13] Traditionally 65 to 70 per cent of Canada's wheat flour exports were sold to Cuba; however, wheat flour exports to Cuba declined dramatically from 794,000 tonnes in 1977/78 to 372,000 tonnes in 1985/86.[14] In response to this loss CIDA increased its flour aid from a low of 82,000 tonnes to over 138,000 tonnes. In 1984 flour aid accounted for 43 per cent of the total wheat flour exports.

Beyond helping to develop and maintain markets, food aid is seen by officials as a "sweetener" leading to the conclusion of other commercial deals. As an example, International Trade and Commerce (IT&C) Minister Jean-Luc Pépin led a trade commission to Morocco in December 1974 "looking for opportunities to improve the level of Canadian exports of goods and services."[15] The same departmental release went on to note that most of Canada's previous exports to that country had consisted of food aid shipments. Similarly, a trade agreement made by Prime Minister Trudeau with Colombia in 1977 was coupled to an agreement to donate 1,800 tons of skim milk powder to the Colombian government.[16]

FOREIGN POLICY OBJECTIVES

As chapter 1 demonstrates, the Canadian food aid program was born in a period when the Cold War was a major preoccupation. Thus, in the early years of the program there was considerable rhetoric about the use of food to win friends and halt the spread of communism. However, since these early years the foreign policy objectives of food aid have generally not been as clearly articulated in public by Canadian policy makers. Perhaps this is because, as Keith Spicer argues, when Canadians examine their foreign aid program "the discussion of political aims becomes slightly indecent."[17] If there is less discussion of such objectives in the public records, the internal policy documents and officials interviewed in the course of this study nevertheless point to a number of political objectives that food aid can serve in the context of both bilateral and multilateral foreign policy.

In the case of bilateral foreign policy, at least six different policy objectives can be identified. First, food aid is perceived by a number of policy makers as an instrument to demonstrate good will to specific countries of foreign-policy interest to Canada. In some cases a food aid allocation may serve as a signal for establishing closer relations with a country. In other cases food aid serves a "diplomatic calling card" function, providing an "initial signal" of Canada's intentions. When Canada wanted to expand its diplomatic relations with francophone Africa as part of its strategy in dealing with the threat of Quebec separation, food aid shipments often proceeded the establishment of a more fully developed aid program. Food aid was clearly used as a "calling card" when Canada sent a food aid shipment to Zambia as a gesture of good will just prior to its participation in the Commonwealth Conference in Lusaka in 1979.[18]

Second, the provision of food aid can provide Canada with a relatively inexpensive and rapid way to demonstrate its political support for certain governments. At least five cases of such use of Canadian food aid can be cited. Officials note, for example, that the main objective of Canada's $4.5 million of food aid shipments to Portugal in 1974/75 was to show its political support for the fragile socialist government after the overthrow of the Caetano regime. Similarly officials mention Canadian food aid allocations to Jamaica, beginning in 1976, as being primarily a demonstration of Prime Minister Trudeau's desire to support the government of Prime Minister Michael Manley at a time when Jamaica was under increased pressure from both the International Monetary Fund and the United States, which had suspended its food aid shipments to Jamaica.[19] More recently shipments of large amounts of food aid to Jamaica under the Seaga government have enabled Canada to provide some visible support for President Reagan's anti-Communist Caribbean Basin Initiative. In both cases Canadian food aid has been considered to be balance-of-payments support, geared not only to easing current financial difficulties but also to providing a visible and highly symbolic gesture of political support to the recipient government. After the assassination of Anwar Sadat, in 1981/82 Canada sent food aid to Egypt, a country that traditionally had not received food aid from Canada.[20] Even more recently Monique Landry, the minister for External Relations, in announcing a grant of $5.5 million of wheat to Pakistan in January 1989, noted that it was intended as a concrete demonstration of Canada's support for the new democratic government of Benazir Bhutto.[21]

Third, food aid is seen as one method available to policy makers to promote internal political stability. Bangladesh is one of the most frequently cited examples of this. CIDA officials have admitted that the distribution system in Bangladesh has an urban bias and food tends to reach elite groups rather than the poorest sectors of the economy,[22] but they have defended this use of food aid by arguing that development can only take place in a stable political environment. To cut off food aid because it was going to urban elites might cause domestic chaos and possibly destroy whatever developmental process currently existed. Noting that food aid to Bangladesh was not really developmental, one official stated in 1979, "if it aids political stability, then we can live with it." Another CIDA document noted that "government action to ensure an adequate supply of food at reasonable prices has become a political necessity."[23] This concern with stability appears to have been an important motive behind sending $9.95 million of food aid to Tunisia and Morocco in 1984/85 after riots broke out there as a result of price increases imposed by the International Monetary Fund.[24]

Fourth, food aid is seen as a useful instrument for fostering better donor-recipient relations. The provision of food aid enables some LDC governments to demonstrate that they have friendly relations with outside powers. This makes local government leaders appear in a positive light to their own people and generates good will toward Canada. This in turn predisposes the recipient toward Canada when the aid relationship goes through more difficult periods. Through being seen as friendly and forthcoming in its food aid transfers, a more satisfactory working relationship is established. This, according to a CIDA official, will hopefully permit franker discussions of more sensitive issues at a later date. One country where CIDA officials maintain that food aid has helped to develop a smoother, friendlier relationship, at least in the past, is Tanzania.[25]

Fifth, recipients may be denied access to Canadian food aid supplies as an expression of Canadian displeasure with the recipient's policies. For example, Canadian wheat aid to Indonesia was withheld from 1964 to 1966 during its confrontation with Malaysia and was restored only when Suharto came to power in 1966. In another case, Canadian bilateral food aid to Vietnam was cut in 1979 after the invasion of Cambodia. In this instance Canada also joined the United States in requesting the WFP to halt all Canadian and American donations of food aid to Vietnam.[26] Canadian multilateral food aid to Afghanistan was halted in 1980, while bilateral food aid to Pakistan, intended in part for the use by Afghanistan refugees, was renewed.[27]

Although Canada has clearly practised a policy of food denial on a number of occasions, these measures have generally been oriented more towards punishment of a recipient for certain actions or policies than towards an effort to bargain for specific concessions. Despite these examples, the use of food aid as a direct, coercive foreign policy weapon has not been a prominent feature of Canadian food aid practice. Indeed in some cases, such as India's explosion of a nuclear device in 1974, food aid was explicitly excluded from the measures contemplated by the federal government.[28] As a general rule the more indirect, non-coercive uses of food aid, as outlined in the four previous objectives, have been a more common feature of Canadian practice.

As well as serving bilateral foreign policy objectives, Canadian food aid fulfils multilateral political objectives. Canadian policy makers, for example, express the view that the relatively large size of Canada's multilateral food contributions "has promoted a positive image of Canada in certain international fora."[29] Given the availability of Canadian surpluses, multilateral food aid is a relatively cheap and quick way to disburse large sums to international organizations. In some cases Canadian officials feel that multilateral food aid contributions may enable Canada to carry more weight in some international discussions than its overall power status would permit. As one External Affairs official put it, in some multilateral agencies "our influence has largely been bought through our food aid concessionality."[30]

An official from the International Affairs Branch of Agriculture Canada also expressed a similar opinion before the Parliamentary Committee on North-South Relations: "In these forums of the United Nations (WFP, WFC, FAO, IFAD), Canada is considered a great power, and not an intermediate power. But at the FAO, at the World Food Council, at the World Food Program, Canada is considered by the countries of the Third World as a great power, not as a super-great, but not far."[31]

Canada's relatively generous shipments of food aid, according to Canadian officials, help to generate the image abroad that Canada is relatively open and forthcoming in its relations with Third World countries.[32]

During the mid-1970s, when there was increased concern about the world food situation, CIDA produced a pamphlet entitled *Food Aid: Fact Sheet on CIDA's Involvement*. The cover and back show a small child drinking milk from a cup. Inside, the document asserts that "in times of drought, flood, famine, civil strife, and general food shortages, food aid is indispensable to the livelihood and survival of millions in developing countries."[33] This example is a good illustration of CIDA's effort to promote humanitarian objectives as being the primary aim of the Canadian food aid program. In its 1975–76 *Annual Report* CIDA notes that "the most apparent objective of food aid programs is to feed hungry people."[34] In its *Food Policy Recommendations* the Interdepartmental Working Group on Food Aid Policy proposed that "the main 'rationale' for food aid is a humanitarian one."[35] Even with cases such as wheat aid to Portugal, where famine or starvation were clearly not present, an article in the CIDA publication *Development Directions* was titled "Humanitarian Assistance: Wheat for Portugal."[36]

It is, of course, difficult to distinguish what constitute humanitarian and developmental uses of food aid. Canadian officials, however, have traditionally referred to humanitarian food aid as food destined for free distribution to and direct consumption by recipient populations. Developmental food aid is seen as the use of food to effect a transfer of resources to the recipient government and is not meant for direct, free distribution.

In 1978 the Interdepartmental Working Group on Food Aid Policy noted that there are two distinct dimensions to the humanitarian objective. One is the use of food aid to provide emergency relief in crisis situations where acute suffering and malnutrition exist. Such situations may result from natural disasters – hurricanes, floods or earthquakes – or may be caused by climatic conditions such as drought. In other cases emergency relief is necessary during civil war or other situations of political turmoil where large numbers of people have been displaced or have had their food supply disrupted. Canadian food aid shipments to countries such as Niger, Mali, Guatemala, Honduras, Nicaragua, and, more recently, Sudan, Ethiopia, and Mozambique have been sent to alleviate shortages stemming from such situations. It is difficult to estimate how much Canadian food aid has been used for these purposes since prior to 1988 CIDA did not provide a breakdown of food aid according to emergency and non-emergency uses.

However, as a whole, emergency food aid appears to have made up only a small percentage of Canada's overall food aid program. During the world food crisis in 1974 only 1.9 per cent of Canada's food aid shipments, as reported to the FAO's Committee on Surplus Disposal, was designated for free direct distribution to recipients.[37] The 1987 parliamentary report *For Whose Benefit?*, without citing its sources, estimates that less than 10 per cent of Canadian food aid goes for emergency famine relief, a figure that corresponds roughly to those cited by CIDA officials in interviews.[38] When it first published such figures in 1988, CIDA contended that 26.4 per cent of its total bilateral food aid, 21.5 per cent of the total multilateral food aid, and 60 per cent of its total NGO food aid, or 26 per cent of the total food aid budget, was destined for emergency relief purposes.[39] In 1991 CIDA reported that 37 per cent of its total 1990/91 food program was being directed toward emergencies. Whatever the exact figure, it is clear that historically a considerably smaller portion of Canadian food aid has been used for direct emergency feeding than is usually believed by the public, although this appears to have changed somewhat in recent years.[40]

The second dimension of the humanitarian objective of food aid is its use in upgrading diet and relieving chronic malnutrition. This is especially directed toward groups considered to be the most "vulnerable," such as young children, pregnant and lactating women, the aged, and the destitute.[41] In some cases feeding programs can assist in other objectives, such as providing an incentive for keeping children in school or ensuring participation in family planning. A relatively small portion of Canada's bilateral food aid is directed to meet this objective. CIDA estimates that only about 15 per cent of Canadian food aid to Bangladesh, Canada's largest recipient, is used in feeding vulnerable groups, for emergency relief, or in food-for-work projects.[42] Most of the Canadian food aid for these purposes has been directed through either the WFP or Canadian NGO's.

In addition, Canadian officials have been very cognizant of the public awareness aspects of humanitarian assistance. This is based on the belief that public support is generated both for food aid in particular, and development assistance more generally, when the public is aware of real human need for food and perceives that food aid is actually reaching and helping those in need. The Task Force on Food Aid and Renewable Resources, for example, speaks of "the public support earned for development aid in general through provision of shiploads of food obviously intended for starving countries."[43] The same document goes on to note that "food satisfies more of the 'humanitarian' instincts of the donor than other potential commodities such as newsprint or machines."[44]

Several members of the Interdepartmental Working Group on Food Aid state that this view of the public's perception of food aid was a decisive factor in giving humanitarian objectives first priority in their policy recommendations. Several of the officials interviewed suggested that the public is generally ill-informed and naive about food aid and sees food aid in straightforward terms in which helping the starving is the primary aim of CIDA's program.[45] As one CIDA official put it, "the image of a child with a bowl most readily sums up food aid for the public, although this conflicts with how the aid planner himself views it." Some officials believe that many people either "do not want to hear about [the] indirect benefits or processes involved," or would not support such indirect objectives even if they were fully understood. In this context humanitarian food aid is a much more easily identifiable symbol than more prosaic uses of food aid or other types of development assistance. As one CIDA official summed up the dilemma, "how do you visually portray a farmer who is given free food while he is being resettled on new farmland? The food may be serving a valuable purpose, but it cannot be portrayed visually at home very easily."[46]

Although the humanitarian objectives of food aid have often received considerable public attention, much of Canada's food aid, especially through bilateral channels, has been directed towards other, longer term objectives. In addition to supplementary feeding of vulnerable groups and emergency relief, a recent CIDA planning document identifies two additional food aid objectives: "increasing the quantities of food available in food deficit countries" and "accelerating the pace of development by freeing foreign exchange and generating domestic resources for investment."[47]

If food aid provides the recipient government with an additional amount of food that it would not have otherwise have been able to import, then it helps to increase the overall availability of food within the recipient country. If however, food aid is a substitute for food which would have been imported commercially, it provides a form of balance-of-payments assistance to the recipient government. Food aid thus indirectly aids development by easing the balance-of-payments constraints on the recipient government and freeing foreign exchange that can then be used for priority development projects. Such balance-of-payments support, one CIDA official contends, "multiplies the effect of Canadian aid."[48]

Officially, according to the rules of surplus disposal that Canada has agreed to under the FAO's Committee on Surplus Disposal, food aid shipments should not displace normal commercial imports. However, Canadian officials have used food aid for balance-of-payments support for years, making it clear as early as 1968 that this was one of the principal objectives of the Canadian program.[49] For some recipients this type of aid may have a significant impact. CIDA estimates that if Bangladesh did not receive food aid it would use up to 25 to 50 per cent of its annual export earnings on food imports.[50]

Many aid administrators like food aid as a form of balance-of-payments support because it can be quickly disbursed and thus is useful in meeting "crisis" objectives. This is particularly the case when economic or political difficulties require a quick response to a recipient's needs. Food aid, because of its nature, can meet these needs more rapidly than other mechanisms, such as lines of credit.[51] A CIDA *Annual Report* notes that when a drop in tea prices led to a 60 per cent decline in Sri Lanka's export earnings, Canada responded by providing "quick disbursing food and commodity aid, in an effort to ease the critical balance of payments problem."[52]

In addition to easing foreign exchange pressures, food aid can provide the recipient government with a form of general budgetary support. Food aid is used this way when a recipient government is able to generate local currency through the sale of food commodities on its domestic markets. The sale of the food aid thus represents a transfer of domestic resources from the private to the public sector. Originally a counterpart mechanism was established to ensure that funds generated this way were used for specific development projects. However, the 1970 Foreign Policy Review endorsed the notion that under "appropriate conditions" the counterpart funds "may be released to the recipient to provide support for its general development programme."[53]

In recent years the use of food aid as balance-of-payments and budgetary support has received renewed emphasis in CIDA policy documents. A 1984 planning document, for example, argues the case for increased food aid in the following terms:

The ability of many nations to import the food they need on commercial terms is substantially less than expected ten years ago ... In an adverse economic climate characterized by stagnating exports, high energy import bills, and sluggish industrialized economies, *they cannot pay for the level of imported food they need without seriously undermining their overall development efforts.* There is little prospect that this will change in this decade and beyond. Food aid can bring welcome, indeed crucial, foreign exchange relief, and it is clear that *food aid will have a major and growing role to play in the foreseeable future.*[54]

The document goes on to note that the provision of bilateral program food aid in these circumstances can simultaneously achieve a number of sub-objectives: "It can respond on a large scale to developing countries' growing need for imported food, it is not administratively intensive for either donors or recipients, and the resources it generates can be used to invest in agriculture, introduce food policy reforms, cover costs associated with targeted food programmes, or support other elements of the recipient's development efforts."[55]

Although the provision of food aid for sale to provide budgetary and balance-of-payments support has increasingly been justified in the context of structural adjustment programs and policy reform, this type of assistance has traditionally constituted the major share of Canada's bilateral food aid. A 1975–76 annual report notes that about 80 per cent of Canadian food aid, or nearly all of Canada's bilateral food aid, is sold to generate revenues for the recipient. About 85 per cent of Canada's total food aid to Bangladesh is sold through its public distribution system. More recently, CIDA estimates that about 75 per cent of its bilateral program for 1986/87 was comprised of this type of "developmental" food aid.[56]

CONCLUSIONS

As this chapter has shown, the Canadian food aid program has attempted simultaneously to meet a number of objectives which I have divided into three groups: humanitarian-developmental, economic, and foreign policy. Canadian food aid has been committed to feeding the poorest and most vulnerable populations. It has been seen as an instrument for promoting national development through such measures as balance-of-payments and general budgetary support. At the same time, it has been used to meet a variety of foreign policy objectives, including the promotion of Canada's international image, the improvement of donor-recipient relations, and the fostering of domestic political stability. Finally, it has been programmed to provide economic benefits to Canada through surplus disposal, value-added by processing, and export market development and maintenance.

The multiplicity of Canadian food aid objectives and the interests that support them create tensions within the food aid program. The food aid strategy that has emerged during the past two decades is in large part an effort to achieve a compromise between the competing demands of the needs of recipient countries and attempts to secure economic and political benefits for the donor. Subsequent chapters will illustrate how efforts to reach this compromise have shaped the strategy and structure of the Canadian food aid program. At the same time, I will show how the institutional environment itself, in which food aid policy is implemented, has played a role in shaping and constraining the objectives which are given priority.

3 Strategic Food Aid Planning: Determining Aid Levels and Delivery Channels

Owing to its complexity and the less than transparent way in which it is administered, Canadian food aid decision making does not readily lend itself to formalized description. As a result the decision-making process by which Canadian food aid is planned and allocated has received little attention in the existing literature. Because of the multi-purpose nature of food aid, and the fact that such allocations have a direct impact on Canada's relations with foreign states, a number of departments share an interest and involvement in the food aid program. The following chapters are concerned with gaining an understanding of how these various interests and objectives are introduced into the allocation process and what weights and priorities are assigned to them.

In seeking to better understand how food aid policies are actually made, it is useful to distinguish, as CIDA does, between two different phases of the policy formulation process: strategic planning and the programming/allocation process. Strategic planning, as defined by CIDA, refers to those decisions which relate to the overall level of food aid, international pledges and commitments, allocations among the various delivery channels, and the commodity composition of the program. Aid programming refers to the process by which the food aid is actually allocated and dispersed to the various recipient agencies, along with attendant issues relating to the terms and conditions of these transfers. This chapter deals with the subject of strategic planning as it relates to the determination of overall food aid levels and the allocation of food aid to different delivery channels.

Selection of food aid commodities will be dealt with in chapter 4, while issues relating to the programming of bilateral programming process will be dealt with in chapters 5 and 6.

DETERMINING OVERALL FOOD AID LEVELS

The first important step in the process of food aid is determining how much food aid Canada will give in a particular year. The overall level of the Canadian food aid program is approved on an annual basis by Parliament as a separate part of CIDA's development assistance budget, expressed in dollar terms, rather than in volume. Since 1978 CIDA has not been able to carry over the unspent portions of its budget. Thus, all food aid allocations approved in a given year must be delivered during that fiscal year or the funds will lapse. Although food aid comes under CIDA's budget, a number of additional departments are involved in making these important decisions. These departments include External Affairs, Agriculture Canada, Finance, Treasury Board, and Fisheries and Oceans.

The actual determination of Canada's overall level of food aid is a complex process which takes into account such variables as the availability of food supplies in Canada, current food prices, the commitment levels of other donors, projected food aid needs, and the overall growth level of the Canadian aid budget. In actual practice the overall size of the Canadian food aid program is largely determined by five variables, several of which are essentially outside the direct control of CIDA itself. These five variables are Canada's international commitments to the Food Aid Convention, pledges to the World Food Program, an internal policy requirement that 25 per cent of the food aid program be made up of non-cereals, the current world price of wheat, and the overall growth of the Canadian development assistance budget.

Canada's international commitments are particularly important in determining the total size of the food aid program. The first of these is Canada's commitment to the Food Aid Convention (FAC), which was first established in 1967 as part of the International Grains Agreement. Since then the FAC has been renewed in 1971, 1980, and 1986. Administered by the Food Aid Committee of the International Wheat Council, the FAC has two primary purposes: (i) to prevent concessional transfers from interfering with normal commercial transactions, and (ii) to share more equitably the burden of food aid among the member countries, including those that are primarily grain-importing countries. The latter objective has been achieved by establishing a global level of total food aid in wheat or coarse grains, agreed on by all members. The contributions of individual donors were negotiated originally as part of the General Agreement on Tariffs and Trade (GATT) Kennedy Round. Each donor's contribution was based on a complex formula which took into account its grain production and consumption levels and per capita GDP. Members who are primarily importers of grain meet their obligations by purchasing grain from other member countries, with priority given to developing members, a requirement designed to benefit Argentina.[1]

Commitments under the FAC are established in terms of a specified volume of grains to be delivered. This provides assurances that food aid levels will not drop drastically during periods of high grain prices and short supply, when many exporters may be tempted to reduce their food aid programs and LDC importers may have difficulty meeting their needs. Under the 1967 FAC, donors agreed to contribute 4,259,000 tonnes of cereals annually. Of this total, the United States had the largest share: 1.9 million tonnes (42 per cent). The next largest donor was the EEC and its member countries with 1 million tonnes (23 per cent), followed by Canada with 495,000 tonnes (11 per cent).[2]

When the FAC was renegotiated in 1980, the overall commitment was increased to 7.6 million tonnes. Although the United States increased its share to 59 per cent of the total (or 4.5 million tonnes), Canada's share fell to 8 per cent (600,000 tonnes).[3] Canada's reluctance to maintain its share of the FAC when the commitment was increased is in part a reflection of concern among Canadian officials that Canada might be forced into a position "where an international commitment has eliminated almost all choice of level for our aid program, and we could be committed to deliver food aid even when it is not appropriate."[4] However, since the 1982 FAC Canada has consistently provided significantly higher levels of cereal aid than called for in the agreement. By 1985/86 it provided 1.2 million tons of cereals, or twice its pledged level, to account for 10 per cent of the total FAC cereal aid.

The second important international commitment is Canada's pledge to the World Food Programme (WFP). Canada's contributions to the WFP are determined during the biennial pledging conferences held for WFP member states. At these conferences Canada commits itself to providing a specified level of commodity and cash donations during the following two years. Unlike the FAC, the WFP pledge is expressed in dollar terms rather than volume. In 1973/74 Canada's pledge to the WFP amounted to only $17 million a year. Following the World Food Conference in 1974 the level increased dramatically to $96.25 million a year in 1975/76. By 1986/87 this amount had nearly doubled to $165 million. As Canada's contributions to the WFP grew, the WFP portion has accounted for an increasingly important share of the Canadian food aid budget, in the range of 40 to 50 per cent of the total food aid budget in recent years.[5]

The process by which Canada's two international commitments are arrived at is clearly a reflection of the origins of Canadian food aid as a surplus disposal mechanism. The marketing of Canadian grains and the international negotiations affecting these markets have historically been the concern of the Grains Marketing Office (GMO).[6] As a result the GMO plays a leading role in coordinating Canada's participation in negotiations regarding the international grains agreements, including those related to the FAC. The decision-making process which determines the level and composition of Canada's WFP pledge revolves around the work of the Interdepartmental World Food Programme Committee (IWFPC). Since the inception of the committee Agriculture Canada has played a leading role in its work, providing both the chairman and secretary. As a result it is the minister of Agriculture who actually announces Canada's pledge at the WFP Pledging Conference. As a subsequent section of this chapter will show, this division of labour has been a source of tension between CIDA and the Department of Agriculture.

The third variable affecting the determination of Canada's food aid levels is an internal policy requirement that 25 per cent of Canadian food aid must be in the form of non-cereals. This requirement, to be discussed in more detail in chapter 4, was imposed on CIDA by cabinet in 1983 as a result of pressures from other departments, particularly Fisheries and Oceans. Since Canada is already obligated to give a designated volume of cereals under the FAC, the minimum value of the Canadian food is determined by a fluctuating variable, the world price of wheat. As a result Canada's FAC commitment, multiplied by the world price in wheat, multiplied by four-thirds (to account for the non-cereal commodities) represents the minimum size of the Canadian food aid program.[7]

In recent years, particularly as a result of the pressing food aid needs in Africa, CIDA has usually provided more food aid than the minimum levels determined by the above formula. Nevertheless there remain lingering concerns about the long-term stability of Canadian food aid shipments. Recipient governments and multilateral agencies such as the WFP have long been concerned that as long as donors continue to make their food aid commitments in dollar terms, the actual volume of food aid delivered is subject to great fluctuation. The most dramatic example of this was the world food crisis of

1974–75. When world grain prices suddenly escalated and world supplies became tight, most exporting countries gave priority to filling their commercial obligations. As a result there was a dramatic fall in global food aid levels just at the moment when greater volumes of food aid were needed by recipient governments. As Table 2 shows, Canadian food aid also declined dramatically in volume during this crucial period, even though spending on the program actually increased. It was only when the government pledged to move one million tons a year for three years at the World Food Conference in Rome that Canadian food aid quantities again began to rise.

The suggestion that donors should make their commitments in volume rather than dollar terms has not been well received in Canada, especially among officials in agencies such as the Treasury Board who are responsible for monitoring government spending. In 1978, when the Interdepartmental Working Group on Food Aid Policy considered the issue, it rejected the notion of making food aid commitments in volume terms as a general principle. Restricting food aid commitments to money values was seen as being "consistent with CIDA's planning process and in accordance with Canadian policy in recent years to limit commitments which entail a maintenance of value obligation."[8] The report did go on to note that in some cases, such as the WFP which plans its projects on a volume basis, volume commitments of food aid would be useful. Such cases, it recommended, should be considered on a case-by-case basis. The Canadian government has never moved toward a broader use of volume commitments. In 1987 the WFP tried to force the hand of donor countries by presenting a pledging target in both volume terms and dollar value. However, Canada joined other donors in refusing to make its commitment in volume terms. As a result the WFP reverted to its traditional policy of asking donors to make pledges in dollar values.

THE CHOICE OF ALTERNATIVE DELIVERY CHANNELS

The selection of the proper delivery system for channeling aid funds to developing countries has been debated at some length in the literature on foreign aid.[9] Each type of delivery system is designed to accomplish a different sent of objectives, involves different techniques of supervision and control, and places a different set of demands on the administrative and analytical resources of the donor agency. The selection of a particular combination of delivery channels is, in part, a reflection of the priority which policy makers attach to certain objectives. But, as I will show, this decision is also at times an attempt to cope with the complex interplay of organizational and bureaucratic constraints within which an aid agency operates.

In the case of food aid the selection of which delivery mechanism to use is particularly complex. Food aid can be delivered through three different "channels" or organizational vehicles: bilateral or government-to-government arrangements, multilateral institutions, or non-government organizations. In addition the food aid may be transferred through two different forms or "mechanisms": program and project food aid. Program food aid consists of bulk shipments of foodstuffs designed primarily as a form of fast-disbursing financial support to recipients. Project food aid generally involves the use of foodstuffs as an input into specific projects, particularly where the desire is to target the benefits to very specific population groups.

In both policy and practice Canadian officials have preferred to specialize by providing all of Canada's program food aid through bilateral channels, while using multilateral channels to deliver project food aid. In addition, a relatively modest NGO food aid program has been undertaken as a more recent alternative.

BILATERAL PROGRAM FOOD AID

With rare exceptions, Canadian bilateral food has been disbursed in program form. These transactions consist of bulk shipments of food aid commodities, in relatively significant volumes, which are made directly to the recipient government. Once the Canadian food aid shipments arrive at the designated port of entry, the commodities are turned over to the recipient government, which assumes full responsibility for their disposition. From this point on Canada exercises no direct control over the ultimate uses of the commodities. The Canadian foodstuffs may in fact be mixed with the commodities of other donors and no longer be identified as uniquely "Canadian."[10]

Bilateral program food aid has attempted to address broad objectives, such a balance-of-payments support. It is expected that by relieving the recipient of the need to import a part of its food commercially, valuable foreign exchange will be freed for other uses. Another objective has been to use bilateral program food aid as a form of budgetary support. In this case the recipient government sells the food aid commodities in order to raise revenues. Thus, through the sale of the food aid, domestic resources are transferred from private to government sectors.

Because it addresses more general developmental objectives, to a large extent program food aid typifies the "trickle-down" theory of aid-giving. The donor expects that its contribution will in fact free resources that will enable the recipient to improve certain structural, economic, and social problems. How this is to be achieved, and what segments of the economy and population are to benefit from the resource transfer, are largely left to the discretion of the recipient government.

In the majority of cases Canadian food aid commodities are sold domestically by the recipient government either on the open market at prevailing market prices or through government-operated public distribution systems at fixed prices which are usually below market prices. During the first thirty years of the program fully 75 per cent of Canada's total bilateral food aid was channelled to only four countries: India, Bangladesh, Pakistan, and Sri Lanka. Each of these countries operates a public distribution system (PDS) which supplies food commodities to various target groups within the recipient population at specially subsidised prices which are often below those prevailing in the market place. Access to the PDS is usually controlled through ration cards or vouchers. This enables the government to give priority access to cheap food supplies to civil servants, military personnel, and other political sensitive groups. Giving subsidized food to government employees is seen as a means of limiting demands for increased wages or other benefits. Governments typically supply the PDS by means of domestic procurement and foreign imports, either on a commercial or concessional basis. By providing food aid for this purpose the donor assists the recipient in meeting its domestic objectives while alleviating the foreign exchange cost of additional commercial food imports. Each of the Asian recipients mentioned above has relied on food aid to supply its system, although in significantly different degrees. For example, food aid has supplied India and Sri Lanka with 12 per cent and 15 per cent respectively of their distribution system needs. In contrast, food aid has been the source of 30 per cent of supplies in Pakistan and 80 to 90 per cent in Bangladesh.[11]

Until the establishment of the WFP in 1961, the entire Canadian food aid package was composed of bilateral program aid. During the sixties, bilateral program food aid still accounted for 90 per cent or more of the disbursements each year. Although the share of bilateral program food aid decreased somewhat between 1968 and 1974, it still accounted for an average of 83.7 per cent of food aid transfers during this period.

However, when CIDA began to implement the pledge made in Rome to deliver one million tons of grains per year for three years, the relative importance of the bilateral program component began to diminish. This trend continued until 1980/81, when bilateral food aid constituted only 38.9 per cent of the total program, a significant reversal of its historically dominant role. However, this appears to have been less the result of an explicit policy decision to downgrade the importance of bilateral program food aid than a pragmatic, operational decision resulting from the austerity cuts in the CIDA budget in 1979 and 1980, when CIDA was obliged to reduce its planned expenditures by $133 million. In making these cuts Michel Dupuy, the president of CIDA, pointed out that the principal aim was to "minimize the disruptions domestically and internationally."[12] As a result, he noted that it would be necessary to make reductions only "where no formal commitment existed, particularly legally binding commitments."[13] As a result bilateral food aid bore the brunt of the cuts in planned spending for that year since Canada's bilateral agreements had traditionally been committed only on a year-to-year basis, while multilateral food aid was already committed as a part of Canada's biennial WFP pledge and therefore could not so easily be slashed. Since then the bilateral share of the program has been restored to more or less equal balance, accounting for just over half the total allocations in recent years (see Table 8).

In examining the evolution of the Canadian food aid program, several factors can be cited to account for the traditional dominance of bilateral program food aid. These factors are derived largely from the fact that the food aid is both bilateral and program in nature. First, bilateral program food aid is more effective in achieving both domestic political objectives and certain specific foreign policy objectives than indirect multilateral food aid. As the bilateral aid involves direct country-to-country interaction, such aid "provides opportunities for many contacts with government and people ... [which] can be most useful to present Canadian viewpoints ... [and] reinforce political relations and generate economy opportunities."[14]

The fact that Canada's bilateral food aid is in program form further facilitates this role. As it is easily and quickly disbursed, it provides policy makers with a flexible mechanism for achieving a number of bilateral objectives: (i) it provides an "opener" for better relations, (ii) it expresses diplomatic support, (iii) it gives support in balance-of-payments crises, and (iv) it improves the donor-recipient relationship. None of these objectives could be achieved as effectively through project or multilateral aid. Due to its flexibility in meeting such a range of objectives, there are frequent pressures from CIDA and External Affairs officials involved with certain countries to initiate certain bilateral programs or maintain others in order not to disrupt a bilateral relationship.

At the same time, bilateral food aid can provide some useful domestic political benefits to CIDA. As the Task Force on Food Aid and Renewable Resources noted, a primary reason for maintaining a substantial bilateral food aid program is, "the high visibility of shiploads of food destined for needy countries, and the public support this generates."[15] No other form of Canadian aid possesses such emotional appeal and is able to elict such a ready response from Canadians.

Second, bilateral program food aid plays a significant role in the achievement of the numerous economic objectives inherent in the program. As it involves direct government-to-government transactions, bilateral food aid is more useful in the development and maintenance of specific markets than more indirect forms of aid. The fact that Canada's bilateral food aid is generally in program form is of particular significance here. Project aid demands a more nutritionally diversified food basket, which requires a more diverse range of products in smaller quantities. In contrast program food aid relies on large shipments of bulk commodities. This permits the shipment of more substantial quantities of surplus commodities such as grains and canola oil than project aid would permit. Canada probably would not be able to fulfill its FAC obligations in cereal aid without large shipments of bulk program food aid. In other cases products such as canola oil have been distributed almost entirely as bilateral program aid since the demand for oil through multilateral channels is significantly lower. Developing new markets and gaining value-added benefits from the disbursement of canola oil is largely dependent on its provision as bilateral program aid.

Third, bilateral program food aid provides CIDA officials with certain administrative advantages. To understand this point more clearly it is necessary to review briefly the difference between project and program food aid from an aid management point of view. Program food aid is the least taxing in administrative terms since it involves the disbursement of only a relatively small number of large bulk shipments. Once the shipments arrive at the point of entry, all responsibility is transferred to the recipient government. Planning and negotiations have therefore traditionally revolved around relatively few issues, such as the nature and volume of the shipment, which are the general conditions under which an agreement is signed. Bulk shipments of program food aid are therefore one of the most rapidly disbursed forms of aid, requiring minimal administrative input and time. Program food aid is thus characterized by a high volume-dispersal rate in relation to administrative input.[16]

This factor is important for Canadian policy makers in deciding which aid mechanism to select. For example, in examining the alternatives open to CIDA the Task Force on Food Aid and Renewable

Resources noted that the US government had carried out a successful project food aid program on the bilateral level. However, the report was also careful to point out that the success of this kind of programming was dependent on an extensive network of over 250 Food-For-Peace officers stationed within the recipient countries. These officials devoted themselves full-time to monitoring American-sponsored food aid projects. The task force concluded that it "would be too costly [for CIDA] in terms of administrative skills, and would not be undertaken at this time as a component of the bilateral program."[17]

Due to its "liquid" nature, program food aid offers aid planners certain advantages in terms of meeting CIDA's administrative requirements. The Task Force on Food Aid and Renewable Resources pointed out that program food aid continued to play a significant part in CIDA's programming because, in part, in this form "large amounts of money can be quickly spent on food aid."[18] As a result program food aid has been important in achieving many of CIDA's organizational objectives, such as relieving disbursement pressures, protecting slower moving projects, and overcoming tying constraints, a role that could not have been as easily played by multilateral project food aid. This will be explored further in chapter 5.

MULTILATERAL PROJECT FOOD AID

Some of Canada's bilateral food aid has been provided in project form, such as the CIDA oilseeds project in India. In general, however, bilateral project aid has constituted only a very small portion of the total bilateral program. Instead most of Canada's project food aid has been provided through multilateral agencies, and more than 95 per cent of it has been dispersed through the World Food Program.

In the case of WFP aid, the recipient government is responsible for the identification, planning, and implementation of projects. The WFP responds to requests for food, coordinates donor contributions, and assures delivery of foodstuffs from donor to recipients. Canada, like other donors, makes a pledge of both cash and commodities to the WFP, on which the secretariat draws to fill the needs of its projects. As a member of the WFP's Committee on Food Aid Policies and Programmes (CFA), Canada participates in discussions relating to the management of the WFP but is not involved in the actual approval and administration of specific food aid projects.

Canada's participation in the WFP is planned through the Interdepartmental World Food Program Committee (IWFPC), a committee composed of representatives from Agriculture Canada, CIDA, External Affairs, Finance, and Fisheries and Oceans, with Agriculture

Canada playing the lead role in the work of the committee. The work of the IWFPC covers three important areas. First, the IWFPC is responsible for proposing both the cash and commodity level of Canada's pledge for the forthcoming biennium. In determining the level of the pledge, a number of factors are taken into account, including (i) the present size and anticipated growth of the total food aid vote; (ii) the requirements of other Canadian food aid programs, especially the bilateral program; (iii) the WFP biennial pledging target recommended by the Committee on Food Aid Policies for member donors; (iv) the absorptive capacity of the WFP and perceived evaluation of its aims and priorities; and (v) the views of various departments of the Canadian government. Once the level of the pledge is determined by the IWFPC, a submission is prepared for Treasury Board approval. The minister of Agriculture then announces the pledge on Canada's behalf at the WFP Pledging Conference. The pledge refers only to a level of commitment in cash and commodities.

Second, the IWFPC is responsible for determining the commodity composition of the Canadian pledge. Here Agriculture Canada takes the lead role in proposing a specific food aid basket for each fiscal year. This decision takes a number of factors into account, including (i) the availability and prices of commodities; (ii) the WFP's commodity needs as requested by the WFP secretariat; (iii) experience with previous years' baskets, especially with regard to development utility and taste acceptability; and (iv) domestic producer interests, especially when certain commodities are in surplus.

The proposed commodities are then discussed by the IWFPC. When agreement on the precise makeup of the food aid basket is reached, the chairman of the committee reports this to the executive director of the WFP. It is generally understood that some changes will be made by Canada to the commodity basket as a result of price changes, commodity shortages, shipping difficulties, or other problems. During the course of the year, when the WFP needs specific commodities, it notifies Agriculture Canada that it intends to draw upon the pledge. Agriculture Canada is then responsible for ensuring that the commodity is available in Canada at acceptable prices, that its purchase will not disrupt Canadian domestic markets, and that the requested time of arrival of the shipment is possible. CIDA, in cooperation where necessary with the Department of Supply and Services, is then responsible for arranging for the procurement and shipment of the commodities.

Third, the IWFPC is responsible for formulating Canada's position on WFP policies and food aid issues in general, as they are discussed at the governing council of the WFP. Although this body deals in large part with the operational policies of the WFP, it has increasingly become a forum for international consultation and action on common food aid problems. After the World Food Conference in 1974, the Intergovernmental Committee of the WFP changed its name to the Committee on Food Aid Policies and Programmes (CFA), to reflect its intention to deal with a broader range of policy issues. Since then, the CFA has emerged as the principal international forum for discussion of general food aid issues by donor and recipient nations.[19]

The fact that food aid is used as a direct input into development projects, and can be more directly targeted at specific population groups, has made the option of project food an attractive alternative, especially among Canadian parliamentarians. In 1980 the Parliamentary Task Force on North-South Relations argued that project food aid, particularly as channeled through multilateral agencies, offered more beneficial developmental results than did bilateral program food aid. As a result the task force recommended "that the Government make increasing use of the multilateral food aid channels and that bilateral food aid be as closely coordinated as possible with those channels."[20] Similarly, the parliamentary committee which reviewed Canadian aid policy in 1987 was critical of bilateral program food aid, noting that "large food aid allocations should not be simply a quick and administratively convenient way of meeting the pressure to disburse lapsing tied aid funds."[21] Instead the committee suggested that "properly designed food aid projects can bring important benefits to developing countries."[22]

Not all of the arguments for multilateral project aid are entirely altruistic in nature. Like bilateral program aid, multilateral food aid can provide a number of political and economic benefits to Canada as a donor, although the benefits provided are slightly different in nature. For example, multilateral aid assists in the attainment of foreign policy objectives of a more general nature. As a major food-exporting nation, certain things are expected of Canada. By providing a significant share of the WFP food aid, Canada is able to play a prominent role in a major international food agency.

In addition the WFP enables the Canadian aid program to increase its geographical spread by indirectly allowing "CIDA to launch a program in priority countries where Canada has not previously had a bilateral food aid program."[23] As an illustration of this point, CIDA was able to provide food aid to fifty-five countries through the WFP in 1979/80, while providing food aid bilaterally to only twelve countries in the same year. Some of the countries receiving Canadian WFP aid, such as Bhutan, Cyprus, Fiji, Western Samoa, Vietnam, the two Yemens, and Panama, were not recipients of any kind of bilateral aid from Canada.[24] The WFP has also enabled CIDA to provide food aid to countries such as Vietnam or Cuba where it would have been impossible to provide it bilaterally for foreign policy reasons.

In terms of economic benefits, multilateral project aid clearly plays as significant a role as bilateral program aid. Unlike other forms of multilateral aid, where Canadian suppliers must compete for contracts with international suppliers, WFP aid is almost 100 per cent tied to the purchase of Canadian products. Shipments to the WFP are smaller and more numerous than bilateral shipments and need a greater mixture of commodities, especially processed commodities which contain a higher proportional of supplementary nutritional components. The WFP has thus served as an important alternative mechanism for channelling commodities that Canada has in exportable surplus quantities. For example, when Canada wanted to dispose of canned beef and dried eggs in 1975, all of it was directed through the WFP. The WFP also absorbs a larger proportion of certain processed Canadian products than do bilateral channels. For example, in some years up to 78 per cent of wheat flour, 100 per cent of powdered eggs, 74 per cent of skim milk powder, and 69 per cent of fish were channelled through the WFP.[25] In 1983/84 CIDA was able to place fish products with only three bilateral recipients while the WFP sent Canadian fish products to twenty-two countries.[26] The WFP has thus, at times, provided Canadian policy makers with a useful additional mechanism for achieving two principal economic objectives (surplus disposal and value-added benefits from the processing of food used for aid) for some commodities that might not have been as easily accommodated in the bilateral program.

Although project aid appears to provide benefits in terms of targetting and control of end uses, observers are generally agreed that, in administrative terms, project food aid places greater demands on the analytical resources of the donor agency. Suitable projects must be identified and viable proposals formulated. Appropriate food aid baskets for each project must be selected. The successful completion of project food aid entails a substantial administrative input to monitor and ensure that stated targets are met. As a consequence project food aid is disbursed at a much slower rate, in considerably smaller volumes, and with lower absorptive capacity than in the program approach and requires a much higher ratio of administrative input to volume of disposal.[27]

These characteristics make the WFP an attractive channel for this type of assistance. The WFP has specialized in the use of project food aid and has established a relatively successful track record. The donor is thus assured that a large degree of control is established over the end-uses of its food aid. At the same time the multilateral channel acts as a "buffer" in the donor-recipient relationship, reducing the appearance of direct donor interference in the affairs of the recipient as recipient use of aid is controlled by regulations jointly developed by donors and recipient through the WFP's governing council.

The WFP also takes responsibility for administration of the program, providing donor governments with significant savings in administrative resources. For example, during recent years Canada has supplied an annual average of $162 million in bilateral food aid and $132 million in multilateral food aid. CIDA has estimated that planning and implementation of the bilateral share used approximately 16–18 person/years in a normal year while the multilateral share required only 4 CIDA person/years. In contrast, it is estimated that the WFP devoted about 150 person/years per year to the administration of Canada's contributions.[28]

Despite the apparent attractiveness of multilateral project food aid, CIDA officials have been reluctant to see this channel continue to expand. In fact a recent CIDA policy statement notes that any further expansion of the food aid program will probably be achieved through bilateral program aid.[29] There are several reasons for CIDA's rejection of continued expansion of multilateral project aid as the major direction for the future.

First, it believes that recipient governments are reaching their absorptive limit for project food aid. This type of aid involves greater administrative inputs from the recipient as well as from the donor and there is growing concern that many recipients, particularly in Africa, do not have the managerial and financial resources available to make effective use of project food aid in the future. Studies have already shown that, although food aid needs have grown most rapidly in Africa, the region's share of global project food aid has actually dropped. Recent projections indicate that this trend will probably continue.[30]

As a result, CIDA officials have begun to play down the benefits of project food aid, despite its acknowledged superiority in targeting the poorest population groups. Thus a recent CIDA document attacks what it sees as the myth "that only project food aid is 'good' food aid, defensible in both humanitarian and developmental terms ... [while] programme food aid is somewhat second-rate development assistance, prompted as much by donor interests as recipient needs."[31] Instead, the document notes, given current economic circumstances, project food aid has a number of disadvantages. In particular, it points out that project food aid (i) places a high demand on technical and managerial skills that are often in short supply because of its

administrative intensiveness; (ii) requires additional inputs of services and equipment, the funding for which is not readily available;
and (iii) involves recurring costs that recipient governments have
difficulty funding.[32]

Second, CIDA has raised questions about the ability of the WFP to
effectively absorb larger amounts of food aid. Since its founding in
1963 the WFP has experienced tremendous growth. By July 1985 it
had funded 1,326 projects with a value of $7.1 billion in 120 countries.
As a source for international development funding, it is now second
only to the World Bank. Constitutionally, the WFP was established as
a joint organ of the FAO and the United Nations.[33] However, the FAO-
WFP relationship has become increasingly contentious as WFP administrators and many donor officials feel that the director-general of the
FAO has attempted to exercise too much control over the operations
of the WFP. Canada's position on this issue has followed a two-
pronged approach. On the one hand the Canadian government has
participated in the Chamberely Group, a coalition of Western donors
including the United States and Great Britain, who have pressed for
reforms within the FAO. When in 1987 Edouard Saouma chose to
run for an unprecedented third six-year term as FAO director-general,
Canada actively campaigned in support of a revival candidate from
Africa. Although Saouma was ultimately successful in his bid for re-
election, Canada's opposition evoked bitter charges from FAO officials
that the Canadian government was conducting a smear campaign
against Saouma. While pressing for changes in the FAO management,
Canada worked with other donors is support of greater WFP
autonomy. In particular, these donors supported the WFP's contention
that it needed greater independence from the FAO in approval for
emergency aid, personnel policies, accounting, contracting, and other
related issues. As a result Canada delayed announcing its biennial
pledge in 1986 in order to have some assurances that the recommendations of a joint FAO/UN Task Force on reform of the WFP were
actually being implemented.[34] In the period leading up to the re-
election of Saouma, the director-general adopted a conciliatory
approach, agreeing to the delegation of authority to the WFP in many
areas dealing with administration and budgeting. However, by the
June 1989 meeting of the WFP's governing council, after Saouma's
successful re-election, tensions between the two agencies had again
escalated as Saouma contended that the delegation of authority to
the WFP had been only temporary. [35]

While supporting reforms in the WFP designed to increase the
agency's administrative efficiency, Canadian officials have opposed
proposals that would expand the mandate of the WFP beyond the

provision of project food aid. One such issue relates to the subject of non-food items. At present, WFP regulations require that it provide only food commodities, either through direct feeding programs or through food-for-work programs, using commodities pledged by donor. WFP officials and many Third World delegations have argued that a major constraint on the implementation of food aid projects is the cost of other important inputs into successful food aid projects, such as tools, seeds, storage and processing facilities, local management personnel, and administrative know-how. Thus they have proposed that the WFP resource base should be expanded to include the collection of non-food items in addition to food commodities. Canada has joined other donors, such as the United States, in arguing against this proposal, contending that such a change would effectively transform the WFP from a food aid facility to a general development assistance organization.[36] More recently the WFP secretariat has raised the issue of constraints on the growth of the WFP in the context of a call for greater authority to "monetize" its food aid: that is, to sell food aid commodities which have been donated to it within recipient countries and use the resulting revenues to support non-food related costs of development projects. From the WFP's standpoint this would reduce the constraints on its absorptive capacity and expand its role, especially in areas where food aid is being linked to structural adjustment programs. Again, Canada has joined the United States in opposing such a move, arguing that it would alter the original mandate of the WFP and would be an indirect means of shifting towards program food aid, in direct competition with bilateral food aid donors.[37]

Third, questions have arisen concerning the structure of the decision-making process itself. The establishment of the IWFPC, with Agriculture Canada playing the leading role, clearly reflected the surplus origins of the food aid program, when commercial concerns were primordial. However, as the share of the WFP allocations in Canada's food aid program increased, this division of responsibility caused frustration within CIDA as some officials questioned whether the agency's development objectives were being adequately represented. In 1975 the CIDA Task Force on Food Aid and Renewable Resources expressed concern that, although CIDA had financial responsibility for the WFP contributions, it played only a "participatory" role in the decision-making process determining Canadian inputs. In particular the task force argued that Agriculture Canada, in its leading role as chairman of the IWFPC, used its position to promote its departmental viewpoint despite opposition from CIDA. As the report summed up the problem: "Although the delegate is accompanied by representatives from other departments, including CIDA, it is solely his prerogative to intervene in the discussion. In fast-paced policy discussion, the delegate is often unable (and sometimes unwilling) to consult with his colleagues on every issue. As a result, the biases of the delegate's department have a tendency to become a Canadian bias in the eyes of the WFP."[38]

Because of this perceived bias, the CIDA task force concluded that "this (interdepartmental) structure is no longer considered adequate" in an era when"the developmental aspects of WFP operations have become paramount."[39] However, the suggestion that Agriculture Canada relinquish its leading role in the IWFPC was viewed by Department of Agriculture officials as a threat to the interests of their department and was strongly opposed. After the Conservative government of Brian Mulroney came to power in 1984, CIDA put forward a proposal that it take the leading role in the IWFPC, only to be rebuffed again by the new minister for Agriculture. As a result the formal structure for deciding Canadian policy on the WFP remains largely unchanged from what it was over two decades ago when the WFP was first established. CIDA has attempted to deal with this by having the vice-president of the multilateral branch take part in the delegation to the CFA meetings. As the top-ranking Canadian official at the meetings, this has de facto placed the CIDA official as the leading spokesperson for Canada at those meetings.

Finally, since Canadian food aid is aimed at achieving a number of foreign policy and economic objectives, there is a clear limit to the extent to which officials will surrender decision-making control over a major share of its aid program. This concern was articulated by CIDA President Margaret Catley-Carlson when she was asked about her views on sending all of Canadian food aid through multilateral channels: "The main difficulty here would really be that we would be missing a food aid bilateral relationship with some countries which basically says that we would be giving up all rights to choose which country ought to be receiving food aid. We would be putting all of our food aid into a process in which we exercise simply a voting right like the others."[40]

NON-GOVERNMENTAL FOOD AID

Although the vast majority of Canadian food aid has been shipped through either bilateral or multilateral channels, a third alternative delivery channel does exist, the use of non-government organizations (NGO's). In contrast to American food aid, where as much as 30 per cent of the total PL 480 budget is channelled through voluntary agencies, Canadian officials have made relatively small use of this alternative. Canada's NGO program began only in 1976 and in its biggest year to date accounted for only 9.9 per cent of the total food aid budget (see Table 8).

Government-assisted NGO food aid has taken two basic forms. One is NGO-skim milk powder (SMP), where surplus milk powder is supplied at no cost to Canadian volunteer agencies. To date seventeen Canadian NGO's have received the milk powder. However, the program has remained very small, averaging about $5–6 million per year. Under the conditions of the program NGO's are required to cover the shipping costs of the aid and milk powder must be used for human consumption within the developing country. Within the framework of these two conditions NGO's are left with very broad latitude as to how they will use the SMP, which is generally used in "on-going" feeding programs (e.g., schools, clinics, day-care centres) or short-term programs (e.g., emergency aid to combat malnutrition or to assist in rehabilitation).[41] In the NGO-SMP program the NGO's play the dominant role in determining needs, targeting recipients, administering the distribution, and monitoring control systems.

The other NGO program is the Canadian Foodgrains Bank (CFB). Initially started in 1976 under the auspices of the Mennonite Central Committee (MCC), the program was expanded in 1983 to include six other Christian development agencies. The CFB gathers contributions from members, largely farmers who tend to contribute food commodities rather than cash. At first the emphasis was on gathering wheat from prairie farmers, but in the early 1980s this was expanded to include contributions of corn from eastern farmers for use in the Horn of Africa. CIDA has funded the value of CFB fund raising on a 3:1 basis up to a maximum of $16 million.

The programming of food aid through NGOs is primarily the responsibility of the special programs branch of CIDA. In this case the identification and formulation of proposals, distribution, and monitoring of projects are the responsibility of the NGO's themselves, with CIDA playing a primarily reactive role. In the case of the SMP program, CIDA pays for the SMP while the NGO arranges and pays for the transportation and distribution costs. CIDA's SMP-NGO allocations are approved on an institutional basis rather than for specific projects.

In selecting which NGO's should receive aid, a number of criteria are taken into account: (i) the recipient country where the aid is to be used must be a developing country, (ii) the priorities, and objectives of the NGO must be compatible with CIDA's policy priorities, and (iii) the programs of the NGO must be seen by CIDA as being basically sound. For example, the projects must be conducive to development, the criteria for selecting them must be clearly stated and acceptable, and the project must be evaluated.

In the case of the Canadian Foodgrains Bank (CFB), CIDA's role again lies primarily in deciding whether or not it will provide institutional support to the program. The CFB acts as an implementing agency for the various church agencies that make up its membership. These member agencies are in turn responsible for programming the resources available to them.

NGO's have generally been viewed by CIDA officials and others as a relatively successful instrument for channelling food aid. In 1975 CIDA's Task Force on Food Aid and Renewable Resources identified several advantages in NGO food aid programs. First, NGO food aid programs appeared to be able to reach those groups who needed the food the most and were not able to procure it at local markets. Consequently the report found that NGO food aid programs, perhaps in part because they are usually small, tended to cause minimum distortion to local food markets. Second, it found that NGO programs were generally well supervised and therefore suffered less leakage to non-targetted groups. Third, the task force pointed out that NGO food programs were often used to encourage local food production, thereby aiding long-term development and avoiding serious distortions in local resource allocations. These conclusions were supported in an evaluative study carried out for CIDA by the North-South Institute. Although more cautious in its findings, the North-South Institute came to the general conclusion that "it is surprising that the NGO/CIDA skim milk powder program has remained so free of the major pitfalls which can arise in food aid programs."[42] In particular it noted that NGO's and their cooperating agencies were able to provide a degree of follow-up and supervision that could not be matched by government bilateral or multilateral programs.

It is perhaps this latter characteristic that has made NGO's an attractive alternative in recent years, particularly in the context of the Ethiopian famine. The famine in Ethiopia has presented a difficult challenge to donors. In such situations success is determined largely by the punctuality of food aid arrival and the ability of the distributors to reach those most in need. However, in the case of the Ethiopian famine, the ability of donors to reach the neediest groups in the population has been complicated by the fighting between the Ethiopian government and insurgency movements in the provinces of Eritrea and Tigre, two of the areas most seriously affected by the drought. Frequent charges have been made that the Ethiopian Relief and Rehabilitation Commission, a government agency which controls the distribution of food aid, has prevented aid from reaching many of those in these northern provinces, resulting in a large movement of refugees into Sudan. As a result CIDA chose to deliver a larger proportion of its food aid to Ethiopia through NGO's and international agencies. Some of these NGOS operated programs aimed at Eritrean and Tigrean populations who were excluded from the normal government distribution programs. In 1985/86 54 per cent of Canadian food aid to Ethiopia was channelled through NGOs, with only 29 per cent being provided directly government to government.[43]

The use of such alternative channels offers the donor several advantages. In some famine situations CIDA officials may lack familiarity and experience with handling food aid, or may not have the time and manpower necessary for careful planning. By relying on NGOs CIDA's field staff is relieved of the more onerous tasks of assessment and overseeing the implementation and distribution of food aid shipments. In circumstances where CIDA lacks confidence in the overall priorities of the recipient government, it can use these alternative channels to ensure that the food is reaching the specific population groups in need.

Despite the relatively good record of NGOs and the obvious advantages that they provide, NGO food aid is likely to remain a relatively small portion of the total food aid budget. Several factors limit the role that this channel plays in the Canadian program. First, compared to their American counterparts, Canadian NGOs operate on a significantly smaller scale. They therefore have a much smaller capacity to distribute large amounts of food aid. Second, the majority of these groups have placed their planning priority on long-term development projects which do not require food commodities as an input rather than on emergency relief programs. Because of this Canadian NGO's have not developed the sophisticated distribution networks that American agencies have. Third, a number of NGOS are generally distrustful of food aid and are concerned about the potentially negative impact that it could have on development. As an umbrella organization for Canadian volunteer agencies, the Canadian Council on International Cooperation has been particularly vocal in its criticism of food aid and has called for its abolition except in cases of emergency.[44] Even though the CFB has generally been seen as a success story, there has been a long history of tension between the bank and its founding agency, the MCC over precisely this issue. Many of MCC's overseas personnel felt that an expanding food-relief program threatened the agency's traditional emphasis on longer-term food production and nutritional programs. Many were also concerned that the more aggressive promotional activities of the CFB, focusing as it does on the more dramatic and tangible famine relief efforts, might undermine constituency support for longer-term, less-glamorous development programs. One MCC official even noted that the CFB was "too preoccupied with the resource and not enough with the need, too supply driven, and too promotion focused."[45] Many of these concerns were addressed in 1985 when a review of the CFB recommended that food grains and cash received by the CFB should be dispensed by the member agencies themselves and not directly by the CFB. Thus the CFB was to act primarily as a "bank," while discretion over the use of resources remained in the hands of the partner agencies.[46]

Some NGOs have complained about CIDA's policy restrictions, which require that they use Canadian food commodities rather than purchasing food grown by local producers in the country where they are working. For example, it was claimed by one NGO that in 1978 it could have purchased three bushels of available grain in Sudan for shipment to Eritrea for the cost of purchasing and shipping one bushel of North American grain.[47] At the same time, NGOs are also wary of becoming too heavily dependent on CIDA funding for fear that their own priorities may be subtly replaced by those of CIDA.[48] Although Canadian NGOs appear to handle food aid in a responsible and developmentally positive manner, it is unlikely that this particular channel for Canadian food aid will ever make up a significant portion of the total food aid program.

THE MIX OF ALTERNATIVE FOOD AID CHANNELS

It has been noted previously that the various channels available for distributing Canadian food aid facilitate the achievement of differing sets of objectives. It is perhaps for this reason that Canadian policy on the proper balance between bilateral and multilateral food aid has been slow to develop. In 1975, when the Task Force on Food Aid and Renewable Resources considered the question of program shares, it came to the vague conclusion that "a growing share" of Canada's food aid should be delivered through the WFP.[49] Later that same year CIDA's *Strategy 1975–1980* was equally nebulous about the exact proportion of program shares. Noting that the interests of both Canada and the recipient can be served by a variety of channels, *Strategy* did not recommend a fixed proportion of funds for each channel. Instead it concluded that this should be determined annually by cabinet. However, *Strategy* did conclude that "an increasing portion" of Canada's food aid would be disbursed through multilateral channels, an affirmation of Allan MacEachen's pledge at the World Food Conference in Rome.[50] When the Interdepartmental Working Group on Food Aid Policy prepared its 1974 recommendations, no decision was made concerning the future role of program shares. However, it was assumed that, as food aid objectives changed and evaluations of various programs were carried out, adjustments would be made in the balance of program shares.

Despite such vague policy statements on program shares, the balance between aid channels underwent significant change in the late 1970s. In 1975–76, as Canada moved toward fulfilling its Rome pledge, multilateral food aid increased from 9.2 to 47.4 per cent of the food aid program in one year. Although this figure decreased somewhat during the next two years, it grew to 50.4 per cent in 1978–79 and by 1980–81 it represented fully 60.2 per cent of the food aid program.

In light of the government's vague policy about program shares, it is interesting to ask whether replacement of the bilateral channel by the multilateral channel was the result of a conscious policy commitment. Evidence suggests that this development was more directly related to the reduction of overall Canadian aid expenditures which occurred at the end of the seventies. In 1979–80, for example, the Canadian government reduced planned development assistance expenditures by $133 million. Since much of Canadian ODA is now planned within a four-to five-year planning cycle, such reductions are not easily made. Thus Michel Dupuy, past president of CIDA explained that the "implementation of a decision to reduce planned ODA expenditures within a short period of time does create operational difficulties."[51]

In making these cuts, Dupuy pointed out that the principal aim was to "minimize disruptions domestically and internationally."[52] In particular, he noted that reductions would have an impact only "where no formal commitment existed, particularly legally binding commitments."[53] In implementing these guidelines, food aid was significantly affected. Since multilateral food aid is committed on a two-year basis, it cannot easily be reduced without breaking commitments. The bilateral food aid program was therefore an easy target for reductions. As Dupuy put it, since the guideline was to safeguard existing commitments, "our reductions bore heavily on liquid commitments and food aid was one of them"[54] (see Table 13). Thus the significant shift in 1980/81 to a multilateral share of nearly 60 per cent of the food aid budget was determined more on the basis of the operational needs to carry out restraints in aid spending that were imposed on CIDA than on a clear policy commitment to a predominantly multilateral program.

Table 13
Canadian aid disbursements, 1977/78, 1980/81 (in millions of Canadian dollars)

	1977/78	1980/81	Change in $	Change in percentage
Total ODA	1,051.1	1,231.0	+180	+17.1%
Total food aid	232.0	182.0	−50	−21.5%
Bilateral food aid	140.1	75.0	−65.1	−46.5%
Multilateral food aid	91.9	107.0	+15.1	+16.4%

Source: CIDA, Annual Report, various years.

The quickly disbursing and "liquid" nature of program food aid took on renewed appeal for Canadian policy makers after this period as increased amounts of Canada's bilateral food aid were channelled to Africa. Historically, Asian countries have dominated Canada's bilateral program. Even during the Sahelian famine of the seventies, Africa never accounted for more than 19 per cent of total bilateral food aid. However, the share of bilateral food aid directed to Africa increased from 17.4 per cent in 1980/81 to 44.4 per cent in 1984/85. From 1980/81 to 1984/85 the total budget of the Canadian food aid program increased by 110 per cent, primarily through an expansion of bilateral food aid. During this period bilateral food aid expanded by 193 per cent, causing the share of multilateral food aid to fall to 32.4 per cent of the program in 1984/85, the lowest point in a decade (see Table 8).

The renewed interest in bilateral program food aid in the mid-1980s has much to do with the changing economic climate in many recipient countries, particularly in Africa, and the way in which food aid assists donor agencies in overcoming some of the constraints they face. The growing level of food imports to Africa is occurring at a time when these countries are least able to finance such increases on a commercial basis. Stagnating exports, falling commodity prices, high energy import bills, and heavy debt repayment loads have all combined to reduce the foreign exchange available to pay for commercial food imports. As John Loxley has pointed out, this growing economic crisis in many recipient countries "enormously complicate(s) the task of aid administration."[55] Goods, services, and local funding are less readily available, thus slowing the rate of project implementation.

At the same time, economic difficulties in industrialized countries have led to additional constraints on donor agencies. There has been increased pressure within donor countries, including Canada, to demonstrate the economic benefits derived domestically from aid programs. Moreover, while there is growing pressure on the global flow of highly concessional resource transfers at home, donor agencies such as CIDA have been under continued pressure to cut budgets, reduce administrative costs, and not expand staff.

In this international and domestic policy environment, program food aid is seen as offering aid administrators a number of important advantages. First, program food aid, as balance-of-payments support, is more politically attractive to central agencies such as the Treasury Board and the Department of Finance since the economic benefits that it provides to Canada are more readily demonstrable compared to the provision of free foreign exchange. Second, food aid has traditionally been seen as an additional element in the Canadian aid program. Thus, there is no guarantee that any significant reductions in food aid would be replaced by equivalent amounts of aid funding, a risk that aid agencies are unlikely to take when aid funding is already tight. Third, only large-scale shipments of quickly dispersing aid will permit CIDA to respond to the projected level of need in Africa without placing significantly increased demands on the administrative resources of both the donor and recipient. Fourth, countries experiencing serious structural problems tend to provide difficult environments for undertaking project aid. At the same time, only program food aid can provide sufficient resources for assisting in the broad policy reforms associated with structural adjustment programs. Thus, as Canadian priorities have shifted toward an emphasis on structural adjustment, particularly in Africa, the attractiveness of program food aid has increased. As a CIDA corporate evaluation of the food aid program noted: "African countries lie closer to the structural adjustment end of the developmental spectrum than do many Asian recipients of CIDA food aid assistance ... program as opposed to project aid is typically required to assist and encourage structural adjustment. Since for program aid, the bilateral channel is the only option, it is likely that as the focus of food aid shifts to Africa, the bilateral channel will absorb an increasingly large share of Canada's food aid dollar, relative to the multilateral one."[56]

Bilateral program food aid is thus likely to continue to play as important a role in the future composition of the Canadian food aid program as it has traditionally, despite its frequent vulnerability to criticism.

CONCLUSIONS

In discussing the relative merits of bilateral and multilateral aid, a CIDA official observed that "the purpose and the means used by the different channels are different and is some ways complementary ... so both are relevant. Does that mean one is more effective than the other? The tradition of over two decades of Canadian aid program indicates that both are relevant."[57] This statement reflects the approach of many Canadian policy makers to the selection of food aid transfer mechanisms. As the Canadian program is designed to meet a multiplicity of objectives, both bilateral programs and multilateral project food aid have been seen as useful instruments in achieving different sets of objectives. What is perhaps most noteworthy is that Canadian policy makers have opted for specialization among aid channels: that is, bilaterally CIDA has concentrated its efforts on shipment of large bulk supplies for open market sales. It has then channelled the food aid it wants to supply for projects via NGOs and multilateral agencies such as the WFP.

Bilateral program food aid places the fewest demands on CIDA's administrative and analytical resources. As earlier chapters have demonstrated, reliance on bilateral program food aid has assisted CIDA to achieving its objectives as an organization actor, such as its concern about building domestic support for aid, easing disbursement problems, protecting slower moving projects, and overcoming the constraints of tied aid.

Parliamentary committees reviewing the Canadian aid program, and development groups lobbying these committees, have consistently expressed support for a more targeted food aid policy that can be achieved only through the use of project food aid. CIDA, however, has lacked the administrative capacity to carry out such a policy. When the Task Force on Food Aid and Renewable Resources carried out its review in 1975, it noted that the US government had carried out a successful project food aid program on a bilateral basis, but only because it relied on an extensive network of Food-For-Peace officers stationed within the recipient countries. The task force concluded that it "would be too costly (for CIDA) in terms of administrative skills, and should not be undertaken at this time as a component of the bilateral program."[58]

This view has remained as the conventional wisdom within CIDA. As pressure increased in the 1970s for a more targeted food aid policy in the wake of the world food crisis, CIDA lacked the administrative capacity to implement such an approach bilaterally without making a drastic reduction in the amount of food aid that it was able to handle. As a result the goal of more carefully targeting food aid to recipient populations was increasingly administered through intermediary agencies such as the WFP and NGO's. This enabled CIDA to meet the demand for more carefully targeted food aid, while displacing the additional administrative responsibility to other agencies. This shift towards alternative channels was reinforced at the end of the 1970s by the need for CIDA to carry out cuts in spending imposed on it by cabinet. Bilateral food aid, being the most "liquid" of all forms of development assistance, bore the major brunt of these cuts.

However, in the 1980s the emergence of the concept of developmental food aid, with its attendant linkages to structural adjustment and policy dialogue, occurred at the same time that the demand for food aid was growing rapidly in Africa. This shift in focus toward a renewed emphasis on large bulk shipments of program food aid, actually fitted CIDA administrative capacity much better than the demand for targeting specific population groups.

The concept of developmental food aid, which will be discussed in more detail in chapter 6, provided the rationale for shifting the emphasis once more to a larger bilateral program food aid which gave CIDA more control over its food aid program, within the limits of its own administrative capacity. As a CIDA food aid evaluation noted, the bilateral channel gives "greater visibility for Canada, greater flexibility with respect to program design, more direct control over the allocation of food aid to particular countries and finally, it affords the opportunity to engage in policy dialogue."[59] Thus CIDA has attempted to design a food aid distribution strategy that gives it flexibility within the range of its objectives while fitting within its own administrative constraints.

4 The Politics of Food Aid Commodity Selection

A very important decision that directly affects the quality of Canada's food aid program is the selection of food aid products to be sent to recipient countries. The nature and characteristics of these commodities and their impact on the recipient vary significantly. Selection of food aid commodities is an important reflection of the type of objectives being pursued in the aid program. Since the 1960s the composition of Canada's food aid basket has become increasingly diversified, with at least twenty different food products included in the program at one time or another.[1] This chapter focuses on the process by which agricultural commodities are selected for the Canadian food aid program.

DOMESTIC ECONOMIC INTERESTS

Although CIDA officials have frequently stated their desire to assure that food aid commodities are suitable from a developmental point of view, there are nevertheless a number of countervailing pressures that enter into the decision-making process. As CIDA's 1978 *Annual Review* pointed out, food aid must also take into account "Canada's economic interest, through surplus disposal and increased value added to agricultural commodities."[2] Surplus disposal provides economic benefits by reducing costly investments in carrying excess inventories over long periods of time. Industries involved in the processing of commodities destined for food aid derive economic benefits, particularly if their current processing capacity is under-utilised.

Thus both producers and processors stand to profit directly from the choice of which particular products to include in the food aid program.

Since the 1960s a number of identifiable groups within the general public have taken an active interest in the Canadian food aid program and its composition. The two largest farm organizations in Canada, the Canadian Federation of Agriculture (CFA) and the National Farmers Union (NFU) have been consistent supporters of an expanded food aid program. These groups have also pressed for the inclusion of specific commodities, such as skim milk powder, and have frequently identified the World Food Program (WFP) as a ready customer for these products. Indeed both the CFA and the NFU have argued for the continuation and expansion of the WFP since its founding in 1963.[3]

Other farm organizations have voiced similar requests. The Dairy Farmers of Canada asked the government "that a major portion of our surplus milk powder production be utilized in foreign aid program."[4] Another producer group, the Union des Cultivateurs Catholiques, also requested that "specific amounts of these [dairy] products be immediately made available to the CIDA."[5]

Not only were these groups specific in stating what commodities should be included in the program but they were clear about the prices they should be paid for the products. For example, David Kirk, executive secretary of the Dairy Farmers of Canada, argued that Canadian farmers should not be paid the lower world price for products included in the aid program since this would transfer a major portion of the cost of the aid to the producers. Although Kirk acknowledged that the use of domestic support prices to value food aid made it less attractive to recipients and caused international accounting problems, he argued that "we think the government should work those out."[6]

Agricultural processors have lobbied the government for greater processing of food aid commodities within Canada. While some organizations have made their requests known before the Standing Committee on Agriculture, others, such as the Canadian Millers Association and the Canadian Rapeseed Crushers Association, have approached either CIDA or the Grains Marketing Office directly. As one CIDA document puts it: "As rapeseed-processing facilities are developed in Western Canada, pressure grows to provide rapeseed oil in preference to unprocessed rapeseed. This results in an aid item with all value-added (and the meal as well) remaining in Canada. Much the same pressures are exerted on CIDA by flour millers."[7]

It is significant to note that this pressure has frequently been applied through other government agencies acting on behalf of their client groups. Thus Canadian trade officials lobbied CIDA on behalf of millers and processors to use greater amounts of rapeseed oil and flour.[8] The Grains Marketing Office was concerned, according to one of its officials, that "the Canadian Wheat Board does not get a disproportionate share of the aid business."[9] The Grains Marketing Office has pressed for the inclusion of such products as flour and soft, white Ontario wheat. Similarly the International Liaison Service has frequently been notified by the deputy minister's office of Agriculture Canada to seek ways to use surpluses identified as problem areas by the department's commercial divisions.

The above examples clearly demonstrate that Canadian farm organizations and food-processing industries are an integral part of the Canadian policy community that promotes the commercial objectives of the food aid program. These groups have consistently promoted their own special interests in commodity selection for some time. These interests have been specific both in the commodities they wish to see selected and the terms under which they should be purchased. It is interesting to note how these interests have affected the actual commodity selection process.

THE SELECTION PROCESS IN PRACTICE: THREE CASE STUDIES FROM THE 1970S

In order to see the impact of these pressures on the selection process more clearly, it is useful to examine briefly three examples of how certain commodities were selected for Canadian food aid.

Powdered Eggs

During the early 1970s agricultural policy under the Liberal government underwent a significant ideological shift away from the use of free and competitive markets towards a regulated marketing structure as a mechanism for establishing prices. Central to this new direction in policy was the establishment of national marketing boards to insure supply management through production controls. This policy, however, was the source of mounting controversy and criticism in 1973 and 1974. Much of this controversy was directed toward the Canadian Egg Marketing Agency (CEMA), the first national marketing authority established under the National Food Product Marketing Act of 1972.

Due to a number of factors, by late 1973 the Marketing Board was faced with the awkward situation of imposing higher prices on eggs at a time when egg surpluses were growing much faster than expected. In August 1974 this problem became acutely embarrassing for the government and for Eugene Whelan, minister of Agriculture, when CEMA's own public relations firm admitted to the destruction by CEMA of nine million rotten eggs in Quebec and three million in Ontario. It eventually became public knowledge that some twenty-eight million eggs had been destroyed in all.[10] Eugene Whelan came under severe attack from several quarters for his mishandling of CEMA. The incongruity of destroying surplus eggs at a time when news reports of starvation and famine in the Third World were prevalent was an embarrassment to the government. Grace Skogstad has noted that the minority position of the Liberal government at that time made the federal cabinet both sensitive to charges of high food prices and "anxious to appease prospective voters."[11] Thus the "rotten egg scandal," as it has been called, was an embarrassment both to Whelan's marketing board strategies and to the Liberal government's handling of the food price issue.

In order to contain some of the mounting criticism, the minister of Agriculture announced on 19 August 1974 that action would be taken to "restore order to national egg markets."[12] As part of this package the federal government would use a portion of the budget allocated for the WFP to purchase egg products from CEMA for use in the food aid program. In all, this program led to the purchase by CIDA of some 575 metric tons of dried egg powder, valued at over $2 million. In testimony later, comments by CIDA President Gérin-Lajoie make it clear that the proposal was initiated by Agriculture Canada and had not been a planned item in the food aid budget.[13] It is interesting to note that the entire amount of the powdered egg aid was distributed through the WFP.

Canned Beef

According to Don Mitchell, from 1973 to 1975 "beef was the most highly politicized and controversial commodity and the most investigated."[14] During this period the Canadian beef market had alternated from apparent surpluses to shortages and from high beef prices to depressed cattle prices. The beef trade had also become an irritant in Canadian-American relations, with each side taking measures to restrict the other's imports.

By the fall of 1974 calf prices were in decline and there was growing concern by many industry and government officials that producers would resort to widespread liquidation of their herds. The NFU was pressing the government to take some significant action to deal with the situation. Among their suggestions, included in a telegram sent to Eugene Whelan shortly before his departure to the World Food Conference in Rome, was the request that beef products be included in the Canadian food aid program.[15]

Whelan's first response was one of scepticism, noting in a speech to the NFU that "India and Bangladesh are the two countries that most urgently need food aid today. Yet, there is no use sending them canned beef. It is against their religion to eat beef ... Canada has twice put beef into a food aid program before. You may know what happened. We couldn't even give it away."[16] Similarly, the minister of state for External Affairs informed the House of Commons that cultural practices limited the possibility of using beef as food aid. Nevertheless Whelan gave into the pressure one month later when he announced a new program to stabilize meat prices by encouraging greater consumption of beef products, especially hamburger meat. Among the proposals was the suggestion that CIDA purchase $10 million in canned meat. This would be essentially low grade beef that would be packed in twelve ounce cans and labelled "Canadian Beef Loaf."[17]

Implementation of the proposal posed some difficulties for the government. Whelan acknowledged later that the government was unable to ship as much beef as expected because of lack of replies to the tender notices issued by Agriculture Canada. Whelan explained this by suggesting that farmers were reluctant to sell their beef at the prices that Agriculture Canada was asking.[18] In all, about $5 million worth of canned meat was shipped in 1975–76, just half of the amount originally announced. Like the powdered eggs, all of the canned beef was supplied through the WFP.

Skim Milk Powder (SMP)

For some time skim milk powder has been a troublesome commodity to both producers and government. The SMP market has been characterized by chronic oversupply and Canadian producers have had great difficulty in maintaining the level of their exports. For example, 1975–76 was characterized by high world stocks of skim milk powder and low world prices. Producers in Ontario and Quebec, who supply about 90 per cent of Canada's milk powder, were particularly hard pressed as other countries expanded milk powder aid programs or undercut export prices.[19]

Various farm organizations, such as the Canadian Federation of Agriculture, the Union des Cultivateurs Catholiques, and the Dairy Farmers of Canada, have at different times called for the expansion of the use of dairy products in the Canadian food aid program. In the face of continued deterioration in their market position, the Dairy Farmers of Canada proposed in 1976 that Canadian food aid to the WFP be expanded to include 100 million pounds of SMP for a period of up to ten years.[20] At its annual meeting in 1976 the Canadian Federation of Agriculture accepted a resolution endorsing the dairy farmer's proposal.[21] Opposition members of Parliament also expressed support for the proposal in the House of Commons.[22]

As in the case of the beef loaf, Agriculture Minister Whelan expressed initial reluctance to the proposal. He noted that "there is just no room for that amount of product at the present time to put into world food aid programs."[23] Whelan also noted the difficulty in finding recipients: "If people are not used to that in their diet, then they cannot use it. There are just certain sections or countries that that [sic] can be used."[24]

Despite his admission of the problems involved in increased use of skim milk powder, only a month later Whelan announced that CIDA had been "instructed to investigate thoroughly the possibility of increasing the skim milk powder component of its food aid program." Whelan went on to note that, as a result of these instructions, "CIDA had decided to buy $20 million worth of skim milk powder, which will eliminate some of the dairy farmers' costs." Although this fell far below the amount proposed by the Dairy Farmers of Canada, it nevertheless represented a 100 per cent increase over the amount of SMP aid shipped in 1974–75. According to CIDA officials, the expansion of the milk powder aid was accepted with great reluctance. Whelan had been able to win cabinet approval for the $20 million program without CIDA's full concurrence. Agency officials argued that it would be difficult to expand the program since the food aid budget had already been committed for the coming year. Because of CIDA's resistance, a compromise was worked out by which cabinet would augment the food aid budget by $10 million if CIDA would realign its planned allocations to make up another $10 million in milk powder aid.[25] Whelan was pleased with the $20 million program, noting that "this amounts to approximately 75 million to 80 million pounds of skim milk powder that the dairy farmers will not have to finance."[26]

However, disposing of this amount of extra skim milk powder was not easy for CIDA. In 1976–77 over $9 million worth of milk powder was shipped to forty-one countries under the auspices of the WFP.[27] But, because of the size of the milk powder program, the WFP could not absorb the full amount. The bilateral milk powder aid was therefore greatly expanded. Instructions were sent to CIDA country desks to inquire if any recipients would be willing to accept the milk powder if it were sent strictly as an additional item to the aid already agreed upon.[28]

Despite this appeal, CIDA was not able to find a sufficient number of bilateral recipients willing or able to absorb Canadian milk powder surpluses.[29] The Asian and African countries which received the vast majority of Canada's food aid have not generally requested milk powder from CIDA. As the milk powder was being purchased by CIDA at prices above the world price, it was a less attractive offer than that being made by other donors, such as the European Economic Community.[30] As a result it was necessary for CIDA officials to find another way to dispose of the milk powder they were committed to using. Thus it was announced that a portion of the skim milk powder would be made available to Canadian NGOs for use in their overseas projects. CIDA would provide the milk powder at no charge to NGOs, who were to pay the shipping and handling costs. The only condition placed on the program was that the milk powder be used in countries recognized by Canada. As one CIDA official noted, the conditions for participation were minimal as "it is a surplus program ... anyone who wants the skim milk powder can get it, if they are willing to pay the administrative costs."[31]

Although these short case studies cover only three of the many commodities included in the Canadian food aid basket, they nevertheless illustrate several important points. While the matching of Canadian foodstuffs to specific recipient needs was theoretically to be made at the desk level, pressure was frequently brought to bear on decision makers to include specific commodities, some of which had not been requested by recipient agencies. Agriculture and Trade officials, on behalf of their client groups, were strong advocates for the inclusion of certain commodities that were either surplus or have value-added benefits for the Canadian economy. In many cases such requests were conveyed from the deputy minister's office of one of the interested departments to the relevant vice-president's office in CIDA.[32]

As the above examples show, when there was no clear agreement the issue was referred to a higher level of decision making, with the cabinet eventually involved in the decision making process. In the case of the skim milk powder and beef, the decision to include them was taken in response to requests made by domestic client groups of the minister of Agriculture. In each of these cases federal supply management policies had become highly politicized domestic issues. The minister of Agriculture was able to take the proposals to cabinet and win support for them, despite the fact that cabinet approval of CIDA estimates normally does not specify the commodity make-up of the food aid program. Since these decisions were taken in a highly politicized climate, there were clear political benefits to cabinet ministers to support the Agriculture minister's appeals, as inclusion of a product had clear appeal to a specific and identifiable public. The two departments interested in agricultural products also had natural allies in the central agencies, the Finance and Treasury Boards, which were both anxious to support measures that retain significant economic benefits from the aid program in Canada.[33]

Analysts have frequently noted that aid agencies such as CIDA lack a distinct constituency.[34] This observation is particularly relevant to the choice of foodstuffs. The intended beneficiaries of the food aid are outside the Canadian political system and cannot effectively express their preference for particular commodities. Development and humanitarian-oriented groups have generally not expressed preference for particular food aid commodities. Instead they have focused on the more general question of whether food aid should be given at all.[35] While academics have criticized certain individual cases, such criticism is sporadic and voiced only after the selection decision is already made.[36] Thus CIDA has no identifiable client groups that create countervailing pressures which would give weight to its interdepartment arguments against the use of certain products.

In each of the cases above, the proposal to use a particular commodity was initiated by the minister of Agriculture with the aim of committing a certain portion of CIDA's food aid budget to the pursuit of policy objectives in Agriculture Canada's own field. CIDA's position was therefore essentially a defensive one, an attempt to preserve its aid program from diversion to non-developmental purposes. CIDA was put into a position of building a case for not using a particular commodity. This is clearly a much more difficult task when the political and economic benefits of Agriculture Canada's proposal are evident to cabinet ministers and there are no other departments which would receive benefits from opposing the choice of specific commodities as vigorously as those arguing for their use. Since the choice of foodstuffs does not have any immediate impact on Canada's relations with recipient governments, the decision is unlikely to be a high priority item for the Department of External Affairs.

Because of these factors CIDA has found it difficult to oppose efforts to intervene in the commodity selection process for domestic political and economic reasons. As a result the composition of Canada's food aid has frequently been made in response to particular commodity problems in Canada and not in the context of the needs of recipient countries. In the above case studies the selection of foodstuffs and the choice of recipients were therefore two separate processes. The effort to match food products with recipient needs was made only after CIDA was already committed to using the product. Consequently the distribution of Canadian food aid was of necessity tailored to suit the needs of Canadian supply management rather than in response to an expression of recipient needs.

THE IMPACT OF COMMODITY SELECTION ON DEVELOPMENT OBJECTIVES

The approach to commodity selection described above has frustrated CIDA's desire to provide food aid that is of optimal benefit to the recipient in a number of ways. First, the emphasis on commercial objectives in commodity selection reinforced the ad hoc, unplanned nature of Canadian food aid allocations in the 1970s. When surplus commodities are inserted into the program to alleviate domestic supply management problems, these unplanned allocations can divert CIDA from the achievement of certain stated objectives. As an illustration, in its *Strategy for International Development Cooperation* CIDA committed itself to greater geographic concentration of aid disbursements in order to maximize the impact of Canadian aid.[37] However, the implementation of the skim milk powder disposal program completely contradicted this objective. The number of food aid recipients increased from twelve in 1975/76 to nineteen in 1976/77 because CIDA had more than doubled its milk powder recipients during that time in order to dispose of the larger amounts of milk. The eight countries to receive milk powder in 1976/77 were Belize, Colombia, Egypt, Guatemala, Guyana, Jamaica, Peru, and Rwanda. None of these countries had received Canadian food aid in the previous year. In fact only Peru and Jamaica had ever been previous recipients of Canadian food aid.[38]

Another example of how commercial concerns can divert from the achievement of development is found in the distributional pattern of these surplus commodities. In point 8 of the 1975–80 *Strategy Paper* CIDA committed itself to directing a major share of its aid to the "poorest countries of the world."[39] As the strategy document notes, "particular attention will continue to be given to the hardcore least developed countries identified by the United Nations." However, as Table 14 shows, the undertaking of the SMP disposal program in 1976 meant that the additional aid went largely to the wealthier developing countries. The increased shipments of SMP to the WFP were not well targeted to reach the poorest countries. Whether one uses the United Nations designation of most seriously affected (MSA) or least developed countries (LLDCs), or CIDA's criterion of countries with less than

Table 14
Distribution of Canadian skim milk powder through the World Food Program
by category of country, 1975–79 (in percentages)

Category	1975/76	1976/77	1977/78	1978/79
MSA[a]	52.4	45.3	15.3	8.2
LLDC[b]	20.9	20.2	3.2	3.7
>$200 GNP	26.5	24.1	25.0	12.0
Number of Recipients	23	41	25	12

Source: Calculated from CIDA, "Statement of Foodstuffs supplied by Canada to UN/FAO World Food Program During Fiscal Years 1963/64 to 30 June 1978"; and "Multilateral Food Aid Program 1978/79."

Notes: [a] "Most seriously affected" countries as identified by the United Nations.
[b] "Least developed" countries as identified by the United Nations.

$200 per capita GNP, it is clear from the table that the distribution of SMP was skewed in favour of the wealthier LDCs.

The disposal of canned beef provides another example of a surplus product which primarily benefited richer recipient countries. A total of ten countries received beef aid in 1975/76, but of this $4.5 million worth of canned beef, 3.9 per cent went to MSA countries and only 1.6 per cent to LLDCs and to countries with a per capita GNP of less than $200. In contrast fully 96.1 per cent of the canned beef was shipped to countries with a per capita GNP of over $520.[40] Thus the distributional pattern of both the milk powder and canned beef clearly contradicted CIDA's commitment to concentrate the major share of its aid on the poorest countries. The bias toward middle and higher income developing countries is the result, in large measure, of the fact that most recipient countries import large amounts of cereals and have therefore developed a capacity for receiving and distributing large amounts of grain. Similar systems, however, do not exist for handling large quantities of other more costly food items, especially in the poorer countries. It is only the wealthier countries which are likely to have the capacity to absorb these food products, or the WFP which can assume responsibility for distributing them as part of a food-for-work project.

Second, the emphasis on surplus commodities has diverted CIDA from development objectives by leading to the selection of food aid products which are unsuitable from the recipient's standpoint. Recipients requesting food aid from Canada generally have their own specific preferences in mind. These preferences are to a large extent shaped by local dietary habits and the cultural orientation of the recipient population. A problem arises for aid planners when the aid commodities available in Canada are not those in common usage in the recipient country. For example many African countries prefer sorghum, which is not grown in Canada, to wheat and flour. In other cases products offered by Canada, such as powdered eggs, skim milk powder, and canned turkey, have not been compatible with local eating habits, making it difficult to find recipients willing to use them.[41]

This issue is of particular importance in emergency situations where the timely arrival of appropriate foodstuffs is of critical importance. In such situations food aid commodities deemed unsuitable by the recipient population may be given a low distribution priority or not distributed at all. This occurred with Canadian shipments of emergency food aid to Mali and Niger in 1972–73. A Treasury Board evaluation found that the commodities sent by CIDA, such as flour and semolina, were not normally consumed outside the major cities. Thus they were given a low priority by government officials for onward transportation from port storage facilities.[42] The desire to provide a rapid response to an emergency situation was therefore defeated. In addition the report noted that other surplus Canadian products such as egg powder, canned meat, and fish, were poor alternatives because of their expense.

Third, the emphasis on the selection of surplus and processed food items adds to the cost of Canadian food aid to the recipient. This occurs in several ways. Some Canadian products have been very expensive in terms of the protein provided per dollar. CIDA officials have considered canned meat and fish "undesirable food aid commodities ... because they are very expensive sources of protein."[43] CIDA President Gérin-Lajoie has admitted that the use of such protein-rich products and canned beef is "not the best use of CIDA money"[44] as it means that less food aid is provided per dollar.

By processing food aid commodities in Canada, the value of the product is further diminished in value to the recipient. Many recipients who have their own milling facilities would prefer their food as little processed as possible. This enables them to gain further benefits from food aid through the employment provided by the refining of the product, and greater revenues can be derived from the sale of the by-products. Administratively, it is also easier and less expensive for CIDA to transport food commodities in bulk, unprocessed form.[45]

But as Table 15 shows, the surplus disposal programs described in the above case studies led to an increase in the proportion of processed foods in the Canadian food aid program. The ultimate result for the recipient is a smaller quantity of food aid per aid dollar. The recipient also forgoes the opportunity to develop its own food processing technology, expand its capacity, and create local employment.

Table 15
Processed and unprocessed commodities as a share of Canadian food aid program, 1973–80

	1973/74		1975/76		1977/78		1979/80	
	Q(MTN)	$(000)	Q(MTN)	$(000)	Q(MTN)	$(000)	Q(MTN)	$(000)
Total	712,094	124.885	1,033,163	226,475	971,519	200,907	558,430	185,481
Percentage processed	10.3	20.6	14.6	31.0	31.1	51.2	23.3	46.0
Percentage unprocessed	89.7	79.4	85.5	69.0	68.9	48.8	76.7	54.0

Source: Calculated from Agriculture Canada, International Liaison Service, "Canadian Food Aid Shipments-Fiscal Years 1972/73 to 1977/78," and CIDA, "1978/80 Food Aid Program."

The real value of food aid has also been further reduced in cases where the product is valued at non-competitive domestic support prices. This occurred in the case of the 1976–77 purchases of skim milk powder described above. The milk powder was purchased at the much higher Canadian domestic support price and, as a result, recipients of Canadian aid received less milk powder for their dollar from Canada than if they had purchased the product at world market prices.[46]

Fourth, the shipment of surplus Canadian foods has raised health concerns, either because of the nature of the food or the way it is used by the recipient. One food aid product that has frequently been criticized as an unsuitable aid item is dried milk powder which raises a number of problems in both its use and distribution. Gastro-intestinal ailments may be caused by the use of contaminated water or utensils in the preparation and serving of milk. But, more important, some authors have expressed concern that certain population groups lack the enzyme lactose which is required for the proper digestion of milk. Such a "milk allergy," which is referred to as lactose intolerance, could cause serious illness. It is for this reason that Canadian emergency shipments of milk powder to Guatemala in 1976 came under criticism as a serious health risk to Guatemalans using the product.[47]

CIDA'S SEARCH FOR CONTROL OVER THE COMMODITY SELECTION PROCESS

CIDA officials have not been unaware of the problems posed by giving in to domestic commercial demands. The Task Force on Food Aid and Renewable Resources had already warned in 1975 that unless the agency took more aggressive steps to counter such pressures "CIDA will continue to be merely an outlet for unwanted food as an 'escape valve' for distortions in Canadian markets."[48] As a result the past decade has seen a concentrated effort on CIDA's part to search for a means of gaining greater control over the food aid commodity selection process. This has led the agency to consider a number of alternative proposals which are designed to limit the negative impact of commercially motivated intrusions.

Triangular Supply Arrangements and the Untying of Food Aid

One proposal, first advanced by the Task Force on Food Aid, is the use of triangular purchasing relationships in which Canada procures commodities in one Third World country for shipment to another Third World country. Such arrangements would not only expand the range of commodities provided by Canada but would enable speedier delivery or more appropriate products in emergency situations. The supplying country would benefit by expanding its agricultural exports, thus multiplying the impact of Canadian aid monies. The concept of triangular food aid transactions has been strongly promoted by the secretariat of the WFP, recipient countries, and academic analysts as constituting an important element in an emergent development-oriented food aid regime.

This concept, which is basically an untying mechanism, was given formal endorsement in CIDA's 1975–80 strategy. The policy statement noted that CIDA would untie up to 20 per cent of its food aid for procurement in Third World countries in cases where the "nature of food requirements or the difficulties of transport and supply dictate that such food be purchased outside Canada."[49] Despite CIDA's commitment to what appears to be an innovative and progressive notion, implementation of the concept has not fared well. There have been only a relatively few cases where such arrangements have actually been carried out. For example, $3.5 million was allocated for the purchase of sorghum from LDC exporters in Sahelian Africa for distribution in Chad, Gambia, and Senegal.[50] In another instance CIDA gave Jamaica a balance-of-payments support grant of $11 million, of which $5 million was to be used to purchase rice from Guyana.[51]

Part of the difficulty in making these arrangements is related to the administrative problems in identifying potential participants and negotiating agreements and transportation arrangements between all three parties. Equally important has been the failure of the concept to win strong interdepartmental support. The lack of enthusiasm on the part of Agriculture Canada is not unexpected, given its economic stake in the issue. A Treasury Board official gave two further reasons for the Treasury Board's traditional reluctance concerning such exchanges. First, triangular exchanges tend to blur the objectives of the program by making it difficult to define who is the real client of the program, the recipient or the third party. This diffusion goes against the Treasury Board's desire to have explicit definitions of objectives and clear indicators of program success. Second, since Canada's role would be more indirect and less visible, triangular relationships tend to negate other objectives that food aid can achieve bilaterally, such as the building of "political credits" with the recipient.[52]

Because of such interdepartmental resistance, as well as the administrative difficulties inherent in this concept, the untying of food aid procurement through triangular exchanges has not proven to be an effective way of enabling CIDA to broaden the availability of foodstuffs and become less dependent on surpluses. Instead CIDA's authority has gradually been diminished, despite public interest in the concept. In 1980 the Parliamentary Task Force on North-South Relations recommended that "every effort be made to supply food-deficit developing countries with food aid purchased by Canada from neighbouring food surplus developing countries."[53] Instead of supporting this recommendation, the Treasury Board issued directions that reduced CIDA's untying authority to only 5 per cent and only "under emergency and other special circumstances."[54] The president's committee of CIDA went even further in 1985 by requiring that untying only be used: (1) in cases of emergency where appropriate foods were not available for transportation in sufficient time; (2) as a "one-time" only situation and not a part of an on-going arrangement; and (3) only if it was part of a first phase, limited response to an emergency situation. Even then, it was suggested that "it may be appropriate to seek the approval of the minister for specific untying proposals."[55] Given the Treasury Board restrictions and the desire of CIDA officials to "maintain interdepartmental support for an untying provision," a CIDA manual suggests that the untying authority "will be used in a limited and careful manner."[56]

The issue of untying Canadian food aid was raised again in 1986 when the parliamentary committee reviewing Canadian aid policies suggested that the untying restrictions on CIDA be eased in cases where food aid could be purchased in neighbouring, developing countries that had exportable surpluses.[57] In response the government stated that it would not modify its policy of untying only 5 per cent of Canadian food aid, although it did promise to reduce the portion of untied aid for non-food aid from 80 per cent to 50 per cent for some African and LLDC recipients.[58]

The Use of CIDA's Purchasing Power

A second alternative proposed by the 1975 Task Force was that CIDA use the purchasing power of its food aid budget in a more aggressive manner to encourage the production of new varieties of food grains or other crops that provide a higher nutrient value per dollar. By contracting with farmers to purchase given amounts over a long-term basis, CIDA could thereby ensure itself of an available supply of preferable commodities.[59]

However, interdepartmental resistance to the concept has again been a major factor in preventing implementation of this approach. Agriculture Canada has opposed the licensing of crops designed only for the use in the food aid program. Instead they have argued for continued reliance on products in which Canada already has a comparative advantage and which are readily produced in surplus.[60] Similarly Treasury Board officials have opposed the concept largely for fiscal reasons. First, it is difficult to forecast what particular products will be in high demand, and thus contracting with farmers for production of a food commodity on a long-term basis is seen as a highly risky venture. Second, the Treasury Board is reluctant to have CIDA engage in long-term contracts, which commit the agency to a specific option, thus precluding other options at a later date.[61] Within CIDA itself opinion has been divided, with some officials arguing that it would be unwise to create a market that would be dependent on the food aid program for its continued existence.

The Right of First Refusal

Another alternative explored by CIDA as a means of gaining some control over the food inputs has been the concept of the "right of first refusal." The main purpose of this concept is to maximize the food available for exports to LDC's. These countries would have the first option to purchase wheat before it was made available to other Canadian customers. As a suggested target the task force recommended that 25 per cent of Canadian wheat be held in reserve for LDCS.[62] This concept was included as part of point 18 IN CIDA's 1975–80 strategy paper, although it noted only that a committee of senior officials would be reviewing "the advisability of guaranteeing, on a first refusal basis, a fixed tonnage of cereals for developing country's markets."[63]

Like the other concepts, the right of first refusal was vigorously opposed by Canadian agricultural interests. Otto Lang, the minister responsible for the Wheat Board, informed the president of CIDA that a need for such a policy had never arisen before.[64] Commentators from the business press also reacted negatively to the idea.[65] Treasury Board officials recognized that the concept could potentially be an effective means of accelerating food shipments to the Third World, but they opposed the idea for two reasons. First, it posed a serious threat to Canadian commercial export interests. Second, it would require an cumbersome administrative system of monitoring to schedule shipments and prevent speculation.[66] Confronted by such resistance within the bureaucracy, the "right of first refusal" concept suffered a rather quick and quiet death.

The Development of Selection Criteria

None of the innovative recommendations of the 1975 Task Force gained acceptance with the exception of a limited use of triangular exchanges. Therefore, it is significant to discuss briefly the outcome of commodity selection, an issue which was brought before the Interdepartmental Working Group on Food Aid in 1978. By this time CIDA President Gérin-Lajoie had been replaced by Michel Dupuy, who noted that "priority will be given to the use of Canadian components with a value-added content."[67]

In formulating its food aid policy recommendations CIDA was able to ensure that the working group addressed a few of its concerns about the selection of food products. This included outlining the criteria which would guide the selection of commodities.[68] These were:

1 In the selection of food products, consideration should be given to the ultimate cost of nutrients.
2 The nutritional balance and convenience of distribution should be considered, especially in cases of emergency.
3 CIDA, whenever possible, should confirm with the recipients that the products to be sent are acceptable.
4 When requested by recipients, the nutritional value of aid products can be improved with additives.
5 Food purchased for aid should be bought on the basis of prices comparable to those prevalent on world markets.

These criteria did address CIDA's concerns about the pricing of food products, the nutritive value per dollar, and the suitability of the product to the recipient. To this extent the food aid policy adopted in 1978 from the working group's recommendations marked several gains from CIDA's standpoint. However, the policy on food aid products fell far short of the innovative recommendations of the 1975 task force and the aspirations of many CIDA officials. None of the key recommendations of the 1975 task force which were designed to give CIDA greater control over aid products were included in the 1978 food aid policy.

The emphasis on the use of surplus products and those processed in Canada also remained intact. This is particularly evident in the formulation of Canadian food aid objectives which gave priority to surplus disposal and value-added benefits. Thus the food aid policy that emerged from the interdepartmental discussion of 1978 represented a defeat for CIDA when viewed in the context of its efforts in the mid-1970s to design a more innovative and aggressive strategy for commodity selection. CIDA was forced to compromise on the two most crucial issues – the use of surplus and processed products. According to one CIDA official this compromise was necessary for CIDA to maintain its "credibility" with other departments on other important aid issues.[69]

Despite this seeming setback, CIDA has continued to emphasize the use of commodity selection criteria as a principal means for resisting pressures from producer groups. Recent CIDA policy statements,[70] while not mentioning commercial policy objectives, have emphasized that commodity selection should be determined by three fundamental criteria:

1 *Need*. This relates primarily to the requirement that the food item proposed should be an acceptable part of local diet, and therefore acceptable to local tastes, and should provide adequate nutritional balance. Grains, since they meet both criteria, have long been the major component of the food aid programs of Canada and most other major donors.

2 *Program effectiveness*. According to this second criterion, food items should be selected for which the donor has adequate transportation and distribution facilities. Because cereal grains have been imported in large quantities by Third World countries, most food aid recipients have well-developed mechanisms that can ensure adequately wide distribution of cereal grains. The same is not true of other food aid items however. Skim milk powder, because of the need to mix it with clean water, poses problems that demand careful control of distribution and monitoring systems. In many countries canned meat, fish, and skim milk powder are considered

Table 16
Comparative costs of one kilogram of food aid commodity

Commodity	Price*	Calories per $ ratio	Proteins per $ ratio
Corn	0.19	18283.16	467.79
Wheat	0.22	15200.00	426.00
Wheat flour	0.38	8742.11	439.11
Beans, red	0.60	5716.67	375.00
Skim milk powder	1.06	3418.30	337.89
Canada oil	1.40	8742.11	–
Mackerel	2.20	831.82	87.73
Sardines	3.00	553.67	65.49
Herring	2.40	866.67	82.92

Sources: CIDA, Food Aid Coordination and Evaluation Centre, Food Aid: A Programming Manual, (Hull: mimeographed March 1986), Section D, 12.
Note: * Per kilogram as of August 1985

luxury items and adequate mechanisms do not exist for targetting their distribution to poorer populations without high administrative overhead expenses.

3 *Cost-effectiveness.* Food aid should provide maximum nutritional impact in relation to financial resources. This can be measured in part by the ratio of protein and calories that the food item provides per dollar spent in purchasing the product.[71] As Table 16 shows, food aid commodities can differ significantly in the cost and nutritional value per dollar that they provide. Cereals and pulses provide the most protein and nutritional value per dollar spent on them, while fish is the least cost-effective product.

In order to try to give some weight to these criteria, CIDA created the position of "commodity officer" within the Food Aid Coordination and Evaluation Centre (FACE). The commodity officer is responsible for monitoring domestic availability of food commodities and assessing the appropriateness of products for inclusion in the food aid program. Perhaps most significant, for the first time the commodity officer gave CIDA a direct contact with domestic producer groups. While such groups continue to make representations through the ministerial level, they frequently contact the commodity officer regarding the potential usage of their products in the food aid program. This has enabled FACE to take a more active stance in resisting the selection of some products by making CIDA's selection criteria known directly to producers and placing the onus on those lobbying to demonstrate that their products did meet the criteria of need, program effectiveness, and cost efficiency. CIDA officials believe that this has been instrumental in avoiding the inclusion of more exotic products, such as seal meat.[72]

Despite the adoption of an agreed set of selection criteria and the establishment of a commodity officer, CIDA has still at times been forced to compromise as a result of pressure from other departments. The clearest example of this is the decision by the cabinet in 1983, which required that the food aid basket be composed of at least 25 per cent non-cereals commodities, and the subsequent expansion of fish aid in the 1980s. This policy decision was rooted in an escalating interdepartmental dispute over the nature of the commodity basket in the early 1980s when CIDA was subjected to increasing pressure to include larger amounts of fish in the program. Prior to the 1980s fish had played only a very minor role in the Canadian aid program, but beginning in 1980 the Department of Fisheries and Oceans began lobbying CIDA and Agriculture Canada to increase the level of fish as food aid from the $5.9 million provided in 1980/81. Approaches were made to the Food Aid Centre at CIDA, country program managers, and Agriculture Canada. The support of the ministers of Fisheries and Oceans and Industry, Trade and Commerce in expanding the use of fish was also solicited. Representations were made to CIDA by industry representatives such as the Fisheries Council of Canada and the Fisheries Council of British Columbia, with the assistance of Fisheries and Oceans. Fisheries and Oceans officials saw this as a part of a larger strategy being developed to diversify Canadian fish markets, especially in the Third World, and to protect existing markets in countries such as Jamaica which were experiencing economic difficulties. In particular Fisheries and Oceans officials hoped that CIDA would go beyond its practice of providing fish aid only to current importers of Canadian fish and more aggressively develop new, potential long-term customers.[73]

From CIDA's standpoint fish aid represented a clear contradiction to the selection criteria that it had sought to establish. Fish is generally much more costly than other traditional Canadian food aid products in relation to the nutrient and protein value provided. In some countries it is regarded as a luxury item and may not be a priority or may not meet the criteria of taste acceptability, particularly in landlocked countries where fish is not a regular part of the local diet. Cans of fish are more difficult and costly to transport and distribute than bulk shipments of grains. Since canned fish represents a high value item in a small container, there is greater concern about the possibilities of diversion and hence a need for more careful monitoring and supervision. In addition the WFP is reluctant to see traditional non-fish aid givers expand their programs, since the program already has concerns about absorbing the fish aid provided by donors such as Norway.[74]

The interdepartmental debate over fish aid was complicated by the fact that Agriculture Canada, the Canadian Wheat Board, and dairy and pulse producers were anxious to maintain their share of the food aid market. Thus they were reluctant to accept any expansion of fish food aid if it meant a reduction in the use of their own preferred commodities. Moreover External Affairs officials were concerned that increased amounts of fish or dairy products should not undermine Canada's ability to meet its Food Aid Convention commitment of supplying 600 thousand metric tons of grain a year.

As a result of this dispute approval of CIDA's omnibus food aid submission to the Treasury Board in 1982/83 and 1983/84 was delayed as the various departments struggled unsuccessfully to come up with a compromise. In the absence of an interdepartmental agreement, the issue was finally taken to the cabinet for resolution and it was decided that a quota of at least 25 per cent of the total food aid budget should be spent on non-cereal products.

In a sense the decision was a classic bureaucratic compromise. As Table 17 shows, non-cereals had already been at, or above, 25 per cent for some time. In one way the cabinet requirement only confirmed what had already become a de facto policy within CIDA. This shift in balance in the food aid program was encouraged by the fact that world grain prices were low during this period. Thus CIDA could easily meet Canada's wheat aid obligations under the Food Aid Convention and still have sufficient resources available to fund a sizeable non-cereals component in its aid program. What the 25 per cent requirement did do was provide a minimum binding floor on the level of non-cereal aid to be provided. If grain prices increased, and CIDA was forced to spend more to meet its FAC obligations, it would not be able to make significant cuts to its non-cereal aid without further cabinet approval. Although the formal cabinet requirement of 25 per cent was only for a period of three years, CIDA planners are well aware that, if the percentage of non-cereals was to drop significantly, the composition of the food aid basket would once again become a cabinet issue. Thus the requirement still functions as an informal rule of thumb.

Whatever the nature of the compromise, it is clear that the decision opened the door for a rapid expansion of the fish component of the program. Fish aid increased from $5.8 million (3.25% of the total food aid budget) in 1980/81 to $30.2 million (9.7% of the total) in 1984/85.[75] Although there was a slight decrease during the next two

Table 17
Cereal and non-cereals in the Canadian food aid program, 1970–91

Year	Grains		Non-grains	
	$ Value	Percentage	$ Value	Percentage
1970/71	90.2	87	4.2	13
1971/72	76.4	96	3.4	4
1972/73	67.4	60	45.0	40
1973/74	95.9	83	19.8	17
1974/75	142.5	82	32.3	18
1975/76	175.4	79	47.2	21
1976/77	172.6	72	67.5	28
1977/78	148.3	64	82.1	36
1978/79	141.7	74	49.5	26
1979/80	130.8	70	56.9	30
1980/81	140.4	77	43.0	23
1981/82	161.1	68	74.6	32
1982/83	196.3	72	76.9	28
1983/84	220.9	67	109.1	46
1984/85	208.0	54	177.1	46
1985/86	191.6	67	90.5	32
1986/87	212.3	64	116.9	36
1987/88	256.4	73	94.8	27
1988/89	241.6	71	99.8	29
1989/90	208.5	73	78.7	27
1990/91	199.4	70	86.8	30

Source: CIDA, FACE Centre.

years, fish aid again climbed, reaching its highest point of $37.0 million in 1988/89 (see Table 18). As Table 19 shows, the diversification of food aid into non-cereals enabled CIDA to take into account questions of regional balance in food aid purchases by using products from regions of Canada that had not traditionally participated in the program when it was composed predominantly of wheat aid. With the expansion of the fish aid program, every Canadian province could now supply some share of the Canadian food aid program.

The Procurement of Food Commodities

An additional factor that affects the quality of the Canadian food aid program is the purchase of the commodities themselves. CIDA has long argued that it should be able to procure Canadian food aid commodities in the most cost-effective manner possible, in order to deliver the most value per aid dollar spent. However, the issue of procurement provides an excellent example of how organizational

Table 18
Canadian fish aid, 1972–91

Fiscal year	Volume (thousand tonnes)	Value (millions of Canadian dollars)
1972/73	2.7	1.9
1973/74	1.2	.7
1974/75	1.0	.6
1975/76	3.8	3.2
1976/77	1.0	1.0
1977/78	2.0	2.7
1978/79	4.6	7.5
1979/80	2.5	6.0
1980/81	2.7	5.8
1981/82	5.2	17.3
1982/83	3.8	9.6
1983/84	7.5	20.8
1984/85	12.0	30.2
1985/86	11.5	29.3
1986/87	9.2	27.4
1987/88	10.6	33.2
1988/89	12.8	37.0
1989/90	9.7	29.2
1990/91	10.2	30.2

Source: Agriculture Canada, "Canadian Food Aid Shipments: Fiscal Years 1972–73 to 1977–78.," CIDA, "Food Aid Program by Commodity and Country, 1978/79–1983/84," and CIDA, FACE Centre.

Table 19
Food aid purchases by province, 1986/87 (in tonnes)

Province	Wheat	Flour	Vegetable oil	Skim milk powder	Fish	Pulses	Maize
British Columbia	–	2,395	–	–	–	435	–
Alberta	191,385	34,806	64,646	1,501	–	2,219	–
Sask.	512,958	21,685	9,011	1,876	–	1,188	–
Manitoba	156,587	7,010	37,847	1,877	–	3,989	–
Ontario	120,588	35,106	8,637	1,876	–	3,438	11,761
Quebec	–	63,914	1,224	11,259	860	–	–
New Brunswick	–	–	–	188	4,915	–	–
PEI	–	–	–	–	2401	–	–
Nova Scotia	–	5,288	–	188	1,788	–	–
Nfld.	–	–	–	–	1,477	–	–

Source: CIDA: Sharing our Future: Canadian International Development Assistance (Hull: Supply and Services 1987), 56.

constraints can affect the outcomes of policies, despite the best intentions of policy makers.

Once a memorandum of understanding (MOU) is signed with the recipient government, the bilateral desk concerned requests the procurements division of CIDA to procure the various commodities in the agreement. CIDA has the authority to purchase wheat, dairy products, and mackerel directly from the Canadian Wheat Board, the Canadian Dairy Commission, and the Fisheries Prices Support Board. In all other cases CIDA must request the Department of Supply and Services to obtain the commodities by open public tender.

A 1983 corporate evaluation of the food aid program found that at least three aspects of CIDA's planning process worked against CIDA's goal of making food aid purchases cost effective. First, the lengthy administrative process of acquiring Treasury Board approval and negotiating and approving an MOU for each recipient each year meant that purchases of food aid commodities often did not begin until the winter months when prices for food aid commodities are highest. Second, the lapsing requirement, which required that all aid purchases must be made before the end of the fiscal year, 31 March placed CIDA in a much weaker bargaining position with suppliers. Knowing that aid funds had to be spent by 31 March or would be lost, suppliers were in a position to hold out for higher prices. Third, since each agreement was handled separately, separate purchases of a particular commodity were made for each shipment in a specific project or program and CIDA was therefore unable to take advantage of volume discounts.[76]

Two developments, which were outlined in the previous chapter, were introduced to address some of these issues. The introduction of multi-year agreements and the delegation of Treasury Board authorities to CIDA were intended, at least in part, to permit CIDA planners to engage in more long-term forward planning that would enable the purchase of commodities at times when lower prices prevailed. By streamlining the programming process it was hoped that CIDA officials would have greater flexibility in purchasing in order to purchase more aid for the dollar.[77]

Despite these measures all problems with the procurement process have not been eliminated. For some time CIDA officials have felt that suppliers were taking advantage of the procurement process to the detriment of CIDA. Hard evidence of these suspicions finally became public in the 1984 auditor general's report. According to Treasury Board guidelines, food aid products must be purchased at world prices; however, the auditor general found that the Canadian Dairy Commission had in fact charged CIDA $4.9 million over world prices for skim milk powder between 1979 and 1982. The auditor general also discovered that CIDA was paying $150/tonne for fortifying milk powder with vitamins when the normal commercial price was $20/tonne, representing an overpayment of $3.6 million between 1980 and 1984.[78] Such pricing policies represented an additional transfer of some $8.5 million of the Canadian food aid budget to Canadian producers and processors without increasing the volume of food aid received by recipients.

Another more serious case of over-pricing became evident in 1987. A CIDA procurement officer became suspicious of comments made by a milling industry official in a phone conversation which seemed to suggest collusion among the millers who were supplying CIDA with flour. This was reported to the Bureau of Competition Policy, which carried out an extensive investigation. In March 1990 charges of bid-rigging and conspiracy to lessen competition were laid against eight milling companies under the Competitions Act. The charges involved $500 million in wheat flour contracts over a period between October 1975 and September 1987. According to the charges laid, price-fixing is said to have taken place even in the case of large emergency wheat shipments to Ethiopia, Sudan, and Chad. Subsequently four of the milling companies, including three of Canada's largest, Maple Leaf Mills, Robin Hood Multifoods, and Ogilvie Mills, pleaded guilty to the charges and agreed to pay $1 million each in fines. Investigation revealed that the Canadian National Millers Association had played a key role in operating the scheme. As a result the Millers Association was prohibited from circulating information that could be used to rig bids to its members.[79]

CONCLUSIONS

The selection of food aid products is a key element in determining the quality of Canadian food aid delivered by CIDA, but it is in this area that analysts of Canadian food aid policy have argued that concerns with domestic agricultural interests have been most prevalent. Ted Cohn, in examining the Canadian food aid program of the 1970s, argued that there has been "a persistence tendency to downgrade LDC interests."[80] In particular he noted that the "types of food donated are greatly influenced by availability of surpluses and by pressure from Canadian processors."[81] As the case studies in this chapter have shown, there is ample evidence to support Cohn's description of the politics of commodity selection in the 1970s.

Why did control over the selection process frequently elude CIDA officials, making it difficult for them to provide the products that they felt might be most appropriate? This occurred for two primary reasons. First, there existed a clear and identifiable domestic public which lobbied for the inclusion of specific commodities in the food aid program. Second, the departments and agencies dealing with the marketing of agricultural and fish products responded to such lobbying efforts by supporting the selection of these products. In many cases they were able to gain acceptance of their position by forcing the discussion to a higher level of decision-making, i.e., the cabinet, where CIDA was at a disadvantage in opposing their proposals. This has had a significant impact on the quality of the Canadian food aid program. As I have shown, Canadian food aid products have sometimes been inappropriate to the needs of recipient populations and have frequently been expensive both in terms of protein provided per dollar and in comparison with prevailing world market prices. In other cases concerns have been raised about the impact that certain Canadian food aid products have on the health and nutrition of recipients. As special interest concerns have forced the introduction of particular commodities, certain types of food have been shipped that CIDA would not normally have given high priority.

How has CIDA responded to such pressures? CIDA has employed three different organizational strategies in attempting to gain greater control of the selection of food commodities. First, it has attempted to establish what organizational theorists call a "negotiated environment" in order to establish greater certainty regarding the quantity and quality of the foodstuffs supplied to the food aid program. Proposals emanating from CIDA with regard to contracting with farmers, longer-term contracts with the Canada Wheat Board, the stockpiling of specially prepared products, the right of first refusal, and the establishment of triangular exchanges are all examples of CIDA's attempt to establish more direct control over the selection and availability of commodities.

Second, CIDA has attempted to strengthen its own administrative resources in dealing with the issue of commodity selection. Prior to the creation of the Food Aid Centre in 1978 CIDA had no specialized expertise on food aid and no one specifically responsible for responding to commodity issues. Interest groups promoting the use of particular commodities would generally approach departments first, such as Agriculture Canada, who would then make representations on their behalf to CIDA. CIDA was thus constantly being placed in a largely reactive position on the issue of commodity selection. Since the creation of the Food Aid Centre CIDA has established the position of a commodity officer who is responsible for monitoring Canada commodity availabilities and analysing needs of recipients.

The Food Aid Centre, through its commodity officer, now serves as the primary contact with interest groups. This places CIDA in a much better position to take a more active role by serving as an initial "gatekeeper" to screen out the more inappropriate commodities.

Third, as CIDA has developed greater administrative capacity to deal with food aid it has sought to build a policy consensus within the Canadian government regarding standards of appropriateness and cost effectiveness in commodity selection. It has attempted to develop a set of criteria that are based on principles set out in fora such as the WFP's Committee on Food Aid Policies, as well as by academic analysts. By appealing to these norms CIDA hopes to gain greater legitimacy for its case while putting other departments and interest groups in the defensive position of having to make a case for inclusion of the product.

Even though CIDA has achieved some success in injecting developmental issues into the process of commodity selection, the program has not been totally insulated from other considerations. As has been mentioned, many of the proposals originally put forward in the early 1970s have not been implemented. Some, like the concept of the "right of first refusal," were undoubtedly naive and not well thought out and were floated more or less as trial balloons. Others, such as the notion of contracting directly with farmers, received mixed support even within CIDA itself because of the problems such schemes could raise. Still other ideas, such as the concept of triangular exchanges, have been opposed by both agricultural interests and agencies such as the Treasury Board.

The adoption of selection criteria and the absence in the 1980s of more exotic food commodities such as powdered eggs and canned beef demonstrate that some progress has been made in injecting greater developmental concerns into the selection process. It can no longer be argued, as Cohn showed in the 1970s, that in most cases there is "a persistent tendency to downgrade LDC interests."[82] This does not mean that commercial factors no longer play a role. Although some of the more dramatic surplus disposal cases have been eliminated, an examination of the patterns of commodity composition during the past two decades reveals that export availability continues to be an important determinant of food aid supplies. Indeed, as the case of fish aid in the 1980s demonstrates, when domestic interest groups work in conjunction with other government departments, particularly in the case of a commodity such as fish which has a strong regional political significance, it is still possible to expand the role of a particular commodity in the food aid program despite the developmental concerns raised by CIDA.

5 The Programming of Bilateral Food Aid

In this chapter I will focus on the programming and implementation of Canadian bilateral food aid: that is, the process by which the actual annual allocations of food aid funds are made to specific recipient countries. Despite the critical attention that food aid has often received, the decision-making process by which bilateral food aid is allocated has been given very little attention in the existing literature.[1] However, a more detailed analysis of the organization of the decision-making process is important to this study for two reasons. First, the structure of the decision-making process determines the capabilities that the food aid program will have in such key areas as planning and analysis, data collection and evaluation, and program implementation. Second, the structure of the organization determines what particular perspectives and interests are introduced into the allocation process and what weights and priorities are assigned to them.[2] Administrative structures are intimately linked to the degree of planning and control a donor agency is able to implement, and thus they ultimately affect the type of aid strategy that a donor agency can pursue.[3] In this chapter I will explore these issues by examining the role that the donor and recipient play in the decision process. For example, are there explicit criteria guiding decision makers in allocation planning or are decisions arrived at through a process of ad hoc bargaining based on the exigencies of the given situation? Chapter 6 will examine the nature and scope of the discussions between the recipient and donor and the types of conditions placed on the food aid transfers.

THE BILATERAL PROGRAMMING
AND ALLOCATION PROCESS

The process by which Canadian bilateral food aid is allocated begins when the recipient country makes a request for food aid. This may be made to the Canadian mission within the country, directly to CIDA (e.g., during a visit of their officials to Canada), or at an aid consortium meeting. According to one CIDA official about 90 per cent of food aid proposals are initiated by the recipient. The request, which may be specific as to both the volume of the commodities desired, is then relayed to CIDA headquarters in Ottawa.

In making requests recipients frequently specify both the volume and the commodity make-up of the aid package. The recipient government usually has its own "shopping list," based on its perception of Canada as a food producer and the generosity of its terms. Recipients primarily request those products which they feel are comparatively advantageous. For example, if a recipient government knows that the European Economic Community (EEC) is currently offering skim milk powder at a cheaper price than Canada, it will direct its milk requests to the EEC and request another product, such as canola oil, from Canada. Even though the recipient is not buying the food as such, nevertheless it does recognize that a donor government is willing to grant it only a given dollar level of aid. The recipient is therefore anxious to obtain as large a volume and as high a quality as possible for the aid dollar received.

During the operation of the program in the seventies, the administration of the Canadian response to food aid requests was largely a "desk-based" operation within CIDA. The precise amounts and composition of the initial response were worked out at the country desk level by CIDA planning officers in Ottawa. Having received the request, a CIDA desk officer would begin a series of informal, ongoing discussions with the recipient government in order to determine if the request was justified. Once this was determined the planner would try to match the request with the supply of funds available and with the particular commodities available in Canada.

The task of making a decision based on both the volume and the content of the aid package has frequently been complicated by recipients who have inflated their requests to as much as double that which was actually needed. In addition certain recipients, through years of experience in making aid requests, have become, as one CIDA official noted, very "artful" in manipulating donors. For example, recipients have sometimes exaggerated their description of the difficulties giving rise to their need for aid, or they have presented overly optimistic reports of the reforms that they have made, hoping thereby to demonstrate their serious intentions to increase agricultural production and their merit as a worthy recipient. In some cases the discrepancy between the stated need and the actual situation might not have been the result of deliberate deception but instead the result of inadequate knowledge and expertise within the recipient's bureaucracy which led to inaccurate and misleading assessments of the recipient's needs and capacities.

The process by which the response to a recipient's request for food aid was formulated in the seventies was largely ad hoc, with minimal planning. As one CIDA official put it in 1978, the bilateral food aid was "patently underplanned." Another was careful to point out that "food aid is allocated, not programmed."

There are several reasons for describing Canadian bilateral food aid in the seventies as unplanned and ad hoc. In the majority of cases aid planners were reacting primarily to a specific food aid request for a single year. The response to this request was not based on an overall consideration of the entire development assistance program within a particular country. When planning documents were prepared as part of the country program review, the analysis of the relationship of food aid to other forms of development assistance was largely ignored. Nor was any effort made to evaluate the way in which the food aid transaction fitted into the overall agricultural development strategy of the recipient. Appraisal of the request usually took place in the context of the immediate factors surrounding the specific transaction under consideration. Food aid was thus allocated on an "add-on" basis. It was a distinct decision-making process, completely separate from the programming procedures for other development assistance. As the focus was only on the response to an immediate request, post-hoc evaluations of previous food aid shipments were minimal. As a result little effort was made to determine the impact that past shipments had had on the recipient's economy, whether future shipments were appropriate for development, and whether the recipients had pursued complimentary policies that maximized the developmental impact of the food aid.

In trying to explain why this approach to the management of the bilateral food aid program was pursued, five important factors can be cited: (i) the attitude of CIDA aid planners to food aid; (ii) personnel inadequacies; (iii) disbursement pressures; (iv) lack of food aid allocation criteria, and (v) conflict of bureaucratic interests.

The Attitude of CIDA Planners

Although an abundant literature now exists on the subject of food aid, it is only recently that any consensus has emerged as to the role that food aid should play in the developmental process. Since food aid was conceived as an instrument of surplus disposal, with developmental justifications added only later, CIDA planning officials have often seen food aid as a separate, non-integral part of Canadian overseas development assistance. Consequently food aid has been viewed by some desk officers as being essentially a "nuisance," except in cases of real emergency or balance-of-payments crises. This attitude was clearly illustrated when an aid planner for one of Canada's largest recipients noted in an interview that "food aid is a drag," and that his primary concern was to "get it over with and get on to the real development projects where results are clear." A former CIDA planning officer also recently noted that "desk officers like technical assistance more than food aid. It is long lasting and visible. Food aid is one shot. It goes in and disappears. That is why desk officers don't like to give it a lot of time."[4]

Personnel Inadequacies

This low opinion of food aid among many CIDA planning officers has been further complicated by certain personnel inadequacies related to training and workload. In the seventies there were no CIDA desk officers who were specifically trained to handle food aid as a specialty. Instead the planning of food aid was added to an already heavy workload. Two factors particularly militated against proper attention being paid to food aid planning.

First, the attention of CIDA aid planners is divided. Unlike the American Food-for-Peace officers who concentrate only on food aid, CIDA planning officers are also responsible for programming other developmental assistance to the recipient. A planning officer is generally involved in preparing economic cost-benefit analyses of aid projects, assisting in recommendations for change in the country assistance program, and maintaining a working relationship with the recipient government and institutions. A sampling by Suteera Thompson, published in 1980, showed that the average officer was involved in the planning of at least fourteen projects at any one time.[5] The CIDA planning officers who were interviewed pointed out that a major portion of their administrative time consisted of the preparation and writing of planning reports and recommendations for project aid. Some aid planners indicated that this left them with little time for any serious study of the recipient's domestic agricultural situation and other factors relating to food aid.

Second, the CIDA planning officers who were responsible for food aid were all based in Ottawa. Their only direct contact with the country under their responsibility might come through an annual visit of two to three weeks. In contrast to World Food Program and Food-For-Peace officials who are located in the field, CIDA planners found it difficult to keep in touch with the myriad factors which might have an impact on a food aid decision. Due to their lack of specialized training, their heavy workloads, and their lack of direct contact with the recipient's domestic situation, planning officers were not well equipped to engage in more detailed food aid planning.[6] This situation was further exacerbated in 1976 when a freeze was placed on any increases in CIDA manpower.[7]

Disbursement Pressures

Owing to the low priority given to food aid as a genuine developmental tool and the personnel inadequacies just mentioned, aid planners have frequently seen food aid as a useful device for attaining other objectives. Some planners have also placed a positive value on maintaining the unplanned, ad hoc approach to food aid allocations. This attitude is closely related to the pressure to disburse which is frequently felt by aid agencies. Such pressure stems in part from the tendency to judge the performance of aid donors by the amount of aid dollars that are transferred quickly. In addition, like other bureaucracies funded by annual government appropriations, aid agencies are often under pressure to use up all of their funds by the end of the fiscal year. Appropriation committees may feel that the existence of leftover funds is an indication that the agency does not need as much in subsequent budgets, or the failure to spend the full allocation may raise questions about the competence of the agency. As Desmond McNeill notes, this leads donor agencies to believe that "one of their biggest problems is to find suitable ways of using the budget they are allocated."[8]

Such an attitude creates an environment conducive to what Judith Tendler has aptly called "money-moving decision making."[9] In this situation the perspective of decision makers shifts from the "scarcity of resources," in terms of the needs of the global development effort, to the "organizational abundance."[10] From the aid planners' point of view, in spite of the constraints under which they work, there is an abundance of funds to spend. What is scarce are projects on which funds can be spent and the time in which to spend them. As a result aid agencies and planners use allocation strategies which can overcome these constraints, expand their absorptive capacity, and therefore permit them to "move" a satisfactory amount of money. Many compromises are made in the interest of fulfilling those requirements which are deemed necessary for the well-being of the agency.

The pressure to disburse is felt not only by the agency as a whole but is also a concern to individual aid planners. Studies have shown that the ability to disburse all of the authorized funds which had been allocated was an important criterion in determining career performance and advancement of CIDA planning officers. CIDA planners were frequently under "incredible pressure to spend."[11] This pressure was also felt within entire geographical divisions of the bilateral branch. A division unable to spend its allocated amount in one year might not receive its full request the following year. Thus pressures are generated to ensure that each division maintains its share of allocations.

Food aid became a factor in this situation largely because, next to cash grants, bulk shipments of program food aid are one of the fastest forms of disbursing aid, requiring minimal administration and time. This characteristic made them an attractive alternative for aid planners. Since rate of disbursal is a key element in evaluating an aid planner's ability, the selection of quick-disbursing food aid could be a wise choice in terms of career advancement.

The largely ad hoc, unplanned nature of food aid therefore permitted the aid planner to do several things. First, he could spend fairly large sums of aid money quickly, thereby lessening pressures to increase disbursement and reach volume targets.[12] Second, the aid planner could then spend a larger amount of his administrative time involved in the planning and memo writing required for the slow-dispersing project aid. This, according to one CIDA aid planner, enabled him to maintain his "bureaucratic respectability" within the department.

Third, the "liquid nature" of food aid could assist CIDA planners in relieving other bureaucratic pressures. A planner could provide large amounts of food aid to a country in order to maintain disbursement levels while "protecting slower moving and more intricate projects that have limited absorptive capacity for money."[13] In other words, since large sums were more rapidly transferred through program food aid, the aid planner was under less pressure to speed up or abandon those projects which, while valid in their own right, were more difficult to implement. Moreover, according to a CIDA report, the ability to move large bulk shipments of grains to bilateral recipients was a necessary instrument if the Canadian government was to meet its commitment, made at the World Food Conference in 1975, to provide one million tonnes of food grains during the three subsequent fiscal years.[14]

Fourth, food aid enabled planners to tackle another policy constraint within which they operated: the tying of aid. Although tied aid is not in itself a direct cause of the disbursement problem, it does compound the difficulty. This is particularly true in Canada's case where since 1970 80 per cent of the total ODA, exclusive of transportation costs, has been tied to the procurement of goods and services from Canadian sources. This can slow down many projects or make them totally impractical if Canada cannot supply the goods needed for these projects at a competitive price. The regulations for tied aid apply to the total ODA funds disbursed. Program food aid, as one component of the total ODA, is composed almost entirely of Canadian products. Therefore, as one internal CIDA document noted, "100% Canadian owned wheat or rapeseed builds up important local cost 'credits' that can be used to advantage in projects where tied aid is impractical."[15]

Absence of Allocation Planning Criteria

The negative attitude towards food aid on the part of many CIDA planners was frequently complemented by what one aid official described as an "ambivalent" attitude on the part of senior management. This was evident in the agency's failure before 1984 to develop any meaningful set of criteria which could be used in the evaluation and planning of food aid requests, despite a history of experience with food aid dating back to 1951. When Canadian resources were adequate to meet all requests, the lack of criteria was not an important issue. However, in periods when food aid requests outstripped the availability of funds, it became a very important factor. For example, because of austerity measures introduced by the federal government, the bilateral food aid program was cut from $138 million to $93 million between 1977–78 and 1979.[16] An official involved in the allocation process noted that a total of about $130 million in food aid requests were received from twenty countries.[17] In preparing the omnibus submission for Treasury Board approval, it was necessary to eliminate $37 million and nine countries.

The paring down of requests was done by the Bilateral Programs Advisory Group, which put the individual requests from the country desks together into one total omnibus submission. Aid planners viewing the process from below likened it to a "poker game," with the outcome completely unpredictable. One regional planner noted that it was impossible to discern any coherent set of criteria by which various requests were judged and finally approved or rejected. In light of this absence of a discernable set of criteria it was impossible for country desk officers to foresee with any certainty which type of food aid request was likely to be approved and which was not.

The Conflict of Bureaucratic Interests

John White, in his study *The Politics of Aid*, notes that when aid agencies refer to domestic pressures on decision-making they are often referring to other government departments rather than other domestic groups. Such departments can exert strong pressures and as White says, they see the aid program "almost exclusively as a field in which their own role [lies] in the preservation of non-developmental interests."[18]

The allocation process involves two key decisions: the selection of recipient countries and the determination of the exact type and amount of food aid to be allocated to a specific country.[19] Although CIDA has the formal responsibility for planning bilateral food aid allocations, numerous other departments have, at times, become involved in the process. As one External Affairs official put it, "CIDA does not run its own program." Thus, when other departments feel that a food allocation has an impact on their own interests, there is strong pressure on CIDA to accept their input and to negotiate the details of the program with other departments. These interdepartmental discussions occur in an ad hoc and informal fashion. Who gets involved, and at what point in the process, largely depends on the nature of the particular issue and the degree of importance that a department attaches to it. When conflicts arise over interdepartmental positions an effort is made to work out a compromise at that level. However, if departments feel strongly enough about an issue it may be progressively pushed to a higher level, until the departmental ministers are called upon to "sort it out."[20]

In most cases where a recipient is a "traditional customer," such as Bangladesh, the food aid is planned as a normal part of that country's aid program. The selection of that country as a food aid recipient has been determined at an earlier time in the history of the aid program and is no longer a critical subject of interdepartmental debate. The food aid allocation process may then be a largely internalized affair within CIDA. Other departments may become involved only to express their views about the level of the aid allocation.

In cases where the recipient has not been a traditional user of Canadian food aid, much more interdepartmental discussion and debate is likely to occur. Interdepartmental conflicts are likely to arise for two primary reasons: (i) a country has not received Canadian food aid before but another department wants to make a case for that country as a recipient, or (ii) an appropriate response to an aid request is made difficult by conflicting foreign policy and developmental objectives.

The clearest example of a department presenting a case for CIDA to include a country for foreign policy reasons is Portugal. As a European country Portugal had never received Canadian food aid. However, after a *coup d'état* overthrew the Caetano regime in 1974, External Affairs officials were anxious to demonstrate Canadian support for the new regime. Thus the Canadian ambassador recommended food aid as one way of providing the Portugese government with rapid balance-of-payments support as a demonstration of Canadian good will. According to an External Affairs official, the External Affairs Department's Portugal country desk, with the support of senior officials, pushed hard for the allocation.[21]

CIDA officials opposed the proposal on two grounds. First, they argued that no development objectives at all were involved. Second, since current funds were not readily available, they felt that the allocation should be postponed for one year. However, the issue was pushed to higher levels for resolution, with the External Affairs Department's position finally winning at the cabinet level. Thus in 1977/78 CIDA was prevailed upon to disburse $7.5 million worth of food aid to Portugal, which was not a Third World country, for clearly foreign policy reasons.[22]

Food aid allocations may not only be influenced by certain departments individually but also by what may be referred to as the "mood" of the interdepartmental community. An example of this was the difficulty of approving food aid shipments to India after its government exploded a nuclear device in 1974. The test was an embarrassment to the Canadian policy of exporting nuclear technology and material for "peaceful" purposes. As a result, a number of sanctions were taken against India, including the review of all aid programs with the exception of "food and food production aid."[23]

As a result of this incident the external affairs community in Ottawa felt a lingering resentment against the Indian government for its nuclear policy. According to some CIDA officials this explains why the 1987/79 request by India for $20 million in canola oil was passed only with great difficulty. CIDA aid planners argued in favour of approving the request; to them the canola program was seen as an excellent way of maintaining the Indian aid program until CIDA was able to develop some worthwhile project type of aid program within the following two to three years. Other departments, however, were strongly critical of the proposal. The Finance Department opposed the program because of the favourable balance-of-payments situation in India. The Treasury Board was concerned about a rapid expansion in the Indian aid program, especially in food aid aid. It argued for more project food aid as a way of enhancing the accountability and control of the program. The Treasury Board also criticized the fact that all $20 million would be concentrated on canola oil, rather than being more diversified among other Canadian products.

Not surprisingly, External Affairs showed particular indifference to the proposal. Support was also lacking from Industry, Trade and Commerce, largely because the Indian government was still in a position to buy canola oil commercially if the proposal was not approved. Although the Canadian government had specifically excluded food aid from its sanctions against India, CIDA officials report that it took an uphill battle on the agency's part to get such aid approved. As one CIDA official put it,"the things that tug at people's heart strings are not there" in the case of India.[24]

In some cases CIDA officials have dropped a food aid proposal altogether rather than face a lengthy interdepartmental debate. An example of this was the case of Vietnam. After the reunification of North and South Vietnam, the Vietnamese government was searching for food aid donors. Canada, approached at various times to become a donor, which it had become one primarily through international channels.[25] A CIDA official noted that the Vietnamese government had also requested bilateral food aid. In return it offered to open its books and invited Canadian officials to examine its projects and distribution facilities at first hand. This offer appeared to be a very good one, enabling Canadian officials to monitor food aid to a much greater extent than some other recipients are willing to allow. However, the CIDA official indicated that the agency was not prepared to "waste time" on the interdepartmental politics that such a request would necessitate. The invasion of Cambodia by Vietnam and mistreatment of ethnic Chinese in Vietnam made it politically untenable to support the aid request, especially against the opposition of External Affairs. Thus, as trade-offs were made among the various proposals on the 1978–79 aid list, Vietnam was cut off within CIDA itself before it faced an interdepartmental fight and the likelihood of having the proposal defeated.

In cases where a food aid proposal may face stiff interdepartmental opposition, the policy of allowing unspent funds to lapse at the end of the year adds another element to the thinking of CIDA officials. A rejection and lengthy debate over an alternative proposal could mean that the new project might not be approved and implemented before the deadline. There is therefore some pressure on officials to select projects that can be approved with relative ease. This, along with the previously cited factors, has helped to perpetuate the largely ad hoc, reactive approach to the allocation of Canada's bilateral food aid during the first three decades of the Canadian food aid program.

TOWARDS A MORE PLANNED APPROACH TO CANADIAN BILATERAL FOOD AID PROGRAMMING

The above account of the way in which the planning and programming of the Canadian food aid program was organized during the 1970s provides the basis for several observations. The principal characteristic of Canadian food aid decision-making procedures at that time was their highly dispersed, decentralized nature. There was no single centre for initiating action on food aid issues. Instead, responsibility was dispersed throughout several branches of CIDA and several other departments within the federal government. In each case, food aid was considered to be an adjunct to these units' other activities, and none of them dealt specifically with food aid as their central, on-going, specialized concern.

The bureaucratic structure for planning and administering Canadian food aid policy clearly reflected its origin as a short-term surplus disposal instrument in an era when development considerations were not given high priority. As food aid programs were established in response to particular historical situations, responsibility remained with those departments or branches that had first initiated the program. Although the food aid program was consolidated in a single vote in CIDA's budget, it in fact operated as a conglomeration of separate programs which were poorly coordinated and integrated. There was no centre of authority for initiating policy discussions relating to the food aid program as a whole, nor for monitoring the ways in which other Canadian policies had an impact on the food aid program. As the program began to grow larger in the 1970s, it became evident that this fragmented, ad hoc approach to food aid planning seriously undermined the effectiveness of the program.

In 1975 the auditor general gave special attention in his annual report to the spending and accounting practices of CIDA. In identifying a number of areas of weak administration, he singled out the food aid program as a particular example. Noting the number of "different responsibility centres" involved in food aid, the auditor general stated that "a lack of operational coordination has created confused situations sometimes detrimental to the food aid program."[26]

Further concerns about the negative effect of the fragmentation of decision-making responsibilities were voiced by the CIDA Task Force on Food Aid and Renewable Resources. The task force noted in particular that this fragmentation created delays in decision making and implementation, especially when responding to emergency food aid requests. As the task force said, "the general rule is extensive intra-agency discussion of what to send, in what amounts and how it will be funded. This often takes several weeks. Once these decisions are made, procurement is another lengthy process. As a result, the Agency is often justifiably accused of sending 'too little too late' in emergencies."[27]

The inadequacy of the Canadian decision-making procedures to respond effectively to recipient needs was further confirmed by an evaluation study carried out by the Treasury Board in 1976. In examining Canadian food aid shipments to the Sahel in 1973–74, the Treasury Board concluded that the numerous decision-making phases between the initial request and the final delivery and disbursement had resulted in some cases of inadequate and inappropriate response from Canada.[28]

*The Creation of the Food Aid Coordination
and Evaluation Centre (FACE)*

The general thrust of all these studies was the need for new organizational and administrative procedures that could consolidate and coordinate the various facets of the food aid program. The 1975 auditor general's report suggested that CIDA should establish a project coordinator. This person, according to the auditor general, should be responsible for all stages of food aid projects, putting an end to the fragmentation of food aid administration among a number of different responsibility centres.[29] The CIDA Task Force on Food Aid and Renewable Resources called for the creation of a centralized unit within CIDA to coordinate all aspects of food aid. It was suggested that one officer should be responsible for dealing with all policy issues relating to food aid and for liaison with other departments and that a second officer should coordinate all aspects of emergency food aid. In addition the task force called for CIDA to be given the leading role in the Interdepartmental World Food Program Committee and to act as Canada's official delegate to the WFP's Committee on Food Aid Policies.[30] The idea of centralizing some aspects of decision-making authority on food aid was given support in the Treasury Board evaluation of 1976, although its proposal was much more limited in scale than that proposed by CIDA's own task force.

The need for change in the administrative structures for planning food aid was reaffirmed in a confidential corporate review undertaken by CIDA in 1977.[31] As a result a new departure in food aid administration began in July 1978 with the creation of the Food Aid Coordination and Evaluation Centre (FACE). Although it was placed in the multilateral branch of CIDA the centre was given the broad mandate "to improve the efficiency and effectiveness of Canadian food aid."[32] In order to do this the new centre was given authority to "be involved in policy and financial management issues for all of CIDA's food aid program."[33]

After an initial start-up period personnel was increased to five professional and three support staff. For the first time there was within CIDA a specialized unit responsible for developing the policy framework for the Canadian food aid program and providing a focal point for expressing CIDA's own point of view regarding Canada's participation in the WFP, FAO, the World Food Council, and the International Wheat Agreement. In addition the centre was given responsibility for providing interdepartmental liaison on all food aid related issues, as well as serving as a focal point for contacts with domestic producers and interest groups.

Although the detailed planning and implementation of specific food aid allocations remains the responsibility of the respective branches, FACE has become increasingly involved in the overall coordination and management of the food aid budget and the annual allocation and approval process. For example, the annual allocation process now begins with FACE issuing a call letter requesting food aid proposals to all country desks and to the special programs branch. This call letter sets out the basic financial framework for food aid and any new policy developments relevant to the programming process. Country desks which contemplate putting forward food aid proposals must now establish a project team, which includes a representative from FACE, in order to collaborate in the preparation of the food aid proposal. Draft food aid proposals are then submitted to FACE before they are submitted to the respective vice-presidents for review. FACE is then responsible for drafting a final omnibus submission for approval by the CIDA president and the minister responsible for CIDA.[34] Within a relatively short period of time the centre has established itself as a participant in nearly every aspect of food aid decision making. Since the establishment of FACE several additional initiatives have taken place in an effort to enhance the programming of food aid, especially within the bilateral branch of CIDA. (Table 20 provides an overview of FACE's involvement in the bilateral planning process.)

Guidelines for Evaluating Food Aid Requests

Although FACE's responsibilities have grown since its establishment, its aim is not to supplant the role of the planning officer in food aid planning. Bilateral food aid planning is still essentially the responsibility of the country planning officers. Instead FACE has attempted to create an environment in which more effective food aid planning can take place by developing a firm data base which serves as a resource for planning officers in the food aid decision-making process. Perhaps even more significant has been the formulation of a set of guidelines to be used by planning officers in the preparation of food aid proposals. These guidelines require information regarding the objectives to be pursued, the end uses of the food aid, and an indication of the reporting, monitoring and evaluating procedures required.[35] They have since been incorporated into a much more detailed programming manual which not only gives detailed guidelines for programming food aid but also presents an overview of the major policy issues involved in the use of food aid and provides extensive information about the characteristics of particular food aid commodities.[36]

Interviewees in the bilateral branch of CIDA have indicated that the establishment of such explicit criteria for evaluating food aid requests has had some subtle effects on the way planning officers approach food aid. First, some desk officers have become "sensitized" to the potentially positive uses of food aid. This is partly due to FACE's efforts to provide more information to country desks. Enhancing the analytical resources available allows food aid to be more clearly planned to meet the needs of recipients. At the same time, pressure from FACE for greater justification of food aid requests has required planners to think through the end uses of their food aid allocations.

Second, the establishment of explicit criteria has helped to provide greater coherence to the planning process. One bilateral official noted, for example, that the guidelines helped to clarify the "rules of the game." As a result, the process of selecting among food aid requests was "no longer a poker game." Instead, when planners prepare their requests they now know in advance which factors will be taken into account and which will be given greater priority.

Third, the guidelines discourage what one interviewee referred to as "fly-by-night" requests. As the centre is asking for greater

Table 20
The bilateral food aid allocation process

Stage 1 Identification	Stage 2 Analysis and development	Stage 3 Review
Receipt of food request by country desk officer	each country desk analyses and evaluates:	the proposal is reviewed, modified and refined as follows:
Country program visits to each recipient by the country desk officers	the amount of food aid that the recipient needs to meet its particular needs	review of desk's proposal by a committee of chief planning officers of the Geographic Division
Data is collected on recipient's food requirements, agricultural production, balance-of-payments situation, efforts at self-development, etc.	the recipient's request, in light of the availability of Canadian commodities	joint review of proposals by food aid programme teams (composed of FACE and branch representatives, and chaired by FACE)
Desk collects information from the country mission, FACE, WFP, other donor agencies, other federal government departments	the ability of the recipient to utilise efficiently the amount of commodities requested	
	the assistance being provided by other donors	common agreement on food aid levels by branch
	the Canadian food aid proposal from the above factors that is best suited toward "matching" the recipient's needs	branch decision on country levels

Stage 4 Approval	Stage 5 Implementation
translation of the proposal into an omnibus submission by FACE	procurement arranged through government agencies (e.g., Canadian Wheat Board, Fisheries Prices Support Board, Canadian Dairy Commission, etc.) or competitive tenders
following endorsement by CIDA president, it is sent to the minister for consideration	tender calls to select suppliers
specific country requests sent to Treasury Board for review and approval, if necessary (i.e. those above $15 million)	arrangement for transportation
	verification of safe arrival at recipient government's port of entry
notification of proposed transfers to FAO Committee on Surplus Disposal	
	monitoring and evaluation
signing of "memorandum of understanding" with recipient government	

justification and more background information, greater preparation is required of aid planners if their requests are going to be accepted. Thus they must be willing to take more time in considering and preparing requests. According to several CIDA officials some requests have been withdrawn or not submitted at all because the aid planner did not want to appear in a negative light as the result of an inadequately prepared request.

Multi-Year Agreements

The effort to promote more careful planning of bilateral food aid allocations has been significantly enhanced by authorization for CIDA to enter into long-term agreements with some food aid recipients. It has been argued for some time by food aid experts that food aid can only be used effectively by recipients for developmental purposes when it is planned on a long-term basis.[37] If a donor is willing to make a commitment over a period of several years, then the recipient is assured of secure supplies for a definite period of time. For the recipient this facilitates better integration of food aid into its overall development planning and helps to stabilize its food supplies on a longer-term basis. For the donor longer-term agreements are administratively more efficient because planning officers do not have to wait until the whole approval process is complete each year before moving on to the more time-consuming tasks of negotiating with the recipient over details of the implementation and arranging for the procurement of the foodstuffs.

The concept of forward planning was given some acknowledgment when Canada made its three-year pledge at the World Food Conference in 1974. The idea was picked up by CIDA's Task Force on Food Aid and Renewable Resources, which recommended that CIDA negotiate all bilateral food aid agreements with major recipients on a three-year basis. These agreements involve pledging a minimum figure for the three years, with additional amounts being negotiated as needed on a year-to-year basis.[38]

However, authorization for the implementation of such agreements was slow in coming to CIDA, primarily because of opposition from the Treasury Board and Finance Department. Officials from these departments were reluctant to accept multi-year agreements because they feared a reduction in budgetary flexibility. They pointed out, for example, that because economic conditions at home and abroad can change so rapidly they were reluctant, from a fiscal point of view, to unnecessarily lock themselves into binding commitments.[39]

However, in 1981 CIDA won a major victory when it was granted the authority to negotiate a three-year agreement with the government of Bangladesh. Since then CIDA has entered into similar agreements with Senegal, Ghana, Peru, Sri Lanka, India, and Mali. Within CIDA this is seen as a significant development in overcoming an important constraint on the longer-term planning of food aid. According to a recent policy statement, CIDA notes that when these bilateral agreements are combined with its biennial pledge to the WFP it expects 75 per cent of its total food aid will be provided on a multi-year basis.[40]

Integration of Food Aid with Other Development Assistance

However, CIDA has not been as successful in implementing another important element in the reform of the food aid planning process. In 1978 the Interdepartmental Working Group on Food Aid Policy proposed that all bilateral food aid, other than emergency aid, should no longer be programmed on an "add-on" basis. Instead it should be fully integrated into the overall development assistance planning for each country. As part of this process periodic reviews and evaluations would be built into the planning process so that objectives could be clearly identified and the degree of effectiveness in meeting them could be determined.

In proposing that the planning of food aid be integrated into overall development assistance programming the Interdepartmental Working Group was proposing in effect to extend the concept of country programming to food aid. In applying this concept it was anticipated that CIDA would work towards a food aid program which would be "tailor-made" for each of its recipients. To achieve this the committee proposed a process of periodic review and evaluation which would follow four principal steps:

1 An identification of the specific objectives that the particular food aid program is intended to meet.
2 An identification of other Canadian or international aid programs which may have objectives that are either similar or conflicting in nature.
3 An assessment of the alternative types of aid available and their comparative efficiency in meeting the stated objectives.
4 A review of countries which had received food aid for three consecutive years to determine whether the original objectives of the program had been met and to identify the impact of food aid on the recipient.

Despite the shift in policy and the creation of a new administrative structure, the integration of bilateral food aid planning into the process of country programming has not in fact fully materialized. Interviewees in both FACE and the bilateral branch agree that the two have not yet been successfully integrated. Although the interviewees expressed strong support for the concept, they pointed out that in practice food aid continues to be allocated primarily on an "add-on" basis.

An important obstacle to the implementation of this concept lies in the current budgetary structure for CIDA funding. Once the level of food aid is determined for the year, CIDA is basically committed to disbursing that amount for food aid. CIDA aid planners point out that they are unable to make the kind of trade-offs that country programming would imply. They do not have the flexibility to freely move funds from food aid to development assistance, or the reverse, based on their assessment of the needs of the recipient. If a country has made advances in agricultural production and its need for food aid is reduced, it is not possible to transfer the funds to other types of assistance. Nor is it possible for CIDA officials to use the funds for other related activities, such as the improvement of transportation or port facilities within the country. While such projects may improve the effectiveness of food aid, they are not in themselves using additional foodstuffs and therefore cannot be included in the food aid budget. Consequently the recipient is faced with a decrease in food aid with no concomitant increase in other forms of assistance. Some CIDA officials argue that this penalizes those recipients who have taken measures to increase agricultural production, by reducing the total flow of aid available to them. As a result some CIDA aid planners feel that the two-vote structure reduces their flexibility in making the most effective use of food aid and have argued for its elimination. However, this has received stiff opposition from other departments in various interdepartmental discussions. The Departments of Agriculture, Finance, and the Treasury Board have been particularly adamant in maintaining the separate vote structure. The argument most often cited is the need to maintain tight budgetary control over such a large program as food aid allocations. Officials in all three departments cited both the size of the food aid program and the auditor general's report as reasons for using the separate vote structures to maintain greater financial control.

However, one Treasury Board policy analyst indicated when interviewed that there were differing viewpoints within the Treasury Board on this issue. He pointed out that the conclusions of the Treasury Board evaluation, which emanated from the then-separate policy division of the Treasury Board, were consistent with integrating the two votes; but he also noted that the project division argued that this would involve a move away from line item budgeting which is easier to carry out from an accounting point of view. Thus the project division's desire to maintain stricter control over food aid won out as the Treasury Board's position in interdepartmental discussions.[41]

Opposition to the notion of integrating the two votes essentially revolves around the question of "additionality." Food aid has generally been based on the concept that food aid is pledged in "addition" to the development assistance that is given. In other words, if food aid were to be eliminated the same amount of funds would not automatically be allocated to other types of development assistance. The removal of separate budgetary votes would assume the opposite: that is, aid planners would have the choice of channelling aid funds into whichever program was deemed the most appropriate. There are domestic forces which favour maintaining the additionality of food aid and consequently the two-vote structure. Agriculture Canada, for example, wants to satisfy domestic producer interests by maintaining as high a level of food aid as possible. Elimination of food aid as a separate activity would make it more difficult to tailor the program to serve Canadian domestic interests and to ensure that food aid levels are maintained.[42]

CONCLUSIONS

As my analysis has shown, Canadian officials took a passive, ad hoc approach to the management of bilateral food aid in the seventies. This unplanned approach to the allocation of bilateral food aid emerged as a natural response on the part of CIDA planners to a variety of environmental influences. In the absence of a clear rationale for a developmental use of food aid, CIDA planners found that food aid could serve a variety of other useful purposes. Since program food aid was not administratively demanding, it played a useful role in dealing with disbursements pressures and the constraints of tied aid. In essence, because of an organizational environment which stressed the necessity of "moving money," CIDA planners had an interest in keeping food aid planning as simple and as uninvolved as possible. There was no clear incentive for planners to spend greater time on planning food aid allocations because such planning cut into what they perceived as the "real" development task before them.

However, as the events of the "food crisis" in the seventies provoked greater scrutiny of food aid programs, CIDA officials became aware of the need to put food aid planning on a sounder basis. The early seventies had been a period of significant growth within CIDA but by the mid-seventies, with a budget of over $1 billion and a president known for his flamboyant management style, CIDA's administrative practices increasingly attracted attention. Reports of the mishandling of food aid distribution overseas only served to fuel such doubts. In particular, criticisms levelled by such sources as the auditor general threatened to undermine the credibility of CIDA while giving ammunition to those who argued for reductions in aid spending and tighter controls on CIDA. In the absence of any formal food aid policy, it is not surprising that this growing "crisis of confidence" prodded CIDA officials into seeking other ways to give greater coherence to the program and to reduce those uncertainties which made it so vulnerable to domestic criticism.

The principal instrument for achieving this was the Food Aid Co-ordination and Evaluation Centre. The aim of the centre was not to supplant the existing food aid allocation process but to use its role as co-ordinator and disseminator of information to act, in the words of one CIDA official, as the "conscience" of country planners. By introducing criteria for evaluating food aid requirements, taking responsibility for some of the more onerous implementation tasks such as procurement, and emphasizing longer-term agreements, FACE attempted to reduce the incentive to treat food aid as merely a "throw-away" item. It is clear that these reforms were introduced to increase the effectiveness of Canadian food aid. To the extent that such measures have been successful, they are dysfunctional vis-à-vis those interests promoting short-term commercial and foreign policy objectives. Furthermore, by placing emphasis on criteria and the provision of greater information to justify food aid proposals, the increased institutionalization of the food aid program is intended to make food aid less attractive in serving purely bureaucratic objectives.

However, there are limits as to how far such organizational reforms can go. This is reflected in the maintenance of food aid as a separate vote within the CIDA budget. The budget structure is a clear reflection of the program's origins as a surplus disposal instrument with limited links to other development assistance programming and some CIDA officials have felt that the maintenance of the two-vote structure limits the extent to which food aid can be fully integrated into overall country programming. This issue is a clear reminder that, once established, institutional structures are hard to change. Even though the circumstances that existed at the founding of the food aid program have clearly changed, established organizational interests are reluctant to see further modifications that might threaten bureaucratic missions or the allocation of budgetary resources. To those who oppose the integration of food aid into one budget vote, the separate vote structure is seen as a means of maintaining some visible control over future levels of food aid spending.

6 The Control of Food Aid and the Issue of Conditionality

When a donor country decides to grant food aid to a recipient country, it faces two fundamental policy decisions. First, should the donor place conditions on the recipient to control the use of its aid funds and the domestic policies which may determine aid effectiveness? Second, if some degree of donor intervention is deemed necessary, what will the conditions be and how will they be administered? These questions are crucial because the donor's attitude toward control and intervention shapes the relationship that exists between the two countries. The donor's attitude also determines the type of administrative machinery and instruments that are necessary to give operational meaning and content to the donor-recipient relationship.

The question of how interventionist a donor should be is particularly sensitive in the case of food aid. Those who have agricultural interests may be concerned that indiscriminate allocations of food aid will have a harmful effect on the structure of commercial market shares. Aid critics point to the negative effects that unregulated food aid can have on a recipient's domestic agricultural production policies and press reports have frequently decried the corruption of recipient officials and the diversion of food commodities for illicit purposes. Such concerns have frequently led aid officials to establish greater control over the use of food aid.[1]

The demand for more conditions on food aid allocations has created a dilemma for aid administrators. Conditions that are aimed primarily at meeting the interests of the donor can weaken the developmental impact of the food aid. In contrast, a program with minimal control of the recipient's use of food transfers may leave the donor agency open to charges of mismanagement by domestic critics. A program containing too many conditions, although these are intended to enhance developmental impact, may create serious friction in the donor-recipient relationship. This chapter examines how Canadian policy makers have attempted to resolve this dilemma. I will analyse the "hands-off" approach to food aid control that has typified the Canadian food aid program in the past and then go on to examine recent efforts to shift Canadian food aid strategies towards a much more activist approach on the part of the donor.

THE AID-GIVING PROCESS AND DONOR CONTROL

In order to understand more clearly the approach that the Canadian government has taken to aid control, it is useful to put the issue into the broader context of the aid-giving process. The donor-recipient relationship is highly complex. Contrary to what dependency theorists might suggest, the process of giving food aid is not simply a unilateral transfer of resources in which a dependent recipient government plays an essentially passive role while the donor defines the nature and terms of their relationship. Instead the donor-recipient relationship is one of mutual dependence in which officials on both sides of the relationship seek to attain certain objectives whose achievement depends to some extent on the actions of the other.[2]

The organisational objectives of donor and recipient agencies have been outlined by Jeffrey Pressman in his model of the aid-giving process.[3] According to Pressman, donor agencies frequently pursue five principal objectives:

1 Moving money   Since the success of a donor agency is often measured by its ability to spend its budget, donors are anxious to find projects that successfully move money through the organization.
2 Information   In carrying out its programs the donor needs information about how the recipient is utilizing its aid funds and the activities of other donors in the field.
3 Control   To assure that its projects are being properly implemented the donor needs to establish some degree of control.
4 Justification   To justify its program with sponsoring agencies at home, the donor seeks information to prove that its projects are worthwhile.

5 Recipient stability and support   To ensure a steady flow of aid funds, the donor tries to establish a stable relationship with the recipient and seeks allies that support its aims within the local government.

At the same time the recipient agency may be pursuing its own set of objectives. These may be any of the following:

1 Attracting Money   The recipient, since it is competing with a number of developing countries for relatively scarce resources, must be able to attract money.
2 Achieving a steady flow of money   The recipient's development planning is facilitated by a steady and predictable flow of aid funds.
3 Autonomy   The recipient has clear preferences as to how aid funds should be used and does not want to appear too dependent on foreign governments.
4 Donor stability and support   The recipient, in order to keep a steady flow of aid funds, is interested in establishing a stable, supportive, and predictable relationship with the donor.

The ability of each side to achieve its objectives is limited by certain basic constraints. First, problems of distance and communication often create an information gap in which key decisions in the aid-giving process must be made in a climate of uncertainty. Second, there are a large number of participants in the aid-giving process. Not only can there be a large number of donors dealing with a single recipient, but the relationship between donors and recipients takes place through groups and units that have varying responsibilities and objectives in the aid process. The aid process is thus characterized by institutional fragmentation and administrative complexity.

These basic constraints in the aid-giving environment limit the type of organizational objectives that participants can accomplish. As well, in attempting to overcome these constraints one participant may place a priority on objectives which conflict directly with the objectives of other participants. For example, the donor's preference for greater control may threaten the recipient's desire for autonomy. Pressman concludes that "as the aid process takes shape, the elements of the model interact with each other to produce difficulties for both donors and recipients and to generate conflicts between these groups."[4] The type of aid relationship between a donor and recipient emerges as an outcome of a bargaining process over conflicting objectives and efforts to overcome environmental constraints.

THE CANADIAN APPROACH TO FOOD AID

Pressman's model of the aid-giving process provides a useful perspective from which to analyse the Canadian approach to the food aid relationship and the issue of conditionality. It is important to remember, however, that Canadian food aid has been disbursed largely in program form which consists of bulk shipments of food commodities in significant volumes. Once the food shipments arrive at the designated port of entry, commodities are turned over to the recipient government, which then assumes full responsibility for their disposition. The recipient government is free to sell the food on the open market or through state-run public distribution systems. Canadian officials have generally felt that their responsibility ended once the commodities reached the recipient's port of entry.

Compared with other types of aid, program food aid is characterized by a high volume-dispersal to administrative input ratio, since it involves the disbursement of only a relatively small number of large bulk shipments.[5] The role of the aid planner is little more than that of a commodity broker. The planner's task is to receive the food aid requests, match them with the availability of Canadian supplies, and recommend their approval. For CIDA, the relative ease of sending large shipments of food aid makes program food aid an attractive instrument for meeting several donor objectives. As chapter 5 has shown, bilateral food aid has enabled CIDA planners to "move money," meet disbursement targets, and cope with other constraints such as aid-tying requirements. Moreover, food aid has been seen as an effective way to build domestic public support for the total aid budget. An internal CIDA document published in 1975 referred to "the public support earned [for] development aid in general through provision of shiploads of food obviously intended for starving countries."[6] The same document notes elsewhere that "food satisfies more of the 'humanitarian' instincts of the donor than other potential commodities such as newsprint or machines."[7]

Furthermore, food aid has been seen as an effective way of building a more stable relationship with the aid recipient. First, the provision of food aid has enabled some LDC governments to demonstrate that they have friendly outside powers upon whom they can call. This helps local government leaders to appear in a positive light to their own people and generates good will toward Canada. This in turn predisposes the recipient toward Canada when the aid relationship goes through difficult periods. Being seen as a friendly and forthcoming country in its food aid transfers helps establish a more satisfactory working relationship and, according to CIDA officials, may permit franker discussion of more sensitive issues at a later date.[8] As one CIDA document has stated, "historically CIDA has established a reputation as a sympathetic donor."[9] In the same vein a number of the officials who were interviewed cited CIDA's reputation for attaching minimal conditions on its food aid as a positive feature in comparison with American Food-for-Peace program, where long debates over counterpart funds and self-help measures have created serious tensions in the donor-recipient relationship.

In addition CIDA officials have acknowledged that providing access to cheap food supplies is often seen as a key to insuring domestic political stability. This is most clearly evident in the way Canadian food aid has been used to support government-sponsored public distribution systems (PDS). During the first thirty years of the bilateral food aid program fully 75 per cent of Canada's total food aid was channelled to only four countries: India, Bangladesh, Pakistan, and Sri Lanka. Each of these countries operates a PDS which supplies food commodities to various target groups within the population at specially subsidized prices often below those prevailing in the market place. Access to the PDS is usually controlled through rationing cards or vouchers. This enables the government to give priority access to cheap food supplies to civil servants, military personnel, and other politically sensitive urban groups. Giving subsidized food to government employees is seen as a means of limiting demands for increased wages or other benefits. Governments typically supply the PDS through domestic procurement and foreign imports on either a commercial or concessional basis. By providing food aid for this purpose the donor assists the recipient in meeting its domestic political objectives while alleviating the foreign exchange cost of additional commercial food imports.[10]

CIDA officials have defended this use of food aid by arguing that development can only take place in stable political environment. To cut off food aid because it is being used by urban elites could potentially cause domestic chaos and possibly destroy whatever developmental processes already exist. Noting that food aid to Bangladesh was not really developmental, one official stated in 1979 that "if it aids political stability, then we can live with it."[11] Similar sentiments have been expressed by other CIDA officials who are involved in giving food aid to Bangladesh. A CIDA document entitled "Food Aid and Food Policies in Bangladesh" gives a further elaboration of this viewpoint. It notes that "there is ample evidence that the country's stability depends to a great extent on the politically volatile and articulate urban population ... it would be very difficult to withdraw a form of government assistance which urban residents have depended on for more than thirty-five years. Government action to ensure an adequate supply of food at reasonable prices has become a political necessity."[12]

As a result of this attitude toward the use of food aid Canadian officials have not developed an extensive arsenal of policy devices for controlling the use of its food aid once it is in the hands of the recipient government. The only "control" instrument consistently used is the memorandum of understanding (MOU), an agreement signed by Canada and each of its aid recipients which outlines the basic requirements that the recipient must fulfil in accepting Canadian food aid.

The MOU has traditionally included three requirements. The first, a safeguard clause, prohibits the recipient from directing its food aid to another country or exporting certain commodities for an agreed amount of time, generally for six months to a year. This ban on exports applies not only to the specific food aid commodity but also to improved products (i.e., wheat flour for those receiving wheat) or replacement products (i.e., a recipient of canola oil cannot export any edible oil).

The second requirement is the usual marketing requirement (UMR), which requires the recipient to maintain a specified level of commercial imports in addition to imports of the same commodity as food aid.[13] This measure is intended to maintain the principle of additionality: by specifying the level of commercial imports that the recipient is required to maintain, the donor ensures that its food aid is not in fact replacing commercial transfers which would take place with it or other exporting countries. The donor is largely responsible, in consultation with other exporting countries, for determining at what level the UMR should be set, generally on the basis of the average level of imports of the particular commodity during the five previous years. Canada's approach to the UMR has been relatively flexible. For example, Canada has frequently exempted countries from the requirement in cases where the country is experiencing severe balance-of-payments difficulties or other serious economic problems, or where the food aid is being supplied as part of an emergency relief program.[14]

Canadian officials have also opposed the use of tied UMR's. Normally a recipient may make commercial purchases in fulfilment of its requirements from any exporting country. American officials, however, have frequently favoured the use of tied UMR's which require that a minimum portion, or perhaps all, of the recipients commercial requirements be purchased from the donor. Canada has used the Food and Agriculture Organization Sub-Committee on Surplus Disposal to protest vigorously against the practice of tied UMR's. Clearly

Canadian officials were concerned about the damage that such measures could do to Canada's traditional commercial markets if the United States used tied UMR's as leverage to improve its share of the recipient's markets, but they also argued that it limited the ability of recipients to shift suppliers and seek the best prices available for a particular commodity.[15]

The third requirement is that the recipient establish a counterpart fund. Revenues from the sale of Canadian food aid are placed in the fund and Canadian and recipient officials jointly agree to development projects to be funded out of these monies. The counterpart funds are seen as having two functions. First, they help the donor to legitimize its surplus disposal program by allowing it to claim that the revenues from the sale of aid are going to developmentally worthwhile projects. Second, the funds provide the donor with some "leverage" over the recipient. By agreeing to the funding of certain development projects, Canadian officials help to shape the domestic priorities of the recipient.[16]

However, despite such potential advantages, Canadian officials have never taken the counterpart funds seriously. The requirement that funds be set aside in local currency "on the value of the Canadian expenditure" proved to be a major stumbling block. In some cases governments were obliged to print new money or transfer funds from other government departments, thus postponing locally financed development activities. As a result, some recipients resented the counterpart requirements, which they viewed as unnecessary. This in turn generated a policy of indifference among Canadian administrators when it came to enforcing the monitoring procedures. Keith Spicer notes that "for years the frictions and imperfections of the system led Canadian administrators to supervise the funds with at best sporadic attention."[17] In 1961 it was estimated that nearly two-thirds of the funds generated by Canadian food aid remained unallocated.[18]

The 1964–65 Appropriations Act changed the nature of the food aid program by establishing it as a separate budget item distinct from development assistance. Food aid was recognized as a legitimate activity in its own right, thus removing the legal basis for the counterpart fund requirement. Despite this counterpart fund requirements have remained a consistent part of Canadian aid agreements. After the establishment of CIDA in 1968 the foreign policy review conducted by the Trudeau government in 1970 reaffirmed the counterpart fund requirement.[19]

Although the counterpart fund requirement was maintained throughout the seventies, the attitude of CIDA administrators remained predominantly negative. As a CIDA manual noted in 1973, the agency's experience with counterpart funds "has not been entirely successful since there has been a tendency to regard them as a bookkeeping exercises rather than as a means to influence the development strategy of the recipient."[20] Aid administrators for the larger Asian recipients saw the counterpart funds as an unnecessary burden. This was especially true, they argued, in countries such as Bangladesh where food aid was fed into large public distribution systems and the revenues received were used to maintain the distribution system itself. Some officials argued that the strict application of monitoring procedures would be time-consuming and would only lead to increased tension between recipient and donor officials.[21]

This negative attitude led to a very passive approach towards the use of counterpart funds by both Canadian officials and recipients. In Indonesia officials could not agree on the use of counterpart funds and rapid inflation quickly reduced the value of the funds to nearly zero.[22] In other cases where projects were not identified, it was noted that "there has been a substantial buildup of counterpart funds in such countries as India and Pakistan which has been the cause of some embarrassment to both Canada and recipients."[23] Both the 1975 Task Force on Food Aid and Renewable Resources and the 1978 Treasury Board study concluded that CIDA's approach to counterpart funds had been so superficial that they had no real influence over the timing or use of the local sale proceeds of Canadian food aid. A CIDA official summed up the agency's experience in the following words: "I think, in fairness, it is only on few occasions when we do have the assurances that one would normally look for to conclude that the counterpart funds are being used specifically for worthwhile development activities."[24] CIDA's 1975 Task Force on Food Aid and Renewable Resources concluded that "in practice, the system is often so artificial that the donor's credibility in other areas may be undermined."[25]

CIDA also placed little emphasis on the need to obtain detailed information from the recipient or develop control measures over the disposition of its aid because of the high priority given to the use of food aid as a quick-disbursing liquid transfer that both helped the donor agency "move money" and promoted recipient stability. The ad hoc, year-to-year allocations posed some problems for recipients. Canada did not, for example, guarantee a steady flow of food aid allocations. In 1974, when world food prices were rising and many countries were experiencing food shortages, the total volume of Canadian food aid actually dropped. In 1979/80, when CIDA was trying to make austerity cuts in its aid program, the number of food aid recipients dropped to ten from nineteen in the previous year. Because of the short term basis on which food aid was allocated, some recipients complained that procurement procedures did not insure them of the maximum amount of food at the lowest possible prices.[26]

However, these complaints were largely compensated for by the recipients ability to maintain maximum autonomy in the use of food aid. The supply of bulk shipments of food as a general budgetary or balance-of-payments support did not place additional administrative burdens on the recipient government. Since monitoring of the disposition of food aid shipments and evaluation of past allocations were virtually non-existent, the recipient government did not have to worry about the donor meddling in its internal affairs. In cases where other donors withheld food aid from recipients to create pressure for other concessions, such as the Americans have done at various times in India, Bangladesh, and Jamaica, Canada has continued its food aid shipments.[27]

The food aid relationship that emerged in the sixties and seventies was thus, from the point of view of donor and recipient agencies, a mutually beneficial one. Saddled with a surplus disposal program not of its own choosing, bulk shipments of food were seen by CIDA as fulfilling several agency objectives. Food aid helped the agency to cope with disbursement constraints and thereby meet its need to "move money." Its symbolic and humanitarian appeal helped to build domestic support for foreign aid in general. Without food aid the overall level of aid giving would undoubtedly have been lower. Finally, food aid was helpful in building a stable and receptive political environment in recipient countries that enabled other projects of a more "developmental" nature to be carried out. From the recipient's standpoint, although food aid may not have always been their first priority it did at least provide an additional source of resources that had minimal strings attached and could be used with a considerable degree of autonomy. Since CIDA placed greater emphasis on the relationship-building function of food aid than on donor control, the food aid relationship was essentially low key in nature with minimal donor-recipient conflict over divergent views of autonomy and control. In addition, this type of aid relationship placed minimal demands on the participants from an administrative and analytical point of view.

THE FOOD AID CONUNDRUM

By the mid-1970s the passive approach to food aid came to haunt CIDA. The heightened media coverage of the 1974/75 food crisis led to numerous press stories which reported wholesale wastage of food, corruption and smuggling, and political favouritism in the distribution of food aid.[28] Opposition critics attacked Canada's practice of permitting recipients to sell food aid rather than distributing it directly to the neediest population.[29] Instead of building confidence in foreign aid, food aid provided a new set of "horror stories" at a time when the agency was coming under closer public scrutiny.[30] In response to the growing criticisms CIDA President Gérin-Lajoie made a high profile visit to Bangladesh, only to report that "it is indeed a sad fact that part of our food aid does not reach those for whom it is meant."[31]

By the beginning of the 1980s there was a growing crisis of confidence in Canadian food aid. A number of voices expressed concern that the "cheap food" being provided by CIDA discouraged domestic production, enabled governments to postpone costly reforms, and was not equitably distributed. These criticisms appeared to be confirmed by the government's own studies. In 1977 a joint CIDA-Treasury Board study concluded that the five largest recipients of Canadian food aid, who made up 75 per cent of Canada's total food aid program," appeared to accommodate policies discouraging domestic production in both the short term and long term."[32]

Critics of food aid have frequently argued that increased food dependence makes food deficit countries more vulnerable to external influences.[33] However, it now appears that increased levels of minimally controlled food aid can actually make the donor agency increasingly vulnerable from the viewpoint of its own organizational survival. In its desire to provide a quick-disbursing form of aid and build a smoother aid relationship, CIDA left most of the key issues of aid control in the hands of the recipient. But the decisions made by the recipient government concerning the ultimate disposition of this aid now left CIDA open to criticism from the anti-foreign-aid lobby,[34] from other government agencies concerned about financial accountability,[35] and from Canada's development community.[36] Thus CIDA's desire to take a relatively "hands-off" approach to the donor-recipient relationship left it increasingly vulnerable to domestic critics as public attention in the late 1970s focused on the growing aid program.

Like other donors, CIDA faced what one writer has called an "impossible conundrum."[37] If the donor continued to provide food aid as it had in the past, with little supervision or control, then it perpetuated policies that neglected agrarian reform and increased food dependency. CIDA would then be leaving itself open to more "horror stories" in the future. Yet the suggestion by some to abolish food aid, except in the case of emergencies, was not seen as a viable option.

How then could CIDA resolve this "conundrum" of supplying more food aid without perpetuating its negative effects and creating new horror stories about aid mismanagement? This question has received increased attention within CIDA as its aid programs have come under increased scrutiny in recent years CIDA President Margaret Catley-Carlson raised these concerns in an address to the Committee on Food Aid Policies and Programmes of the WFP in October 1985. She began by noting that funding for aid is increasingly limited and, despite global grain surpluses, recipient countries should not take a growing supply of food aid for granted. Instead she argued that "food aid is a scarce resource and we must manage it accordingly."[38] The CIDA president went on to state that "unless we can demonstrate that our food aid is not a disincentive to local farmer, that it supports and complements agricultural development activities, that it is doing something to prevent recurring 'emergencies,' that it assists and encourages recipient governments to invest in their rural areas and maintain a policy framework which will stimulate productivity … unless we can prove all these points, we will not be able to maintain public and parliamentary support for a substantial Canadian food aid programme."[39] Catley-Carlson then concluded that in order for food aid to be a continuing and growing part of Canada's aid program, "we will have to demonstrate convincingly that it is a good 'investment' in future agricultural productivity, a development transfer which is at least as efficient and effective as competing claims for scarce resources."[40]

The CIDA president was clearly signalling to recipient governments that food aid would no longer be simply seen as a "throw-away" item to be added as an afterthought to the rest of Canada's ODA. Instead greater priority would be placed on the need to provide adequate justification and information in order to reassure a sceptical Canadian public and press. The issue of food aid effectiveness was thus clearly linked to the need to satisfy the domestic critics of CIDA who found in food aid a highly visible and symbolic target.

It has been particularly significant for Canada's food aid strategy that this emphasis on the need to demonstrate food aid effectiveness at home has been accompanied by an effort by CIDA to link food aid with policy dialogue and policy conditionality. The intellectual framework for this effort has been largely drawn from World Bank analyses of the African situation, especially the bank's 1981 report *Accelerated Development in Sub-Saharan Africa*.[41] This report, which is sometimes referred to as the Berg report, argues that the root causes of Africa's food problems are primarily internal in origin. African governments have pursued policies that systematically discriminate against the agricultural sector. The report suggests that the solution to Africa's problems is to constrain the role of the state as much as possible and allow the free market to allocate resources and set agricultural prices. Donors can respond by encouraging recipients to adopt policies that give greater scope for market forces.

The influence of the Berg report is clearly evident in recent CIDA policy statements. In *Elements of Canada's Official Development Strategy, 1984*, the agency notes that Canada, like other donors, is under public pressure to demonstrate the effectiveness of its aid programs. Citing the Berg report, the CIDA statement goes on to note that the effectiveness of aid is frequently linked to the policy environment within the recipient country. Thus the report concludes that "for Canada, the questions which obviously arise are how the ODA programme should react to inappropriate policies in recipient countries and the extent to which economic performance conditions should be imposed for the continued provision of ODA."[42]

The report goes on to suggest that the linkage between effective aid and recipient policies be established through greater conditionality in the allocation of Canadian aid. This point was emphasized by the president of CIDA in Rome, when she made it clear that future food aid flows would depend on whether recipient countries were willing to engage in policy dialogue with Canada and undertake structural policy adjustment reform programs deemed to be necessary by the donor community.[43]

In this context food aid is seen as a resource which can be used to influence changes in the recipient's domestic agricultural policies. Recent CIDA documents have identified several ways in which food aid can contribute to this process: (i) food aid, especially if offered on a multi-year basis, can provide a recipient government with assured external support while reforms are being carried out; (ii) the sale of food aid can generate revenues to be used to finance producer incentive schemes agreed to during the dialogue process; (iii) negotiation over counterpart funds can provide CIDA with some measure of control to insure that investments are directed toward the agricultural sector and are not misdirected, and; (iv) the foreign exchange that is saved can be used to import the necessary inputs, such as tools, seeds, and fertilizers, needed to expand agricultural development projects.[44] In outlining this approach CIDA has indicated to recipients that it wishes to take a much more involved approach to the aid relationship and to expand the range of issues which are discussed with recipients when making food aid allocations.

The decision to continue to provide large amounts of program food aid maintains Canada's traditional method of delivering food aid.

What is different is the context in which CIDA plans to deliver this aid. Influenced by a growing literature on food aid, CIDA officials argue that the most important factor in determining the success of food aid transfers is the kind of policy environment provided by the recipient governments.[45] If the recipient government is highly committed to agricultural development and is pursuing a sound food strategy, even large amounts of food aid are unlikely to have a negative effect. If, however, the government is not committed to the agricultural sector, lacks a food strategy, and continues urban-biased, cheap food policies, even the best managed food aid program will fail to have a positive impact.

The logical conclusion of this reasoning is that the donor must concern itself with the broad policy environment of the recipient country. This view was clearly articulated in Catley-Carlson's address to the CFA when she served notice to recipients that the agenda of issues to be discussed in the food aid-giving process would no longer be limited only to the specifics of a particular food aid transaction. Instead Canadian officials now want to be assured that the recipient government is pursuing a range of agricultural, developmental, and fiscal policies which create a policy environment in which food aid can be effectively used. In cases where this is absent, the CIDA president warned that "the future size and orientation of our food aid programme will be very much influenced by ... whether developing country governments are prepared to engage in a dialogue with Canada and other donors ... to ensure that our mutual efforts are not thwarted by inappropriate policies."[46]

This represents a significant departure from the type of aid strategy that Canada pursued in the seventies. CIDA has committed itself to moving away from its traditional passive, "hands-off" approach to food aid to an aid style that calls for much greater donor involvement. CIDA's priorities in the aid relationship have clearly shifted to an emphasis on the need for greater information to justify its food aid shipments and greater donor control over the ultimate impact of the food aid.

STRENGTHENING CIDA'S CAPACITY FOR A MORE ACTIVIST AID STRATEGY

As mentioned at the beginning of this chapter, the aid relationship can be seen as a mutual bargaining process. From this perspective it can be argued that CIDA's emphasis on developmental food aid is an effort to extract greater benefits from the aid relationship. Instead of simply seeing food aid as a means of generating good will and moving money, the agency now wants clear evidence of developmental effectiveness and accountability in order to reassure the Canadian public that its funds are being wisely used. This is reflected in the number of references in recent CIDA policy statements to the need for recipients to enter into a process of dialogue.[47] According to CIDA's own definition, policy dialogue is a "process in which donors and recipients seek to define the development policies most likely to bring success."[48] An additional aspect of this process may be to engage in "conditionality" which "goes a step further by making the provision of assistance conditional on the adoption of certain policies."[49] Although the emphasis is placed on "dialogue," it is clear that the process is intended to persuade recipients to adopt policies that are more in line with donor preferences.

In a sense, this involves a re-negotiation of the terms of the aid relationship. Like any negotiating process the outcome will depend on the relative bargaining strength of the two parties involved. CIDA's case raises the question of whether an agency has the capacity to exercise greater influence and control over recipient policies related to food aid. This can be seen particularly in the area of information and analytical capacity.

As an earlier CIDA document noted, a direct, involved approach to food aid control means that "CIDA has a different evaluation than the recipient of its economic priorities."[50] Similarly Benjamin Higgins notes that efforts to influence a recipient's allocation of resources "implies that the donors are either wiser or more virtuous than the recipients."[51] To be sure that their efforts achieve the desired results "requires penetrating economic and political analysis of each recipient country at each point of time."[52] This observation has been confirmed by recent studies of food aid which have argued that linking policy dialogue to food aid requires an intimate knowledge of the recipient's domestic policy environment that only an extensive field staff can develop.[53] In particular, donors need to go beyond the traditional macro-economic analyses, to understand more fully the political and social forces which shape food policies and which would constrain the implementation of policy reforms.

Beyond the question of analytical capacity there is also the question of whether the quantity of food aid offered by Canada provides it with sufficient leverage to influence the policies of recipients. Globally, Canada's status as a food aid donor appears impressive compared with its position in other issue areas of international politics. Canada is the largest per capita food aid donor in the world. Its contributions to the WFP rank second only to the United States, and it regularly ranks second or third as a bilateral food aid donor.

Table 21
Canada's rank as a donor in selected recipient countries, 1988

Country	Total ODA (millions of $us)	Canada's rank	Canada's percentage of total bilateral ODA
Bangladesh	931.2	3	12.6
India	949.8	9	5.2
Pakistan	1,000.7	4	6.4
Sri Lanka	436.1	6	6.5
Jamaica	173.1	2	25.0
Ghana	235.9	4	8.9
Mali	260.1	6	4.8
Senegal	367.2	5	6.6
Zambia	407.2	6	7.5
Peru	244.4	5	9.2

Source: CIDA, 1989–90 Annual Report, Table U, 121–2. (Hull: Supply and Services, 1991).

However, on a country-to-country basis Canada's status as a donor is much different. Since the early seventies there has been a proliferation of food aid donors and at any one time a recipient government may be negotiating with more than a half dozen bilateral and multilateral food aid agencies over a range of commodities, which are available under varying conditions. Thus Canada's food aid contribution often represents only a small proportion of the total food aid transfers, and an even smaller proportion of the country's total food supply. In Bangladesh, for example, Canadian food aid accounts for only 17 per cent of that country's total cereal food aid.[54]

In terms of overall contribution of development funding to a particular recipient, Canada's position may not be any stronger. As Table 21 shows, Canada is only one of many donors providing aid to a recipient at one time. Even in the case of Canada's largest food aid recipients, Canada provides only a relatively small proportion of the total resources being provided. India, Pakistan, Bangladesh, Tanzania, and Sri Lanka each deal with twenty-nine to thirty-one different multilateral and bilateral aid agencies.[55]

In this fragmented and sometimes competitive "aid market" donors may pursue conflicting objectives, place divergent demands on the recipient, or take actions that undercut other donor initiatives. CIDA officials claim that efforts in the seventies to push for changes in Pakistan's domestic pricing policies were undercut by generous shipments of American food aid which were given for strategic political reasons.[56] Recipients may take advantage of this situation by playing donors off against each other. By cultivating alternative sources of aid the recipient is then in a position to resist pressures by some donors to accept certain policy conditions. Thus the extent to which Canada as a single donor can exercise significant influence over the recipient's policy priorities is questionable.

CIDA officials are well aware of the constraints under which they are operating and in recent years a number of policy initiatives have been undertaken.[57] Viewed in the context of this analysis, each of these areas can be seen as an effort by CIDA to improve its bargaining position vis-à-vis recipient countries in order to ensure that Canadian priorities are being achieved. In particular, I will focus on: (1) multi-year contracts; (2) eligibility criteria; (3) donor co-ordination; (4) counterpart funds; and (5) monitoring.

MULTI-YEAR COMMITMENTS

The expectation that Canada can use its food aid resources to influence recipient policies is predicated on two assumptions. First, Canada must be able to provide a sufficient level of resources to ensure that the recipient will give particular heed to its proposals. Second, Canada must be willing to make a sufficiently long-term commitment, assuring the recipient of a degree of continuity in supplies if it undertakes politically risky policy reforms. In order to address these concerns, CIDA has placed increased emphasis on the need to provide food aid on a multi-year contract basis.

The notion that donors should plan their food aid allocations on a longer-term basis has been widely advocated since the World Food Conference in 1975. From the recipient's perspective, it is much easier to make more effective use of food aid if it can be assured of certain levels in advance. Thus recipients are not faced with erratic year-to-year fluctuations that could disrupt their planning.[58]

From the viewpoint of a process of policy dialogue, multi-year contracts can be seen as serving two useful functions. First, the offer of a multi-year commitment reassures the recipient that a reliable, predictable supply of food resources will be available during a time when it is being asked to undertake sensitive policy changes. It is believed that assurances about continuity of supply will make the recipient more open to suggestions from the donor about possible policy reforms. Second, multi-year contracts provide a means for the donor to enhance its bargaining power with the recipient. As one CIDA official noted, by discussing food aid flows over a longer period the negotiators are automatically dealing with larger sums of money. For example, negotiations with Bangladesh now involve a three-year commitment of $180 million instead of a one-year allocation of $60 million. By focusing on the larger, multi-year contract, it is hoped that the recipient will take Canada's commitment more seriously and be more willing to discuss a broader range of policy issues with Canada.

The concept that Canada should provide food aid on a multi-year basis was proposed as early as 1975 by the Task Force in Food Aid and Renewable Resources. It was argued at that time that such contracts would enhance CIDA's bargaining power. For example, the Task Force argued that CIDA could "play its cards close to the chest" by making the fulfilment of each year's commitment conditional on the recipient's performance in agriculture or proper distribution of the food aid.[59] However, when the Interdepartmental Working Group on Food Aid Policy prepared its recommendations on food aid in 1978 CIDA was not successful in getting interdepartmental approval for the idea of multi-year contracts. Both the Department of Finance and the Treasury Board opposed the idea, arguing that to allow the government to maintain greater fiscal flexibility it was unwise to unnecessarily lock itself into binding commitments.[60] Nevertheless CIDA was able to win a significant victory in 1981 when it received authority to negotiate a three-year agreement with Bangladesh. Since then approval has also been given to enter into similar agreements with India, Sri Lanka, Mali, Senegal, Ghana, and Peru.[61]

The multi-year agreement provides CIDA with a basis for negotiating certain conditions on the use of its aid. In the case of Bangladesh the agreement requires that a portion of Canada's food aid be used in feeding programs aimed at vulnerable groups. An interviewee involved in the negotiation of the agreement noted that this condition was included primarily to demonstrate to the Canadian public that their perception of food aid as going directly to the starving is being fulfilled.[62] The multi-year commitment to India is specifically linked to the use of canola oil for a project intended to strengthen India's domestic oilseed production and marketing. Finally, the commitment with Mali was been made conditional on the government's pursuit of policies proposed by the multi-donor group's "Cereal Marketing Restructuring Project."[63] Similarly, agreements with Senegal, Peru, and Sri Lanka have been contingent on the successful implementation of a structural adjustment program negotiated with the donor community.

ELIGIBILITY CRITERIA

Chapter 5 illustrated that in the past there was no specific set of criteria for the allocation of food aid. Instead any country that was eligible to receive Canadian foreign aid was automatically a potential candidate. As a result recipients were often added to the food aid program for a variety of political, commercial, and humanitarian reasons. Nevertheless the Canadian food aid program has historically been significantly concentrated in terms of the volume directed at certain countries. For example, from 1951 to 1981 81 per cent of Canada's bilateral food aid went to only six countries, with India and Bangladesh alone accounting for 62 per cent of the total.[64] Since its independence Bangladesh has been the largest recipient of Canadian food aid, in some years accounting for more than 50 per cent of the total. However, as food "emergencies" became more prevalent in the seventies and the Canadian government engaged in the surplus disposal of newer aid commodities such as skim milk powder, the number of recipients expanded rapidly. With growing emphasis on the need to meet food needs in Africa, the number of recipients has continued to escalate, reaching twenty-six in 1984/85, the highest total in the history of the food aid program.

Canada's food aid shipments to Africa, unlike those to Asia, have consisted of a greater number of shipments of smaller amounts of food to a larger number of recipients. For example, in 1984/85 CIDA delivered $102.05 million worth of food aid to four Asian recipients. Bangladesh alone accounted for $61 million while none of the others were below $10 million. In contrast, in Africa $95 million worth of food aid was delivered to nineteen countries. With the exception of Ethiopia (which received $12 million), all received less that $10 million. A total of fourteen countries received $5 million or less. Thus in Africa Canada's food aid resources are much more widely disbursed. In many individual cases Canada's food aid is either a small percentage of the total food aid being received or represents a small contribution to the overall food available in the country. For example, in 1984, although ranked fifth out of twenty-three food aid donors to Senegal, Canada supplied only 9.8 per cent of that country's total food aid imports. The largest donor, the United States Agency for International Development (USAID), accounted for 26 per cent of the total supplies.[65]

In recent years there has been growing criticism of the facility with which donors often grant emergency food aid, particularly in cases where chronic shortages have emerged because of the recipient's urban-biased food policies.[66] Officials within CIDA see two dangers in this approach. First, giving emergency food aid too readily can make it a long-term form of program food aid without sufficient analysis of its broader implications and without linkages to other aid efforts ever having been undertaken. When the food aid is not linked to policy reforms the root causes of the chronic shortages will not be dealt with. Second, "if emergency food aid is provided more readily than developmental food assistance, it could penalize those countries making serious efforts to achieve agricultural and rural improvements."[67]

CIDA has responded to this problem by attempting to move towards a policy of greater concentration of food aid transfers. Thus the agency has decided to provide developmental food aid through multi-year contracts to countries that are classified by cabinet as category I aid recipients.[68] Within this group food aid is concentrated on "those countries which have in place developmentally sound policies and programmes for their agricultural sectors, or which undertake to make a serious commitment to introduce such measures."[69]

From the donor's perspective this policy of concentration offers several advantages. Engaging in long-term developmental food aid requires much greater analysis and understanding of the recipient's economy and policies. As a CIDA food aid manual notes, "effective programming of multi-year commitments of bilateral program food aid requires sound analysis, careful planning, regular monitoring of food trends and policy developments in the recipient country, consultation with other donors, and on-going policy dialogue. At present, CIDA does not have the staff resources to undertake such a programming effort in a large number of countries."[70]

Since CIDA's analytical capacity remains limited, the policy of concentration permits the agency to focus primarily on those countries where Canada has established a presence and has already developed some knowledge and understanding. Limiting the number of recipients will therefore reduce the analytical and administrative demands on the agency. By concentrating on fewer recipients it is hoped that CIDA will be able to channel larger amounts of food aid to those countries chosen, thus giving the agency a larger base for influencing the recipient.

However, even in cases where Canadian food transfers are significant, there is no firm evidence that this will translate into any degree of influence over recipient policies. For example, during the seventies Tanzania was one of the largest recipients of Canadian food aid in Africa. From 1975 to 1980 Canada provided about half of Tanzania's wheat imports.[71] Despite this CIDA was not successful in its attempts to link continued food aid supplies with policy changes in Tanzania's agricultural pricing policy. As a result Canada has discontinued its food aid shipments to Tanzania.[72]

Evidence from Asia does not provide any more convincing indications that food aid provides a good source for leverage. Despite

Bangladesh's very great dependence on food aid after independence, and a concerted effort by donors to bring about policy changes, Roger Ehrhardt has concluded that "donors were able to extract only marginal policy concessions from the Government of Bangladesh."[73] Analysts generally agree that Bangladesh's food policies changed only when the government itself saw the necessity for change, not when donors tried to bring pressure to bear.[74]

As a result it is perhaps not surprising that Canadian aid officials have emphasized that their approach will focus more on what they refer to as "positive conditionality." This has been defined by one official interviewed as "being supportive of a government when it is taking a policy direction that we can support." CIDA officials have justified this on the basis that the agency wants to avoid the kind of confrontations that have frequently characterized the policy-dialogue process with the International Monetary Fund (IMF) or the USAID. A policy of "positive conditionality," by pre-selecting recipients which have already shown a willingness to pursue its preferred policy, relieves the donor from the need to engage in the application of more direct and rigid forms of conditionality that are likely to generate greater conflict between the donor and recipient. As a CIDA food aid manual notes, "when recipients themselves are genuinely committed to the policy adjustments necessary to achieve their food objectives, as has been the case in Mali, Sri Lanka, and Bangladesh, it may be necessary for donors only to monitor food-related development and to encourage and assist national governments to maintain their efforts."[75]

To some extent the concept of positive conditionality may be interpreted as part of the agency's recent preoccupation with minimizing risk-taking and error-making.[76] Thus positive conditionality suggests that food aid will be concentrated on countries that have already demonstrated a willingness to fall into line with current IMF/World Bank prescriptions. A CIDA list of policy reforms that could be linked to food aid ("the revising of urban-oriented cheap food policies, adjusting overvalued exchange rates, reducing the preponderant marketing and transport role of inefficient parastatal government agencies that set prices for, purchase and resell agricultural commodities, and directing a larger portion of national investments to rural rather than urban enterprises")[77] follows closely the current IMF/World Bank prescriptions.[78]

A recent CIDA policy paper indicated that it will use a combination of the carrot and the stick in ensuring that approved policies are pursued by the recipient government. In this context it is noted that "positive conditionality" implies that "the country is informed before deciding on a adjustment package that Canadian balance-of-payment aid will be available if a satisfactory adjustment package is adopted."[79] An incentive is thus provided to the recipient to agree to a structural adjustment program on the promise that Canadian food aid, as a form of balance-of-payments support, will be forthcoming.

Selecting recipients who appear to be on the "politically correct" path does help guarantee success. However, the implementation of structural adjustment programs can never be taken for granted and the performance of recipient governments frequently falls short of expectations. In such cases, the policy paper notes, it may be necessary to also use "negative conditionality" in which "there is an understanding with the recipient country that Canadian resources will not be disbursed if the country deviates in a major way from the macroeconomic adjustment program."[80] Such a strategy has its downside, particularly when negotiated in the context of a multi-year food aid agreement, since "CIDA must consider the potential adverse political consequences of withdrawing from subsequent years of a multi-year commitment if the policy reforms do not proceed in a satisfactory way."[81]

CIDA appears to have already had to face this issue with Sri Lanka, one of the longest-standing recipients of Canadian food aid, when it failed to live up to the conditions of a structural adjustment agreement negotiated with the World Bank and other donors. When Canadian officials were unable to identify alternative channels that they felt could successfully target food aid in direct feeding programs, CIDA decided to discontinue the bilateral food aid program to Sri Lanka completely.[82] Similarly, Canada's fish aid program to Zaïre was suspended when evaluations showed that the aid was primarily benefitting urban elites while the government had not demonstrated any significant effort in promoting agricultural reform. It is likely that in the future Canadian food aid disbursements will vary much more significantly as governments are dropped or added to the list on the basis of their performance in structural adjustment programs or demonstrated commitment to agricultural development.

DONOR COORDINATION

Despite the move to multi-year contracts and stricter eligibility criteria, CIDA's ability to participate in policy dialogue remains limited by its small analytical capacity and the highly fragmented donor environment. As one solution to these constraints, CIDA has become a vocal supporter of the need for donors to work together in their food aid strategies. This cooperation can take place at two levels.

First, donors may meet to discuss issues of mutual concern. These may range from more technical issues of the timing and logistics of food aid deliveries to the exchange of information on recipient policies and food aid impact. In this regard CIDA has supported recent efforts to establish mechanisms for sharing information regarding food aid flows.

Second, donors may work together in a donor consortium which involves the recipient. These groups not only provide a means of coordinating the logistics of aid deliveries but serve as a forum in which policy dialogue can take place. The experience of donor groups with policy dialogue is still relatively limited. However, Canada is participating in donor working groups in Bangladesh, Sri Lanka, and Mali, with the Mali group cited by CIDA as an example of how it will engage in policy dialogue. Canada is a participant in the multi-donor Cereals Marketing Restructuring Project which is pressing the Mali government to end the monopoly held by the state cereals marketing board and increase producer prices for grains to stimulate production. This group is only part of a much broader effort led by the IMF, the World Bank, and the United States to make future assistance to Mali conditional on the reform of public finances and enterprises and a switch to greater emphasis on private sector activities. These efforts include strong pressures by the United States on Mali to partially dismantle its public sector through fiscal reforms and reductions in public sector employment.[83]

From the point of view of the donor agencies such donor coordination is seen as having several advantages. First, the policy dialogue efforts of some agencies are not undercut by large inflows of unconditional food aid by other donors, sometimes under pretext of emergency food aid. Second, by coordinating donor efforts recipients are less able to play donors off against each and seek alternative aid sources. Third, smaller donors such as Canada can overcome their limited analytical and monitoring capacity by relying on the more detailed and sophisticated analyses performed by larger agencies such as the World Bank or USAID. Fourth, in cases where jointly managed counterpart funds are established as part of the dialogue process, administrative demands on both the recipient and individual donors may be reduced. Fifth, by participating in a broad inter-donor effort sensitive policy issues can be raised without the smaller donors bearing the brunt of any recipient resentment that might be generated.

Nevertheless such donor efforts raise important questions about policy dialogue and the role that food aid donors such as Canada might play in it. In principle, at least, Canadian officials have emphasized the mutuality of the process in order that "we may understand each other's perspectives and problems, work within a framework of shared priorities, and ensure that our mutual efforts are not thwarted by inappropriate policies."[84] Another CIDA document suggests that "Canada's generally positive image on North-South issues, and its credibility with both the more radical donors and the more conservative donors, allows for an influence on these issues that goes beyond the relative volume of our contributions."[85]

However, the impact of smaller donors may in fact be limited. After a thorough study of the experience of donor-coordination in Bangladesh, Nurul Islam suggests that "once an economic forum was established the more aggressive and active donors would dominate and, unless underlying differences were very strong, individual donors would seldom stand out against the general view."[86] Indeed Canada may well be a dependent participant in the "dialogue process," since it is highly dependent on other agencies forming their own assessment of recipient needs and may not be able to credibly put forward an alternative judgment of its own. Canada's role may also be restricted by its limited field staff. Two cases, which the agency cites as examples of how food aid can be linked to policy dialogue, are illustrative of this. In Mali Canada has a field staff of only two people devoted to aid issues, compared to the USAID's staff of forty. Similarly in Bangladesh USAID has a field staff of some forty officials while Canada has only five.

An unpublished report of the North-South Institute summarizing the findings of its evaluation studies of four country programs argues that because Canada generally has a smaller field staff than many other donors, Canadian aid personnel are frequently dependent on the expertise of others, "without of course the benefit of a particular Canadian view."[87] Similarly Cranford Pratt has argued that there is a "marked tendency for government officials in the Departments of External Affairs and Finance to accept as professionally unquestionable the analysis offered by the IMF and the World Bank."[88] In light of such evidence the recently released parliamentary review of foreign aid concludes "as things stand now, Canada is in the position of preaching co-ordination and dialogue while not being able to practice it."[89]

The commitment by the Canadian government in 1988 to develop and implement a plan to decentralize more decision-making to the field level may help to address these weaknesses. However, given Canada's overall smaller contribution of resources there remains the danger that is some cases Canadian food aid may be no more than part of a "fire brigade" operation when the dialogue process led by other donors runs into trouble. This appeared to be the case in both Tunisia and Morocco, where the removal of food subsidies as part of an "economic stabilisation" program approved by the IMF and the World Bank led to rioting.[90] Canada responded by sending $9.95 million worth of food aid to the two countries, which then rolled back the price increases in order to restore political order.

COUNTERPART FUNDS

As attention within CIDA has shifted to a more activist aid strategy, the role of counterpart funds has continued to be debated within the agency. In the seventies this debate largely pitted those officials in CIDA who saw counterpart funds as an unnecessary imposition on recipients against officials in the Treasury Board and Department of Finance who wanted to maintain at least "perceived control" over the disposition of funds.[91] After two internal reviews of this issue, in 1984 CIDA adopted a flexible approach which no longer requires the recipient to establish a counterpart fund.

The decision concerning counterpart funds now rests ultimately on the confidence that CIDA has in the recipient government. In some cases Canadian officials may already be satisfied with the policies being pursued and feel that the recipient government is making sound resource allocations. The recipient may then be given complete responsibility for the allocation of resources generated by the sale of Canadian food aid. In other cases, however, where CIDA officials believe that appropriate policies are not being pursued or that the recipient does not have sufficient administrative capacity to efficiently handle the counterpart fund, CIDA may take a more active role in the administration of the funds. In this way the counterpart fund mechanism can be used to ensure that the funds support only those projects preferred by Canada.

The concept of the counterpart fund has been enjoying a "renaissance" in the case of Canada's African recipients. It is felt that in this region recipient governments are frequently less committed to agricultural development and more likely to pursue urban-biased food policies. Thus in some cases, where a process of policy dialogue has not yet been established, the counterpart fund mechanism is seen as a means of gaining some assurance that the funds are being used for agricultural development.[92] At a time when development funding is increasingly scarce in Africa, counterpart funds may be used to meet local cost funding requirements. They thus enable CIDA to overcome a policy constraint in order to advance some projects that might not otherwise be implemented. In other cases, such as Mali, negotiations over the use of the counterpart are seen as an integral part of the policy-dialogue process. Here the counterpart fund is used to cover the expenses of restructuring Mali's cereal markets and providing more attractive prices to food producers.

Equally important, counterpart funds continue to be a useful device in justifying the "developmental" type of food aid which CIDA officials fear is not well understood by the public. In a recent document designed to explain CIDA's response to the African food crisis, the use of counterpart funds for agricultural development projects was repeatedly mentioned in order to explain why Canadian food aid to Senegal, Ghana, Zambia, and others is in fact being sold.[93] But despite these glowing reports in CIDA public relations brochures, the agency has had continuing difficulty in effectively monitoring the use of its counterpart funds. A corporate review of the food aid program concluded in 1986 found that in five out of nine cases problems were discovered with the counterpart fund mechanism. In some cases it was not possible to establish any direct link between the fund and specific individual projects. More recently problems of fraud and mismanagement have been discovered in the use of counterpart funds in Zaïre.[94]

MONITORING AND THE DILEMMA OF EMERGENCY FOOD AID

The desire for greater information and control frequently manifests itself in the demand for greater monitoring of aid programs. For example, the auditor general has cited the lack of adequate monitoring procedures as evidence that CIDA has not built sufficient accountability into its food aid program. In the past CIDA officials have resisted establishing extensive monitoring procedures for a number of reasons. First, they argue that once the food is delivered to the recipient's port it is the legal responsibility of the receiving government. To impose strict monitoring procedures beyond this point threatens the political sovereignty of the recipient government and can be an irritant in the donor-recipient relationship. Second, since most Canadian food aid is program aid, Canadian foodstuffs are mixed with other donations, commercial imports, and domestically procured products. The Canadian food loses its identity and is impossible to trace as it moves through the food pipeline. Third, CIDA officials contend that, given the financial and administrative constraints under which CIDA operates, it is too expensive to maintain the kind of field staff that extensive monitoring requires.[95]

The issue of monitoring is closely related to the distinction CIDA now makes between developmental and emergency food aid. In the case of developmental food aid it has been argued that the main benefit derived is the contribution that the food aid makes as a balance-of-payments and budgetary support to the recipient government. The crucial judgment must be made when the country is initially selected as a candidate for program food aid. If CIDA is satisfied that the recipient is allocating its resources wisely, then there is no need for further monitoring.

However, emergency situations present the agency with a more complex set of problems. Emergency food aid must be delivered to specific population groups in a short period of time. Climatic conditions, rough topography, and inadequate transportation infrastructures can greatly complicate that distribution process. In such cases food aid is highly susceptible to damage and misuse. With the glare of public attention on what is perceived as a life and death situation, the issue of monitoring becomes more politicized, as demonstrated by the attention given to it during hearings before the Standing Committee on External Affairs and National Defence on the Canadian response to the Ethiopian famine.[96]

In this case the decision to channel an increasing amount of emergency food aid through Canadian non-government organizations (NGO's) and the International Emergency Food Reserve (IEFR) can be seen as an attempt by CIDA to overcome the double constraints of an Ottawa-based administration and a limited field staff. These agencies generally have more staff members in the field and are more capable of monitoring the distribution of food. By using these agencies as intermediaries CIDA can ensure that monitoring of food aid is taking place, while relieving itself of the administrative burden of carrying it out. CIDA's administrative task is then limited to the less onerous one of assessing the general effectiveness of these intermediary agencies, a job that can be done just as easily in Ottawa.

The Ethiopian famines of 1984–85 and 1987–88, with their extensive media coverage and large Canadian response, presented the Canadian government with a unique challenge. As the earlier food crises of the seventies have shown, such high profile emergencies can become public relations disasters for aid agencies. For example, in 1974 Canada rapidly increased its food aid allocations to Bangladesh following the emergence of famine conditions following that country's independence. By 1974–75 Bangladesh accounted for $68 million dollars or 43 per cent of the Canadian bilateral food aid budget. Although Canada's contribution was only a small part of a larger international undertaking, by the end of 1974 Canada's large food transfers to Bangladesh were beginning to cause concern at home. The instability of the Bangladeshi government led to a breakdown in domestic order with a concomitant increase in hoarding, smuggling, and black marketeering. This led to press reports in Canada that Canadian food aid was being distributed to elite groups rather than to the poorest groups and that it was also being frequently smuggled.[97] At home critics expressed surprise that Canadian food aid was being sold. Questions were asked as to why Canadian food was not being distributed to the truly needy, and concern was expressed as to whether CIDA was really in control of its food aid program.[98] Faced with growing criticism of the Bangladesh food aid program, CIDA President Gérin-Lajoie made a highly publicized trip to Bangladesh in March 1975 to review the situation. However, on his return Lajoie had to admit that "despite some recent improvements, the rural landless – most of them without work – get an extremely meagre share of rationed food, while the system takes care of the urban areas, and within rural areas, gives priority to the army, teachers, and public servants."[99] Gérin-Lajoie explained to a Canadian reporter that there was little Canada could do about this since the use of the food aid raised important questions concerning the recipients political sovereignty: "De la même façon que le Canada ne veut pas subir d'atteinte à sa propre autonomie nationale ... il faut respecter la souvraineté nationale des gouvernements avec lesquels nous faisons affaire."[100]

Although the government would later claim that some improvements had been made based on representations from the Canadian government, the damage had already been done to the credibility of the Canadian food aid program. When a parliamentary committee reviewed Canadian aid policies in 1980, it was the Bangladesh experience that provided the critics of food aid with ammunition for attacking the program.[101] The director of CIDA's Food Aid Centre steadfastly maintained that there was little more that could have been done because "by introducing greater elements of control, namely introducing more conditionality with aid transfers, there is a danger in increasing the risk of being accused of interfering in sovereign decisions."[102]

One decade after the Bangladeshi famine Ethiopia burst into the Canadian consciousness in October 1984 with the broadcast of a BBC news documentary on the famine in Ethiopia. The famine immediately captured public attention and Canadians demanded to know what they could do to respond. In November 1984 the Canadian government announced that it was creating a $65 million special fund for Africa, $15 million of which was to be set aside to match donations from individual Canadians. The response was dramatic. A Decima poll later revealed that one out of every three Canadians reported that they had made a personal donation to Ethiopian famine projects.

By February 1985 the Canadian government announced that it was giving another $15 million in matching funds for relief, and in April it set aside an additional $18 million in matching funds for NGO recovery projects.[103]

The Ethiopian famine posed a unique challenge to the Canadian government. Ethiopia did not have a well-developed distribution system for handling grain imports as Bangladesh had had. In fact Canada had cut back food aid shipments to Ethiopia in the 1970s because of concerns about inadequate distribution and transportation facilities. Furthermore, unlike Bangladesh, the Marxist government of Ethiopia was not a priority recipient of Canadian development assistance. As a result the Canadian government had only limited presence and experience in Ethiopia. Given the rugged terrain, weak infrastructure, continuing domestic civil war, and tenuous political ties with the West, the Ethiopian famine provided donors with an even more difficult environment than the Bangladesh famine of a decade before. Nevertheless the evident scope of the famine and the resulting public response in North America made it clear that a massive response by Western donors was necessary.

In addition to significantly augmenting the availability of funds for Ethiopian famine relief, the Canadian government took two significant organizational steps. First, as the extent and nature of the famine became evident Joe Clark, the minister of External Affairs, appointed David MacDonald as an emergency coordinator for the African Famine. MacDonald was a former Conservative cabinet minister in Joe Clark's brief government in 1979 and enjoyed a reputation within the Canadian development community as a sympathetic supporter of Third World issues. Second, a joint government/voluntary sector body, called Africa Emergency Aid, was created in November 1984 to co-ordinate NGO interventions in the Ethiopian famine. Both agencies were unique in the sense that it was the first time that such ad hoc agencies had been created in response to a specific famine, and they both effectively took some of the decision-making process outside normal bureaucratic channels.

The Canadian famine coordinator's mandate was essentially to "assess the food crisis in Africa and particular in Ethiopia" and "to propose concrete steps for the government to take in providing assistance."[104] To carry out this role MacDonald was given direct access to the ministers of External Affairs and Supply and Services and could waive normal tendering requirements for food aid purchases when it was deemed necessary. Word was sent out to CIDA that the coordinator's decisions should not be questioned. All of this was designed to enable him to bypass the normal bureaucratic channels and speed up the food aid disbursement process.[105]

However, the coordinator also had a wider mandate than simply managing the delivery of foodstuffs to famine victims, a mandate directed as much to the Canadian public as to the victims of the famine. It was hoped that his office would serve as what MacDonald himself labelled as the "symbolic focal point" or "chief cheerleader" of Canadian famine relief efforts. Thus MacDonald acknowledged that an important part of his mission was "to make sure that we avoided the horror stories of the seventies."[106]

To this end MacDonald undertook several missions to Africa accompanied by journalists, members of Parliament, and NGO representatives. These trips were specifically focused on monitoring and were widely covered by the Canadian press. But, most important, they were partly directed at neutralizing growing criticism of the Ethiopian government's handling of the famine. Several groups were concerned that the Ethiopian government was using the famine as a means of promoting its battle against anti-government forces in Eritrea and Tigre and was limiting access to food aid to government supporters. MacDonald argued, however, that the missions found no evidence that Canada's food aid was being misused by the Ethiopian government. In particular he contended that there was no substance to claims by group such as Cultural Survival and Médecins sans Frontières that the Ethiopian government was using food aid to support a resettlement program designed to win the war against Eritrea and Tigre through a policy of genocide.[107]

In another case two Canadians, one of them a professional journalist, were hired by MacDonald to accompany a shipload of CIDA and NGO food aid from Montreal to its final distribution points in Sudan. MacDonald then sent a letter to members of the Canadian public who had contributed to the special fund for Africa explaining the monitoring procedures.[108] Some NGO officials close to these operations, however, felt that the public relations dimension of the missions was beginning to dominate the task of field monitoring. An administrator of one of the largest Canadian NGOs involved in the Ethiopian famine felt that the head of his organization had made a mistake in taking part in one of MacDonald's missions. He felt that the organization, by taking part in the official missions, had tacitly approved MacDonald's description of events, particularly those relating to the resettlement program, and that this subsequently made it difficult for other members of the organization to publicly state other, alternative evaluations of the situation.[109]

The debate over the Ethiopian famine, and particularly the issue of the resettlement policy, reflected a serious rift among the agencies who were involved in Ethiopia. Some felt that the Ethiopian government was pursuing a genocidal and coercive policy and that aid agencies should withdraw their support until the human rights situation improved. Others felt that strong public criticism of the Ethiopian government could only jeopardize programs and possibly endanger more lives. The Canadian government appeared to side with this latter viewpoint. On the surface, the famine coordinator presented a reassuring view to the Canadian public, but at the same time his office took steps to provide food aid to NGO's who were channelling some of the aid through Sudan into Eritea and Tigre provinces, keeping a double set of books to minimize the embarrassment and wrath of the Ethiopian government.[110] MacDonald argued that he used his access to the Ethiopian government to raise the resettlement issue with Mengistu himself. Later MacDonald claimed that such "quiet diplomacy" had been successful in getting the Ethiopian government to suspend its resettlement program.[111]

While it is not possible to verify MacDonald's claim, it is clear that the government did successfully defuse much of the public criticism of the famine relief program. Thus, although the emergency coordinator's office was a temporary creation (it was disbanded in March 1986) and not a normal part of CIDA's food aid decision-making process, it did serve the purpose of defusing criticism of Canadian food aid operations during a critical period. As a result press coverage of the Ethiopian famine generated less critical scrutiny of the agency than had the food crisis of the seventies. Although a Decima poll revealed that from July 1985 to February 1986 the number of Canadians who believed that Canadian aid was not effective increased slightly from 30 per cent to 34 per cent, the number who favoured an increase in aid spending actually rose from 24 per cent to 30 per cent.[112] The government was thus able to avoid the type of "crisis of confidence" that followed in the wake of the Bangladeshi famine in 1984.

Despite the success of the "public relations" aspect of the Ethiopian famine relief effort, there has still been lingering controversy over the Canadian approach of "quiet diplomacy" in famine situations, particularly where there is evidence that food aid is being used as a political weapon. The Canadian government and most Canadian NGO's have argued that the largest number of persons can be assisted only if efforts are made to work with the Ethiopian government, despite what reservations they might have. While not unsympathetic to the plight of the Eritreans and Tigreans, it is argued that they should be assisted in a low-key way that does not disrupt relations with the Ethiopian government.

Others, particularly Oxfam Canada, have adopted a more assertive approach, especially after the Ethiopian government expelled the Red Cross and other NGOs from the northern areas of Ethiopia. With all voluntary workers expelled from the region it was no longer possible for donors such as Canada to rely on these agencies to monitor the distribution of food aid. Given this situation Oxfam argued that it was imperative that the Canadian government make resources available to finance "transborder shipments" of food aid into the north. NGO's operating in Sudan could then channel food supplies to the Eritrean and Tigrean relief societies who would distribute them in the areas which were under rebel control. Oxfam argued that the expulsion of voluntary workers from the north was only a further indication that the Ethiopian government was intent on controlling all food aid distribution, using food as a weapon in the prosecution of its campaign against the insurgents. Only by using back-door channels directly into rebel-held areas could more extensive starvation in Northern Ethiopia be avoided.[113]

Despite this plea CIDA's initial position was to oppose the use of Canadian government monies to fund increased transborder shipments. While some technical arguments have been given, two fundamental foreign policy reasons were cited by CIDA officials. First, it was argued that relations between Sudan and Ethiopia were delicate and that the Sudanese government had expressed to donors its opposition to transborder shipments through Sudan as being a violation of national sovereignty. Second, it was argued that, since the Ethiopian government saw the conflict solely as an internal matter, it could use transborder shipments as an excuse to "ban all Canadian NGOs from functioning in Ethiopia."[114] Underlying these arguments was a strong reluctance on the part of the Canadian government to take any action that would appear to undermine the sovereignty of the Ethiopian government and give de facto recognition to the opposition forces.

Nevertheless, following a parliamentary report that recommended increased support for transborder shipments, CIDA did make more food aid available for such shipments. However, the determination of the exact level of such funding continued to be a sensitive issue. When the level of Canadian food aid to Ethiopia declined in 1989, some members of the Canadian NGO community expressed concern that the government had seriously underestimated emergency food needs in areas of the country outside government control. According to one NGO estimate 67 per cent of Canadian food aid was targeted to civilians in government-controlled areas, while 80 per cent of the most seriously affected population lived in areas outside government control. The main issue here was how emergency needs were being determined. Since CIDA was reluctant to disclose how these estimates were arrived at, some NGOs believed that the government had relied too extensively on estimates of the World Food Programme (WFP) and those of the Ethiopian government which were biased in favour of the interests of the central government. NGOs argued that there needed to be a more systematic independent assessment of needs outside government-controlled areas in order to ensure that the needs of the most seriously affected population groups were actually being met.

This situation, and the Canadian response to it, demonstrates the basic dilemma in emergency aid situations.[115] In cases where it does not fully trust the recipient's capacity or will to distribute its food supplies in a fair and equitable manner, the donor must rely on alternative channels for monitoring or distribution, but these organizations work within the country only with the permission of the recipient government and many who have on-going development projects are reluctant to take actions that might threaten their presence in the future. As an intergovernmental organization the WFP is committed to recognizing the sovereignty of all governments, and therefore is prohibited from supporting such activities as unofficial transborder shipments.[116] In addition it must often rely on the official estimate of need put forward by the recipient government. Thus, while a donor may wish to circumvent direct government control by using channels such as NGOs and WFP, the recipient government still ultimately controls the situation. As a CIDA vice-president noted, "I am left with this uncomfortable feeling that they will retaliate, because this is a very visceral thing for them. This is territory. They do not see this in any way as we see it ... Maybe they would not do a blanket rejection of Canadian assistance or of Canadian NGOs. Maybe they would single out individual NGOs. Maybe they would do nothing. It is the whole problem of trying not to get yourself into a situation where the only arms that you have to use are cut off. Where does that leave you?"[117]

CONCLUSIONS

In this chapter, I have attempted to examine the aid-giving process from the perspective of donor agency objectives, particularly focusing on the issue of donor control. Because of its surplus disposal origins and questionable developmental rationale, Canadian policy makers have found food aid useful in meeting three organizational objectives: (1) it helps CIDA to "move money" and overcome certain organizational constraints; (2) it builds public support for CIDA and foreign aid in general; and (3) it generates good will with recipient governments and contributes to a stable political environment that "protects" CIDA's ability to carry out other development projects.

Because of these priorities CIDA gave little attention to the issue of donor control over the ultimate use of Canadian food aid. This passive style of aid-giving had two implications for CIDA. First, minimal administrative demands were placed on the agency. Desk officers functioned as little more than commodity brokers. Since Canadian involvement ended at the recipient's port, there was no need for a more specialized knowledge of the recipient's domestic policies or for a more complex administrative structure. Second, recipients were accorded considerable autonomy in using food aid resources according to their own domestic political priorities. Consequently donor-recipient conflict was kept to a minimum.

In the 1970s and early 1980 recurring food emergencies in various parts of the world focused public attention on the Canadian response. Subsequently Canadian food aid was the subject of numerous media reports and two reports by the auditor general. The Committee on North-South Relations, the Committee on Public Accounts, and the Committee on External Affairs and National Defence also held hearings on food aid policy at that time. No other aspect of Canadian aid policy received as much critical attention as food aid. Such reputable individuals as David Hopper, former head of the International Development Research Centre, joined in the call that "we tie our food aid with some pretty strong strings."[118] It was clear that CIDA's passive approach to food aid control made it increasingly vulnerable to criticism.

As recent policy statements have shown, CIDA has become increasingly sensitive to the need to provide reassurance to both the Canadian public and political leaders that Canadian food aid is being used "effectively." This is particularly evident in CIDA's new emphasis on using food aid as a resource to encourage recipients to pursue domestic policies that give priority to agricultural production. Policy dialogue, counterpart funds, and multi-year agreements with conditional clauses are the mechanisms by which CIDA has attempted to gain greater control over the uses of its food aid.

However, as I have shown, CIDA has not been in a position to unilaterally impose changes on recipient behaviour which affect the uses of its food aid allocations. CIDA's own bargaining position vis-à-vis recipients is limited by the tight strictures on CIDA's administrative resources, by the comparatively small role that Canadian food aid plays in most recipient economies, and by the fragmented donor environment in which aid is given. CIDA has sought to counter these constraints by concentrating on fewer recipients, encouraging inter-donor cooperation, and using intermediary agencies such as Canadian NGO's and the World Food Programme.

Conclusions:
The Determinants of
Canadian Food Aid Policy

In times of drought, flood, famine, civil strife, and general food
shortages, food aid is indispensable to the livelihood and survival
of millions in developing countries.[1]

(CIDA publication)

There are only a few circumstances in the world where food aid
makes good sense.[2]

(CIDA official)

Its ability to produce an abundance of food supplies in an era of
dwindling resources makes Canada what James Eayrs calls a "foremost nation" in an important area of contemporary international
relations.[3] It is not surprising that from its modest beginnings in
1951 the Canadian food aid program has grown into a large and
complex part of Canada's overseas development assistance. During
the past three decades over three billion dollars worth, or fully one-
fifth of all Canadian foreign aid, has been offered in the form of
foodstuffs. Although Canada's relations with the Third World have
become more complex as issues such as trade and monetary reform
have risen on the international policy agenda, food aid remains the
largest single component of Canada's development assistance
strategy.

Despite four decades of operation the Canadian food aid program
is no less controversial than it was in its initial years. As the above
quotes remind us, CIDA officials themselves express widely divergent
views of the role that food aid can and should play in Canada's
relations with the Third World. The debate over food aid as a form
of foreign aid reflects the more general debate over the proper objectives of Canadian development assistance and the proper strategy
for its allocation. By studying the evolution of the food aid program
and the way it is administered, some useful insights can be gained
into the overall priorities and objectives of Canadian foreign policy
in relating to the Third World.

THE EVOLUTION OF CANADIAN
FOOD AID POLICY

The evidence presented in this study has clearly shown that until the late 1970s Canada pursued an essentially passive, reactive approach to food aid management. Organizational responsibility for the food aid program was dispersed among a number of bureaucratic actors. Long-term planning played a minimal role in the determination of food aid allocations and responses to food aid requests were formulated on an ad hoc, case-by-case basis, with allocations frequently dependant on a balance between interdepartmental interests. Once the food aid was delivered, the Canadian government took a "hands-off" approach in which minimal conditions and supervision requirements were placed on the recipient government.[4]

However, this approach to giving food aid has undergone substantial changes in the past two decades. The critical turning point appears to have been the world food crisis of 1972–74 and the subsequent politicization of food policy issues. Like other donors, at that time Canada began a period of extensive review and reassessment of its programs. This resulted in a number of new policy initiatives that were designed to establish a more active, developmentally oriented food aid policy. The 1980s was a period of consolidation and restructuring as many of the policy themes introduced in the 1970s were elaborated and refined. This study has shown that there have been three substantive changes made to Canadian food aid strategies since the early 1970s.

First, there has been a significant organizational change with the first formal institutionalization of the food aid program since its founding. The creation of the Food Aid Centre (FACE) and its involvement in every phase of Canadian food aid planning, programming and implementation established for the first time an institutional basis for the operation of a coordinated food aid program. It can no longer be said, as was the case in the 1970s, that the Canadian food aid program is nothing more than a diverse collection of unconnected programs pursuing disparate objectives. By establishing an institutional basis for specialization in food aid, CIDA has been able to take a more active role not only in planning and implementing food aid projects but also in responding to food aid policy issues raised both domestically and internationally.

Second, there has been a significant evolution in the policy rationale for the Canadian food aid program. Since the mid 1970s there has been at least a rhetorical commitment to bringing Canadian food aid policies and programs into line with the emerging concepts and norms of a developmental food aid regime.[5] Canada has joined other donors in elaborating policy statements which emphasize the need to promote agricultural development and food production in developing countries, and has also linked Canadian food aid contributions to the food strategies and development plans of recipient countries. While recipient needs and developmental criteria have received greater priority in Canadian policy statements, the most significant shift in the 1980s has been the elaboration of the concept of developmental food aid, linking food aid to structural adjustment and policy dialogue.

Third, there have been significant substantive changes to the nature of Canadian food aid programs themselves. These changes have been evident in a number of dimensions: a much greater multilateralization of Canadian food aid, the greater use of alternative channels such as NGO's and multilateral institutions in responding to emergencies, the elaboration of more objective criteria for allocating bilateral food aid, greater use of multi-year programming, and increased monitoring and evaluation of food aid transfers. In many ways Canadian officials have moved a significant distance towards implementation of many of the proposals advocated by Canadian analysts in the late 1970s and early 1980s as well as those embraced in international statements issued by the WFP's Committee on Food Aid Policies.[6] However, such comments must be tempered by the recognition that the tensions between the various objectives underlying the program still exist. Tying requirements for the food aid program have been tightened rather than relaxed and the expansion of fish aid suggests that export and surplus disposal considerations can still some times override developmental considerations. Despite the rhetorical commitment to the concept of triangular food aid exchanges, Canadian practice lags far behind that of other donors. In surveying the nature and extent of these changes, the following conclusions can be drawn about the "determinants" of Canadian food aid policy.

THE IMPACT OF ECONOMIC INTERESTS

For many students of Canadian aid policy domestic economic interests provide the primary explanation for Canadian aid policies. Pointing to the fact that tied aid generates government expenditures that benefit the domestic economy, analysts argue that aid policies are designed primarily to serve the needs of economic interests within Canada. Dominant class theorists such as Cranford Pratt have cited the privileged access of the business class to Canadian policy makers and the integration of the values and interests of the dominant class into the government bureaucratic elite as the primary explanation for the commercially oriented nature of many Canadian aid policies.[7] How adequate are such explanations in accounting for the evolution of Canadian food aid policy?

At first glance it appears that food aid provides a good example of an aid policy driven almost entirely by domestic economic considerations. There is little question that the existence of domestic grain surpluses was the primary motivating factor in establishing the food aid program in the first place. It is equally evident, as has been demonstrated in chapter 1, that surplus conditions were an important reason for the selection of particular commodities, the choice of recipient, and the fluctuations of overall levels of food aid giving during the first three decades of the program. Chapter 4 provided several vivid examples from the 1970s which illustrated the ways in which economic considerations frequently overrode development considerations in the area of commodity selection.

Having stated this it is also important to point out that the influence of commercial motives has also been tempered by Canada's status in world grain markets. Being a smaller agricultural producer than the United States, Canada has always been in a weaker position in competing in world agricultural markets, and the desire of Canadian policy makers to use food aid as an outlet for Canadian surpluses has therefore been tempered by a fear that it could not compete directly in an outright trade war with the United States. Thus, with the exception of canola oil, there is little evidence that Canada has used its food aid as a strategic market-development mechanism in the same way that the United States has used its PL 480 program. Instead Canadian policy makers have turned to food aid primarily in reaction to politically embarrassing surpluses or lost markets. Rather than being an active market development tool, Canadian food aid has been more a crisis-oriented, defensive mechanism for dealing with specific short-term difficulties experienced by particular commodities.

In this regard it is interesting to note that the politics of commodity selection are in many regards similar to those of trade protectionism. Students of trade policy have wondered why governments which are ideologically committed to trade liberalization frequently adopt protectionist policies. David Protheroe and Margaret Biggs, in studying the Canadian case, argue that specific business groups demanding protection have a much greater incentive to organize and lobby aggressively than those groups committed to liberalization.[8] They are able to point to specific short-term economic and political benefits and to identify specific groups or industries who will suffer if action is not taken. Those supporting liberalization are at a disadvantage because they can only appeal to longer-term, more abstract benefits that may emerge. Similarly those appealing for the inclusion of a particular commodity in the food aid program can point to immediate benefits that will accrue to an identifiable group within Canada. CIDA has been left in a defensive position, trying to make the longer-term, more abstract case for the rejection of the commodity. The role of inter-bureaucratic politics appears to be especially important here.

This study suggests that commercial considerations have greater weight when other bureaucratic actors play a role in initiating and promoting commodity proposals on the behalf of client groups. While CIDA has frequently attempted to oppose such proposals, it is apparent that when they are "kicked upstairs" for political resolution at the cabinet level CIDA has frequently come out the loser. This was particularly the case in the 1970s when domestic agricultural issues became increasing politicized at a time when the federal government had committed itself to pursing a more aggressive policy of supply management. In such circumstances domestic surpluses were an acute embarrassment to the government, raising serious questions about its competence to implement supply-management policies. In such circumstances CIDA was clearly weakly placed to defend its position.

This raises the question of how CIDA has attempted to deal with these commercial pressures in the context of its efforts to reform the Canadian food aid program. From an organizational point of view CIDA has employed three different strategies in attempting to gain greater control of the selection of the primary input into the food aid program, i.e., food commodities. First, it has attempted to establish what is known by organizational theorists as a "negotiated environment" in order to create greater certainty regarding the quantity and quality of the foodstuffs which are supplied to the food aid program.[9] Proposals emanating from CIDA with regard to making contracts with farmers, longer-term contracts with the Canada Wheat Board, the stockpiling of specially prepared products, the right of first refusal, and the establishment of triangular exchanges are all examples of CIDA's attempt to establish more direct control over the selection and availability of commodities.

Second, CIDA has attempted to strengthen its own administrative resources in dealing with the issue of commodity selection. Prior to the creation of the Food Aid Centre in 1978 CIDA had no specialized expertise in food aid and no one specifically responsible for responding to commodity issues. Interest groups promoting the use of particular commodities would generally approach departments such as Agriculture Canada first and those departments would then make representations on their behalf to CIDA. CIDA was thus constantly being placed in a largely reactive position on the issue of commodity selection. Since the creation of the Food Aid Centre CIDA has established the position of commodity officer, responsible for monitoring the availability of Canadian commodities and analysing the needs of recipients. Through its commodity officer, the Food Aid Centre now serves as the primary contact with interest groups. In many ways this officer plays a role which organizational theorists refer to as "boundary-spanning."[10] Boundary-spanners can help an organization cope with uncertainty by representing the organization to outside actors, defending the organization from external threats, and monitoring the environment for events that are relevant to the organization. By monitoring recipient needs and the Canadian market and serving as the primary contact with domestic interest groups, the FACE commodity officer places CIDA in a much better position to take a more active role in response to external pressures. The commodity officer, by acting as an initial "gatekeeper," attempts to screen out the more inappropriate commodities and defends CIDA's decisions to outside actors.

Third, as CIDA has developed greater administrative capacity to deal with food aid, it has sought to build a policy consensus within the Canadian government regarding standards of appropriateness and cost effectiveness in commodity selection. CIDA has developed a set of criteria that are based on principles articulated in fora such as the WFP's Committee on Food Aid Policies and by academic analysts. By appealing to these norms CIDA hopes to gain greater legitimacy for its case while putting other departments and interest groups in the defensive position of having to make a case for inclusion of products which violate these criteria.

The adoption of selection criteria and the absence of more exotic food commodities such as powdered eggs and canned beef in the 1980s, demonstrate that some progress has been made in injecting greater developmental concerns into the selection process. This does not mean that commercial factors no longer play a role. Although some of the more dramatic surplus disposal cases have been eliminated, an examination of the patterns of commodity composition during the past two decades reveals that export availability continues to be an important determinant of food aid supplies. Indeed, as the case of fish aid in the 1980s shows, when domestic interest groups work in conjunction with other government departments it is still possible to expand the role of a particular commodity in the food aid program despite the developmental concerns raised by CIDA, particularly for a commodity, such fish, which has strong regional political significance. The maintenance of a regional balance in the procurement of food aid commodities appears to be a continuing, if subtle, factor in the selection of commodities for the program.[11]

THE CANADIAN PUBLIC PHILOSOPHY AND POLICY PARADIGMS

In examining the contradictions between competing objectives of the Canadian aid program, most analysts have focused on the ways in which political and economic interests tend to take precedence over developmental and humanitarian concerns. The terms "humanitarian" and "developmental" are taken to be virtually synonymous and mutually reinforcing. What is of concern here are the ways in which these objectives are undermined by non-developmental interests. Little attention has been given to the possibility that humanitarian and developmental objectives may actually represent quite different visions of how aid should be distributed. In fact much of the public debate over food aid, I suggest, reflects the inherent contradiction between humanitarian and developmental objectives and the difficulties of reconciling these within the food aid program.

In examining this issue it is useful to note that food aid policies and strategies can be categorized into two basic approaches to defining and responding to food aid needs.[12]

Hunger-responsive food aid. The need for this type of aid is identified in terms of nutritional deficiencies of specific population groups. The aim of such food aid is to alleviate chronic hunger and acute deprivation by providing food directly to the affected populations and to vulnerable groups such as women and children. This type of food aid gives priority to emergency food aid, feeding programs for vulnerable groups, and food-for-work programs where the distribution of food aid can serve as a dietary supplement for recipient populations.

Supply-stabilization food aid. This type of aid is used primarily to stabilize market prices in the recipient country. Need is identified in terms of the "resource gap" between production and consumption. Stabilization food aid is thus targeted at much broader objectives, which include promoting the growth of the recipient economy, providing balance-of-payments relief, generating local revenues, and ensuring domestic economic stability. Little attention is given to targeting specific local population groups. Instead the donor relies on governmental and commercial food distribution systems to pass benefits on to these groups.

From this study it is evident that both types of aid-giving have been present in the Canadian food aid strategy. The interdepartmental 1978 *Food Aid Policy Recommendations* gave clear support to the hunger-responsive food aid strategy when it noted that "the main 'rationale' for food aid is a humanitarian one. Food aid should be provided primarily to address the nutritional needs of the poorer segments of recipient-country populations."[13] The 1984 Food Aid Strategic Plan shifted the emphasis to stabilization food aid, noting that the primary objectives of the program were "increasing the quantities of food available in food deficit countries" and "accelerating the pace of development by freeing foreign exchange and generating domestic resources for investment."[14] Providing supplementary food to nutritionally vulnerable groups and emergency food aid were listed as the third and fourth objectives of the food aid program.

In order to understand the differing emphasis placed on these two types of aid giving, it is necessary to look at the relationship between aid strategies and the domestic political culture of donor countries. A recent study of Western middle powers concluded that the dominant socio-political values of the domestic environments of donor states were the most important determinant of aid policies.[15] For example, those countries where values connected with the welfare state were most strongly rooted in domestic political culture were more likely to pursue a poverty-oriented aid policy, placing greater emphasis on targetting the poorest population groups because of their commitment to principles of equity and social justice.

Influenced by the findings of this study of middle powers, Cranford Pratt has argued that much greater attention needs to be given to examining the impact of domestic political culture on the formulation of Canadian aid policies. Pratt suggests that it is important to understand the dominant public philosophy underlying Canadian policies towards the Third World. Drawing on the work of Ronald Manzer, he proposes that public philosophies are important because they provide "the set of ideas that give definition to the problems which public policies address and direction to the search for a solution to them."[16] Liberalism, the dominant public philosophy of Canada, is, Pratt contends, expressed internationally by a commitment to liberal internationalism. This has provided a "strong and broadly based support for a substantial aid programme."[17]

In examining the influence of liberal values on the formulation of Canadian public policies, Manzer suggests that Canadian liberalism has at its core a fundamental contradiction between two strands of liberalism: ethical liberalism and economic liberalism. Ethical liberalism places emphasis on the "alleviation of hardships due to circumstances beyond one's control,"[18] while economic liberalism emphasizes the primacy of market forces and the need to maintain the effective functioning of the market. In some instances these two strands can be mutually reinforcing – Keynesian economics may be considered to be an attempt to bring these two strands of thinking together within a common policy paradigm – but in other instances they contradict each other.

In this study it is evident that the tension between these two stands of liberalism provides an important basis for understanding some of the crucial debates regarding the nature of Canada's food aid strategy and the priority given to alternative types of food aid. The presence of ethical liberalism in Canadian political culture helps to explain the generally strong support found among the Canadian public for Canadian aid programs. A 1980 poll found that the majority of respondents argued that Canada should give aid for "humanitarian purposes" (59 per cent) or accepted the fact that "Canada is rich" as a justification for giving aid (29 per cent). Only 4 per cent suggested that provision of "trade benefits for Canada" was a basis for aid giving.[19] Other polls have produced very similar results. For example a 1985 Decima research poll showed that 81 per cent of the respondents felt that Canada had a moral responsibility to give aid, while only 18 per cent felt that aid should be given because it could lead to more trade for Canada.[20]

Ethical liberal ideas also help to explain the strong interest shown in Canadian food aid, especially in responding to emergency food crises abroad. This was never more evident than in the overwhelming Canadian response to the Ethiopian famine. When the Canadian government announced that it would match private Canadian contributions on an three to one basis, polls revealed that 56 per cent of Canadians had personally contributed to the Ethiopian famine relief effort.[21] As food aid is such a highly visible and emotive form of aid, Canadians feel that Canada, as one of the breadbasket regions of the world, should share generously of its surpluses with those who are suffering "due to circumstances beyond one's control."

For this reason the Canadian public generally has a "hunger-responsive" model of aid-giving in mind when they think of food aid. This has raised expectations that the Canadian government will respond quickly and generously to food crises and will take steps to ensure that food aid is indeed reaching those in genuine need. A recent poll which revealed a high level of support for Canadian aid to relieve "hunger and poverty" also showed that 75 per cent of the public felt that the government should give directions to the recipient governments concerning the ways in which the aid could most effectively reach the neediest population.[22] For the public food aid is most commonly perceived as being destined to feed malnourished people directly, not to provide general support to governments, which is clearly an indication of the ethical liberalism underlying support for this type of aid.

However, as this study has also shown, when it comes to the actual implementation of the food aid program Canadian policy makers have more frequently been influenced by the policy paradigms rooted in the second strand of the Canadian public philosophy: economic liberalism. From the very beginning of the program Canadian aid officials were sceptical of the developmental rationale for food aid. Donation of foodstuffs for public consumption was seen as nothing more than a welfare subsidy for unproductive, short-term consumption. Only if food aid could somehow be linked to longer-term investments that promoted economic growth could food aid be seen as playing a useful developmental role. Thus, rather than distribute food aid for immediate consumption, Canadian officials preferred to sell food aid through governmental or commercial channels in order to generate counterpart funds. These funds could then be used to finance investments in more productive, long-term, "real" development projects. Canadian policy makers felt that it was less important to target specific population groups than to assist governments in overcoming those constraints that inhibited economic growth within recipient economies. Broader objectives such as balance-of-payments relief, generation of local revenues, or the stabilization of domestic supplies and prices were pursued in implementing food aid programs. Canadian policy makers tended to follow a dualistic strategy: justifying food aid policies in terms of appeals to the values of ethical liberalism, reinforcing public perceptions of Canadian aid associated with hunger-responsive food aid, while implementing Canadian food aid within the economic liberalism framework of stabilization food aid.

This explains in part the commitment Canadian policy makers have made to using food aid to support the domestic political stability of recipients. Economic liberalism places emphasis on the need to maintain a stable environment in which economic growth can take place. As has been seen, Canadian policy makers were not concerned with supporting specific regimes which had a particular political bias, but they frequently justified food aid policies in terms of their contribution to political stability. This approach to food aid clearly reflects the predominant political culture within the Canadian policy-making community. The Canadian International Image Study has shown that the bureaucratic elite which determines Canadian foreign policy defines the aid program in primarily altruistic terms, while rejecting the use of aid to resist communism or support national liberation movements. At the same time Canadian bureaucrats rank "stability in recipient countries" as the most important of eleven potential objectives of Canadian aid, even outranking "need" as an objective.[23]

It is apparent that political stability has been a recurrent theme throughout the history of the Canadian food aid program. It was a prominent justification for the large food aid allocations to Bangladesh and the reluctance of Canadian officials to apply more stringent controls on the use of the food aid. More recently it has been the rationale for providing food aid support to the governments of Tunisia, Morocco, Jamacia, and Egypt. By enabling governments to consolidate political support and demonstrate their external legitimacy, the generous provision of food aid with minimal strings attached has been seen as a way of creating a stable environment that would allow "real" development projects to be implemented and economic growth to be promoted.

CIDA officials are quick to assert that development assistance, whatever form it takes, is ultimately humanitarian in nature. For them, there is no contradiction between ethical liberalism and economic liberalism. Stabilization food aid, if it ultimately improves living standards within the recipient economy, is considered to be as humanitarian as hunger-responsive food aid. Nevertheless the notion of aiding governments rather than people still runs counter to most public perceptions of what the aims of food aid really are. Many of the groups outside the government that were concerned with food aid issues in the 1970s and 1980s stated their positions primarily within a hunger-responsive framework. At the centre of concerns raised by MP's such as Douglas Roche and Father Bob Ogle, and encapsulated in the recommendations of the report of the Task Force on North-South Relations, was the argument that food aid should be more carefully planned to aid needy population groups and less to support governments. This placed CIDA in a difficult position since it clearly lacked the administrative resources to implement targetted food aid on a large-scale basis. Nevertheless the government responded to some of these concerns. In some cases, such as Bangladesh, efforts were made to ensure that the specified levels of food aid would reach the most vulnerable groups.

The move towards greater multilateralization of Canadian food aid which began in the mid 1970s was based on the assumption that this aid was more directly aimed toward specific population groups. The rapid and large-scale response to Ethiopia and the use of alternative channels, especially NGOS, also reflected these humanitarian concerns. In the case of the Ethiopian famine the high profile role of David MacDonald as famine relief coordinator and his efforts to reassure Canadians that food was reaching those in need showed that the government had become increasing sensitive to the public demand for hunger-responsive food aid. Changing country distribution patterns in the late 1980s, with increasingly large amounts of food aid going to countries like Ethiopia, Sudan, Mozambique, and Angola, also reflected a greater sensitivity to needs defined in humanitarian terms.

However, the hunger-responsive model of food aid-giving has not totally replaced stabilization food aid and the 1980s have seen a strengthening of the policy paradigm underlying the stabilization approach to aid-giving. Two developments reinforced this trend in the 1980s. First, the economic crises faced by many Third World countries have made the implementation of targetted food aid much more difficult. Since this type of food aid is more demanding administratively and places more demands on the the recipient, the absorptive capacity for this type of food aid among recipient governments is greatly limited. Stabilization food aid, with its promise of balance-of-payments support, generation of local revenues, and quick disbursement, became increasingly attractive as a way of overcoming some of the difficulties facing recipients and encouraging renewed economic growth. At a time when financial resources for Third World countries have become increasingly limited, the advantages provided by stabilization food aid have become more attractive.

The second development has been an ideological reorientation of Western governments since the late 1970s towards more strongly held orthodox liberal values. In the aid field this liberalist orthodoxy has been most evident in the various reports of the World Bank, which in turn have heavily influenced development thinking among bilateral donor agencies. This has led to a growing emphasis on the need to link aid-giving to policy dialogue and structural adjustment programs that give priority to the importance of the private sector, seek reduction in public expenditures, and generally diminish the role of the state. Within this framework food aid targeted for direct public consumption is clearly seen as a liability. It requires a larger bureaucratic apparatus to administer and is frequently a part of the public subsidies that such adjustment programs seek to eliminate.

The influence of this liberalist orthodoxy on the evolution of Canadian food aid policy is most clearly evident in the 1983 corporate review of the Canadian food aid program. From this study two primary rationales for Canadian food aid emerged. First, it could support balanced economic growth by providing additional resources to recipient governments in countries "setting sound economic policies and promoting sectorally equitable growth."[24] Second, in cases where such "balanced growth" policies were not being followed, it was recommended that "policy dialogue to bring about key structural reforms in the recipient country is an indispensable proviso to any food aid assistance."[25] The growing importance of this emphasis in Canadian food aid has been reflected in the greater priority given to bilateral, government-to-government food aid, the curtailment of the expansion of the multilateral program, and the downplaying of the merits of project food aid in CIDA policy statements. Greater emphasis has been placed on selecting the "right" countries to receive food aid based on the track record of their domestic policy performance. Since his installation as CIDA president in 1989 Marcel Massé has aggressively proclaimed the philosophy of structural adjustment as the dominant focus of Canadian aid policy.[26] The dominant policy paradigm guiding the making of Canadian food aid policy is thus still firmly rooted in the same strand of economic liberalism that has shaped the program from the beginning.

THE BUREAUCRATIC DIMENSION

Some students of aid policy have suggested that the formulation of aid strategies can best be explained by focusing more narrowly on the aid agency itself and the interests of those administering the programs. John White, for example, has suggested that "the makings of an aid policy lie in the hands of those who actually administer it."[27] Similarly, in his critique of the traditional "mixed motives" explanation of Canadian aid policy, Kim Nossal points to the interests of "the organization which effects the transfer of resources between them – the state" as the primary explanatory factor.[28] In particular Nossal argues that once an agency for the administration of an aid program is established, a strong bureaucratic interest develops which demands that the organization "be nurtured and maintained for its own sake."[29] Thus he contends that CIDA officials tend to adopt aid policies which justify larger administrative resources. According to Nossal this explains why CIDA officials prefer "a capital-intensive, project-oriented, tied-aid programme [which] demands high person-year allocations for administration, both within Canada and in the field."[30]

Nossal's conception of the way in which an aid strategy is developed is similar to the explanation that public-choice theorists have put forward to explain the politics of budgetary decisions. This is based on the idea that state officials are motivated primarily by self-interest. Since prestige and salary levels are associated with larger budgets and staffs, bureaucratic officials will always seek to maximize the size of their budgets and organizations. As a result bureaucrats will opt for policies which inevitably require large organizations to administer, thereby building demand for organizational growth into the design of policies themselves. For this reason Nossal suggests that "other types of development assistance strategies that would have the effect of reducing sharply the number of state officials needed to plan, administer, assess and monitor project aid have been persistently avoided."[31]

But what keeps CIDA from designing an aid strategy that consumes an ever-larger amount of government resources? Why does the level of aid actually given often fall short of stated targets? Nossal suggests that while aid officials are seeking to maximize their budgets, other state officials, particularly those charged with overseeing government spending, have a strong interest in limiting the real cost of the aid program to the Canadian economy. This latter interest, which stems from the "intra-state conflict over resources and the relative power of the foreign affairs bureaucracy," is what places a brake on "unbounded growth" stemming from the self-interested designs of aid bureaucrats.[32]

Nossal's conception of the aid strategy formulation process is essentially a restatement of the "guardian-spender" framework common in public policy analysis.[33] Certainly there is much in this study that gives credence to this view. There are numerous cases where the Treasury Board secretariat, as the "guardian" of the public purse, has played an influential role in shaping Canadian food aid strategy. It was the Treasury Board's call for an evaluation of the food aid program in 1977 which initiated the series of reappraisals of the whole food aid strategy. It has also been noted that the Treasury Board secretariat, in its role of approving food aid expenditures, has raised questions about the commodity composition and value-added components of the program in an effort to ensure that the real costs of the program are reduced. This role was particularly illustrated in its delay of approval of the food aid budget for two years in the dispute over the amount of non-cereal commodities in the program. Many of the inter-departmental disagreements alluded to in this study have stemmed from the Treasury Board secretariat's concern with maintaining a degree of budgetary control and accountability over the food aid program. Its support of counterpart funds, its criticism of the concept of triangular food aid transactions, and its desire to maintain a separate vote for food aid in the aid budget also reflect this desire for accountability. Further, its opposition to budgeting for food aid in volume rather than dollar amounts and its reluctance to accept multi-year food aid programs reflects the board's desire to avoid commitments that unnecessarily reduce the government's budgetary flexibility. Such disputes seem to fit the expectations of the "guardian-spender" framework very nicely. CIDA (the spender) is pressing for larger spending authority and more flexibility in its spending, while the Treasury Board (the guardian) attempts to maintain firm control on departmental spending practices. At the same time CIDA must face the challenges of other spenders, whether it be Agriculture Canada, the Department of External Affairs, or the Department of Fisheries and Oceans, who wish to see that food aid expenditures benefit objectives in their policy domains.

As useful as the "guardian-spender" framework may appear, it does not provide a complete explanation for the formulation of Canadian food aid strategy. In fact in the case of food aid Nossal's suggestion that officials adopt strategies that demand high person-year allocations for administration can be reversed. Time and again in this study I have shown that Canadian aid officials have sought to design a food aid strategy which would be suited to their limited administrative resources. "Administrative convenience" has been a much stronger motivating factor in policy design than "bureaucratic expansion." Part of the justification for channelling more aid through the World Food Program (WFP) and non-government organization's (NGOS) was to permit better targeting of food aid while significantly reducing the administrative burden on CIDA. Reliance on the WFP and NGOS for monitoring activities during emergencies was also cited by the CIDA president as a less administratively costly alternative for CIDA. It has also been noted that the traditional preference within CIDA for program food aid was a way of meeting disbursement targets that minimized administrative demands and that the adoption of a policy of greater concentration on fewer recipients, particularly those that were already pursuing policies amenable to Canada ("positive conditionality"), was partly influenced by the lack of resources to engage in more serious forms of policy dialogue. All of these policies were selected and justified to some extent on the basis of an appeal to administrative convenience. As such they reflect an attempt to adopt an aid strategy appropriate to existing administrative resources.[34]

Such evidence suggests that in elaborating an aid strategy officials may not always be seeking primarily bureaucratic expansion, as Nossal suggests. In a recent study of the politics of public spending in Canada, Donald Savoie maintains that bureaucrats are more concerned with maintaining the status quo and job security than with necessarily expanding budgets.[35] This observation is similar to those made by organizational theorists who argue that organizational managers are primarily concerned with reducing the uncertainties in their task environment which threaten the survival of the organization.[36] In the case of aid programs analysts such as Jeffrey Pressman and Judith Tendler have argued that the complex environment in which aid agencies work makes it difficult for them to spend the budgets that have been allocated to them. The problem is not that they do not have enough money but that administratively they have too much. The challenge then is to find ways to "move money" in such a way that the organization meets the criteria of efficiency and effectiveness by which spending authorities and the public evaluate its performance. Thus from the organization's point of view the problem is primarily one of having an abundance of funds which must be spent in ways considered sufficiently appropriate that they do not threaten credibility, and hence future levels of budgeting. This was certainly the problem faced by CIDA in the early 1970s when the agency was unable to spend its allocated budget each year and began to carry over large surpluses from year to year. This became focus for criticism of the agency, leading Parliament to withdraw CIDA's authority to carry over funds from one year to the next. It was noted in chapter 4 that this interest in spending all allocated funds helped to reinforce the preference for program food aid and made its administrative convenience an attractive way to "move money" and reach disbursement targets. In response to these disbursement pressures, the clear incentive in the 1970s was to keep the food aid program as uncomplicated and simple as possible.

Initially this seemed to be an effective strategy in dealing with food aid, especially since many within CIDA's management doubted its developmental validity. However, this line of thought had begun to change significantly by the late 1970s. In recent years Canadian food aid has been dealt with in numerous media reports, in at least two reports by the auditor general, and in hearings before the Committee on North-South Relations, the Committee on Public Accounts, and the Committee on External Affairs and National Defence. Few aspects of Canadian aid policy have received as much critical attention as food aid. In these fora it became increasingly clear that CIDA's traditional "hands-off" approach to food aid had left the agency vulnerable to criticism from both financial agencies and the media that it was not in firm control of its aid program.

In discussing CIDA's response to these criticisms it is useful to draw on Judith Tendler's application of organizational theories to the behaviour of aid agencies.[37] Tendler argues that aid agencies, like private firms, cannot live with a high degree of uncertainty in their task environment. Consequently they attempt to establish some control over the contingencies prevalent in their uncertain environment. By engaging in contingency-reducing actions such organizations attempt to build into themselves a certain self-containedness which brings these uncertainties into the realm of the predictable.

This perspective is useful in understanding the nature of the changes that CIDA officials have attempted to implement in food aid policy. Like other organizations CIDA has attempted to establish some degree of control over the many uncertain elements of its food aid program which left the agency vulnerable to much criticism in the 1970s. One method of achieving this was to adapt the organization's technological core in order to bring the contingencies into the realm of predictability. Evidence of this can be seen in CIDA's efforts to reorganize the mechanisms and procedures by which food aid is allocated. The establishment of FACE as a central coordinating unit was intended to integrate the diverse elements of the food aid process into a coherent whole. The technology for allocating food aid was transformed as efforts were made to develop criteria for evaluating food aid requests and integrating bilateral food aid into the country review process. These changes were intended to create the administrative and analytical resources to overcome those organizational constraints that weakened CIDA's capacity for planning food aid allocations.

However, organizations not only adapt their internal structures but also attempt to expand their domains in the direction of crucial contingencies. This is done either by incorporating contingent elements into the design of the organization or arranging a negotiated environment. Business firms regularly engage in the process of vertical integration. Forward integration is intended to establish control over the disposal of products while backward integration establishes control over the firm's inputs or supplies. Continuing this analogy, it is clear that many of the organizational proposals put forward within CIDA were efforts to incorporate certain contingencies through a process of vertical integration. CIDA's dependency on surplus Canadian products, the suitability and availability of which are highly variable, is a source of uncertainty for CIDA, thereby threatening the quality of its output. Thus proposals emanating from CIDA with regard to contracting with farmers, longer-term contracts with the

Canadian Wheat Board, stockpiling of specially prepared products, right of first refusal, and the establishment of triangular exchanges are all examples of CIDA's attempt to establish greater control over an important input into the food aid program. CIDA could then define its needs in terms of recipient interests rather than through the contingencies of the Canadian economy.

Another uncertainty for CIDA involves the disposition of its product–food aid. Reports of corruption within recipient governments, poor administration, and "leakage" of food aid to non-target groups raise questions about CIDA's capability to deliver food aid to its intended recipients. In response to this issue CIDA has struggled with the question of the extent to which it should become involved in trying to influence the recipient's domestic policy. As a result there has been a move on CIDA's part toward the establishment of better monitoring procedures and the imposition of some conditions on the availability of its food aid. Explicit criteria have been established which the recipient is expected to meet if it wishes to continue receiving food aid. CIDA has also expressed growing interest in linking its food aid allocations to a policy dialogue coordinated jointly with other donors. These developments represent an effort by CIDA to establish a negotiated environment in hopes of gaining greater control over the ultimate disposition of its food aid. As a result there has been a noticeable shift away from Canada's traditional passive, "hands-off" approach towards a more active, interventionist style of aid-giving.

Thus in looking at the evolution of the Canadian food aid strategy during the past decade one finds little evidence to support Nossal's contention that aid strategies will be chosen primarily to justify higher budgets and greater administrative resources. Instead the effort has been focused primarily on elaborating a strategy suited to the limited resources at CIDA's disposal that also helps to reduce those uncertainties which threaten the survival of the agency. Such evidence suggests that in elaborating an aid strategy officials may be less concerned with bureaucratic expansion, as Nossal suggests, and more concerned with maintaining the status quo and ensuring organization survival.

THE GLOBAL FOOD AID REGIME

Thus far most of our attention has been focused on the domestic determinants shaping Canadian food aid strategy. However, some analysts have recently noted that international aid-giving is no longer carried out on a strictly individualistic basis but has become increasingly a social process. Donors are now more cognizant of the activities and expectations of other donor states and, as a result, decisions regarding levels of aid-giving and other issues are increasingly influenced by these external expectations. For example, Paul Mosley suggests that the existence of a forum such as the Development Assistance Committee of the OECD, which scrutinizes the quality and quantity of the aid performance of member countries, has been instrumental in persuading Japan to play a larger role as an aid donor.[38]

Despite the growing institutionalization of development assistance, including food aid, on a global basis, relatively little attention has been paid to the impact of the aid regime on donor aid policies. Nossal introduces the concept only briefly in his discussion of the "mixed motives" model. He notes, for example, that "standing, particularly for a lesser power, will in large part depend on the degree to which it adheres to the norms and expectations of acceptable behaviour."[39] He thus argues that to some extent the maintenance of an aid program reflects an interest in the prestige gained by aid officials from participating in an international system of aid. However, Nossal admits that this argument "can only account for the continued existence of a commitment to ODA, not for the nature, type or range of the programmes themselves."[40]

Nevertheless Nossal has touched on an important point: that aid officials, in developing their aid strategy, will be influenced by the norms and expectations placed on them by other participants in the international aid system. This would suggest that it is important to examine the influence of the international "regime" for aid-giving on development of donor aid strategies. The term regime has come to be associated with the "sets of implicit or explicit principles, norms, rules, and decision-making procedures around which actor's expectations converge in a given issue area."[41] The existence of such regimes may have an important impact on the formulation of foreign policy. Robert Keohane argues that by changing transaction costs and providing information such regimes affect the decision-makers' perceptions of self-interest and their calculations of the costs and benefits of alternative choices.[42] Intergovernmental organizations (IGOS) play an important part in the creation and maintenance of regimes. On one hand such IGOS create the opportunity for member states to legitimize certain viewpoints and norms which are central to their foreign policies. But at the same time, as Karns and Mingst contend, IGOS can affect member countries by setting an international agenda, thus "forcing government to take positions on issues."[43] Moreover "they subject states' behavior to surveillance through information sharing ... they embody or facilitate the creation of principles, norms, and rules of behavior with which states must align their policies if they wish to benefit from reciprocity."[44] In addition Karns and Mingst argue that "IGO-created norms and principles may be used by domestic groups to press for change in national policies."[45]

In the case of food aid a global regime oriented to the developmental uses of food aid has emerged only in the the past two decades. Previously the elaboration of a set of principles and norms to regulate the process of food aid giving was primarily focused on protecting commercial grain markets from the adverse affects of food aid. Canada participated in the elaboration of these regime rules largely because of its desire to protect its own interests from the threat that US PL 480 food aid posed to Canadian markets. Thus Canada participated in each of the Food Aid Conventions negotiated since 1967 and has incorporated the rules of the Food and Agriculture Organization's sub-committee on surplus disposal into its food aid agreements.[46]

The 1970s saw the emergence of new principles and norms which were designed to move food aid in a direction that better served the developmental goals and needs of the recipients. These principles were first articulated at the Rome World Food Conference in 1974 and have been restated and elaborated on in subsequent guidelines developed by the Committee on Food Aid Policies and Programmes (CFA).[47] Since its mandate was expanded in 1975, the CFA has been the principal focus for the discussion of the principles and norms of the food aid regime. Among those principles promoted by the CFA have been multi-year programming of food aid, linkage of food aid to the promotion of agricultural and rural development, greater use of triangular food aid transactions, larger use of multilateral channels for food aid, more objective criteria for allocating bilateral food aid and greater use of evaluations as a basis for programming additional quantities of food aid.

There are several ways in which the global food aid regime and the institutions associated with it have had an impact on Canadian food aid decision making. First, the pledging process of the WFP, whereby the WFP's executive director makes known the needs of the agency and recommends pledging levels, serves to set targets for food aid levels which must be taken into account in the domestic budget-making process. As the pledge to the WFP is made on a biennial basis, Canada's response to the director's call for pledges has an important impact on decisions regarding other elements of the food aid budget during the two-year period.

Second, the CFA meetings provide a forum for discussion of food aid policies and practices of both donors and recipients. It has now become common practice for one donor and one recipient government to have their food aid policies and programs reviewed each year by CFA members. Although donors expressed initial reluctance about this proposal, they have now accepted it. Canada's food aid policies were first reviewed before the CFA in 1985. Although these sessions are generally far from being "hard-hitting," they nevertheless force donors to define and defend their programs within the general framework of norms and principles for food aid giving set out by the CFA.

Third, as the global food aid regime has become more institutionalized, the body of knowledge concerning food aid practices has grown significantly. This is partly as a result of the efforts of donors to encourage information sharing among themselves. Canada has played a role in the development of a computer program which allows information sharing directly between donor agencies. The knowledge among donors about the existing needs and responses of other donors is now at a much higher level than it was even a decade ago. More important, there is an emergent body of consensual knowledge concerning the use of food aid transfers. As noted in chapter 5 aid officials themselves often held food aid in low regard, in part because very little literature existed on the developmental rationale and use of food aid as a development resource. The 1970s and early 1980s saw the rapid growth of a more popularly oriented literature that launched a vigorous, if at times polemical, assault on food aid. The FAO and the WFP have been active in promoting the development of a stronger theoretical basis for food aid decision making that more clearly defines its relationship to development programming. This has led to the gradual emergence of a small group of private scholars who have played an influential role in the formulation of regime principles and norms. Scholars such as Hans Singer, Hannan Ezekiel, Edward Clay, and Raymond Hopkins have written policy papers for the WFP secretariat or the CFA and have participated in the WFP seminars. The Institute for Development Studies (IDS), where Singer and Clay are based has, jointly with the WFP, organized seminars on food aid for aid administrators, including representatives from CIDA. At least one director of CIDA's Food Aid Centre has spent time studying at the IDS, while scholars from the IDS have conducted training sessions at CIDA.[48] CIDA's corporate review in 1983 included not only a comprehensive literature review but also interviews with the IDS, the WFP, and other principal food aid donors. The rationale for developmental food aid that was outlined in the corporate report and included in subsequent CIDA food aid manuals as representing the "emerging consensus" reflects to a large extent the views of this community of aid administrators and scholars. There is little doubt that this emergent body of "consensual knowledge" has had an important effect on the evolution of Canadian food aid strategy in both rhetoric and practice, even if it still falls short of expectations in a number of areas.

The emergence of an "epistemic community" which promotes a body of "consensual knowledge" regarding the uses of food aid as a development resource provides a useful basis for understanding how developmental and humanitarian concerns may become incorporated into government aid policy.[49] Most students of aid policy, focusing on its domestic determinants, argue that developmental and humanitarian interests are consistently downgraded because the intended beneficiaries, recipient governments or populations, are outside the domestic political process and therefore there are few means for these interests to be given adequate expression in the policy process. Thus much attention has been given to issues such as development education or the funding of non-governmental development groups as ways of building a stronger domestic constituency attuned to development concerns. The general assumption is that developmental considerations will be inserted into the policy process only in a "bottom-up" fashion as the influence of the business interests is curtailed by a strong pro-development domestic lobby.

However, it is apparent that development considerations may also enter into the policy process through the influence of "epistemic communities" and the body of "consensual knowledge" that they promote. The influence of the scholars and analysts forming such a community may not operate directly on the domestic policy process of donors but the body of knowledge promulgated by this community is influential in defining the norms and principles of the international regime. This provides domestic policy makers with a basis for pressing for changes in national policies and challenging the assumptions of existing policies or those of their critics. Domestic groups can use these norms and principles as a benchmark for judging their government's performance. Thus, in order to maintain its standing within the international community, the donor may feel compelled to demonstrate that, using Nossal's words, "it adheres to the norms and expectations of acceptable behaviour."[50] This would suggest that those wishing to advocate the emergence of a more developmentally oriented aid policy should give greater attention than they have in the past to the ways in which epistemic communities are formed and influence regime norms and principles on the international level, and how these norms and principles in turn shape national policy decisions.

IMPLICATIONS FOR THE FUTURE

What are the implications of this study for the future directions of Canadian food aid policy? As I have shown, food aid remains a controversial aspect of the Canadian aid program. In many ways Canadian food aid can be described as increasingly internationalist as a result of many of the reforms that I have described. The program has been gradually restructured to accord with international guidelines on food assistance, especially as they have been defined at the World Food Conference and subsequent meetings of the Committee on Food Aid Policies and Programmes. Nevertheless there still are many who question the legitimacy of food aid as a component of development assistance. As one recent CIDA document noted, "attitudes concerning the role and impact of food aid remain strongly influenced by the conventional wisdom concerning food aid as it was during the 1960s and early 1970s."[51] Thus, while few doubt the necessity of food aid in genuine emergency situations, the concept of using food aid as a developmental resource has only gradually taken root. What should be the future direction of the Canadian food aid program? The answer to this question raises two fundamental issues.

More Or Less Food Aid In the Future?

One issue regarding the future direction of the Canadian food aid program concerns appropriate levels of food aid-giving. When the parliamentary Task Force on North-South Relations was carrying out its study in 1980, such reputable groups as the Science Council of Canada and the Canadian Council on International Co-operation called for the elimination of long-term food aid, with the exception of emergency food aid. While these recommendations were not accepted, serious thought has continued to be given to the idea of at least placing a ceiling on future levels of Canadian food aid-giving. This position was most clearly articulated in the 1987 report of the Winegard committee, which recommended that future levels of non-emergency food aid should not exceed 10 per cent of the total ODA budget.[52] Although the government rejected this recommendation, food aid levels, as we have seen, have dropped recently as a result of budget-cutting measures imposed by the federal government. It is now evident that CIDA management has clearly targeted food aid as one area which should bear an important share of future aid cuts.

Given the controversies over food aid, would it be wiser to simply shift priorities to other types of development assistance and permit the food aid program to take the brunt of budget-cutting exercises? If recipient need is a primary criterion for answering this question, then a good case can be made for resisting this option and actually increasing food aid levels significantly during the next decade. In the late 1980s numerous food-monitoring agencies attempted to develop estimates of projected food aid needs of the least developed countries (LDCs) until the year 2000. The United States National Research Council then brought these various research centres together to compare estimates. Using "modest growth" assumptions it was projected that LDC food import needs would rise from 83 million tons in 1989/90 to 163 million tons or even higher by the year 2000. As many of these countries were experiencing ongoing economic and political crises, it was estimated that a growing portion of these needs could only be met by food aid transfers rather than purely commercial transactions. Thus, even using moderate growth assumptions, most agencies projected that future food aid levels would need to rise from the current 10 to 13 million tons a year to 30 to 40 million tons, or even higher, to meet projected needs.[53] Given the vagaries of variable weather conditions and uncertainties associated with civil turmoil, food aid needs could rise even higher in some regions, such as Africa. Thus, if need is used as a criterion to determine future Canadian food aid levels, then a strong case can be made for increasing future food aid levels and avoiding the temptation to use it as an administratively convenient means of budget cutting.

Making Stabilization Food Aid More Hunger-Responsive

If more food aid, rather than less, is likely to be needed during the next decade, what form should this aid take? On the surface the choice appears to be a simple one. As Raymond Hopkins has remarked, "there are only two useful things to do with food: eat it or sell it."[54] As I have shown, Canadian support for food aid, rooted as it is in ethical liberalism, has tended to favour a hunger-responsive approach to food aid. Canadians expect that Canadian foodstuffs which are sent abroad as part of the aid program relieve hunger and malnutrition by directly feeding people. Nevertheless there is growing awareness among analysts that traditional forms of famine relief may do little to relieve long-term hunger and may in fact be a contributing factor to perpetuating poverty and malnutrition. With the continued deterioration of economic conditions in the Third World, the demand for stabilization food aid will continue to grow.

To the extent that these economic problems are seen to be caused, or as least exacerbated by, recipient government policies, there will also be strong demand within the donor community to link food aid programs to structural adjustment programs. Future Canadian food aid programming is thus likely to continue to move towards even greater emphasis on stabilization food aid.

This shift towards more stabilization food aid linked to structural adjustment programs could generate continuing distrust and cynicism among the public concerning the "real" uses of Canadian food aid. Public support for Canadian food aid will depend in large part on public perceptions of CIDA's ability to administer the food aid program in an effective and efficient manner, defined largely in terms of its "hunger-responsiveness." Although CIDA has clearly attempted to portray more accurately the multiple uses to which food aid can be put, the notion that food aid is primarily to support governments runs fundamentally counter to those values of ethical liberalism which hold that our aid should help the genuinely needy. How do we reconcile these two seemingly incompatible approaches?

The key to this question lies largely in the kind of conditionality that is attached to Canadian food aid transfers. Much of the discussion regarding "developmental" food aid has focused on macro-conditionality, i.e., the types of policies that recipient governments should pursue in order to continue receiving food aid. An alternative approach is to give greater attention to issues related to micro-conditionality, that is, looking at "demand ... not so much directed to policy changes, as to the effects of aid on target groups, such as the poor or women."[55] There are three essential ways in which Canadian food aid may be used to promote structural adjustments within an essentially hunger-responsive framework.

Providing additional macro-resources to fewer countries. Currently global food aid transfers represent only about 10 per cent of total financial aid to the LDC countries. Hence, on a global level, the doubling or even trebling of food aid is unlikely to have a significant impact on the compelling capital needs of the Third World. However, an increase in food aid, which is concentrated on a few poor countries who are trying to adopt a more hunger-responsive strategy of structural adjustment, could make an important difference. In order to avoid past problems with disruption of local markets, such assistance should be concentrated on those countries which are already heavy importers of food and are likely to remain so, at least in the medium term.[56] Thus, while it is wise to concentrate food aid on fewer bilateral recipients in order to maximize impact, the willingness of the recipient to undertake a structural adjustment program should not be the only criterion for concentration. Instead preference should be given to those countries which are committed to what has been dubbed "adjustment with a human face," which takes the distributional implications of structural adjustment programs into account in the very beginning and plans into them some protection for the weaker and more vulnerable groups within society.[57] By concentrating more food aid on a smaller number of countries committed to this type of program, sufficient resources may be provided to have a positive effect.

Providing compensation to the "losers" of structural adjustment programs. It has now become widely evident that structural adjustment programs create obvious winners and losers during the implementation process. Low-income families are frequently dealt a triple blow. Austerity policies implemented as part of such programs often result in cutbacks in employment and pay restrictions. At the same time food prices may rise as a result of devaluation and pricing policies, and cutbacks in government expenditures may lead to decreases in the provision of health and education services. Recent studies have chronicled the decline in standards of health, nutrition, and education among the more vulnerable groups, particularly in urban areas. In such circumstances food aid can be used to provide compensation to the losers of structural adjustment in two ways. 1 *Public works programs*, using food aid as a form of compensation, can be designed to provide employment for the victims of austerity programs who are suffering unemployment and salary loss. Such programs can have the dual benefit of producing employment at relatively low cost while assisting in the construction or maintenance of the economic infrastructure necessary for long-term economic growth. 2 *Feeding schemes* can be used to direct additional food resources to particularly vulnerable groups, such as children and pregnant or lactating women.

Maintaining social services. The reduction of government services is a common feature of adjustment programs aimed at deficit reduction. Such cuts are inevitably most severe in relation to social services in rural areas, especially rural health services and mother-and-child health clinics. In some cases food may be used directly to keep such services running. In other cases food aid may be sold (monetized) to generate revenues for the continuation of such services.

While such proposals are not new, they have not generally been considered to be an important element in the discussion and negotiation of structural adjustment programs. As we have seen Canada has been ready, like other donors, to inject food aid in cases such as Morocco where food aid is provided as a quick remedy for an adjustment program which has gone wrong. Food aid should instead be seen as a resource, which needs to be planned as part of a structural adjustment program from the very beginning. This opens up an area where Canadian officials can genuinely play the "middle" role that they have at times referred to in official publications. Canada should take a much more activist role in raising questions concerning the distributional implications of structural adjustment programs and ensuring that the potentially positive role that food aid can play in terms of micro-conditionality is planned from the beginning.

The Canadian government could also move towards a greater emphasis on a hunger-responsive approach to food aid policy by immediately doing three things. First, it could commit itself to taking a more active role in ensuring that the distributional implications of structural adjustment programs and the potential role of food aid to assist the "victims" of such programs are raised at the earliest possible stage in appropriate bilateral and multilateral fora.

Second, the Canadian government should support the relaxation of a number of the rules currently part of the global food aid regime. For example, regulations such as the usual marketing requirements, which require recipients to import an equivalent amount of food at commercial prices, and regulations that prohibit the re-export of food aid commodities are increasing irrelevant and should be abandoned. In addition the Canadian government should relax its position on prohibiting the World Food Program and Non-Government Organizations from "monetizing" (or selling) their food aid. A relaxation of these rules would give such agencies greater flexibility in the use of their aid resources and enable them to direct more of their aid to specific target groups.

Third, the Canadian government should give greater practical support to the idea of third country purchases and trilateral commodity exchanges. While not without some management difficulties, studies have shown that such exchanges can provide useful additional benefits to the developing countries involved. Although the Canadian government has given rhetorical support to the idea, Canadian practice falls far behind international trends in this area. In the 1980s 7 per cent of global food aid was purchased in developing countries through such exchanges. The food aid program of the European Economic Community purchased fully 11.3 per cent its food aid through these exchanges. In sharp contrast, developing country purchases and trilateral exchanges accounted for only 1.8 per cent of Canadian food aid.[58]

After four decades of experience food aid remains a resource that has great potential for powerful positive or negative impacts on recipient countries. To grasp the opportunity to use food aid positively requires both a strong political will and careful attention to the planning and management of this resource. As this study has shown, CIDA has taken a number of important steps to improve the planning and administration of the food aid program. Following the crisis of confidence in the food aid of the 1970s, Canadian officials have succeeded in making food aid more respectable. However, future support for the food aid program will be maintained only if Canadian officials are able to demonstrate that the shift to "developmental" food aid does not just mean more resources being made available for governments to carry out macro-adjustment policies. Future political support for a growing food aid program will be gained only to the extent that CIDA is able to demonstrate that the benefits of food aid transfers are genuinely targetted towards hungry people, not just resource-hungry governments.

Notes

INTRODUCTION

1 An excellent summary of the literature on food aid can be found in S.J. Maxwell and H.W. Singer, "Food Aid to Developing Countries: A Survey," *World Development* 73 (1979): 225–47, and E.J. Clay and H.W. Singer, *Food Aid and Development: Issues and Evidence* (Rome: World Food Programme Occasional Paper no. 3, September 1985).

2 Science Council of Canada, *Collaboration for Self-Reliance: Canada's Scientific and Technological Contributions to the Food Supply of Developing Countries* (Ottawa: Supply and Services Canada 1981), 11.

3 Canadian Council on International Co-operation, "Background Discussion Paper," Appendix "RNSR-9" in Canada, Parliament, House of Commons, *Minutes and Proceedings and Evidence of the Special Committee on North-South Relations*, 1st Session, 32nd Parliament, Issue No. 10 (1 October 1980) 10A:31.

4 Robert Carty and Virginia Smith, *Perpetuating Poverty: The Political Economy of Canadian Foreign Aid* (Toronto: Between the Lines 1981), 114.

5 Paul Fromm and James Hull, *Down the Drain? A Critical Re-Examination of Canadian Foreign Aid* (Toronto: Griffin House 1981), 155.

6 Douglas Williams and Roger Young, *Taking Stock: World Food Security in the Eighties* (Ottawa: North-South Institute 1981), 52–7.

7 Theodore Cohn, *Canadian Food Aid: Domestic and Foreign Policy Implications* (Denver: University of Denver, Graduate School of International Studies 1979).

8 Canada, Parliament, House of Commons, *Minutes and Proceedings and Evidence of the Special Committee on North-South Relations*, 1st Session, 32nd Parliament, Issue no. 19 (28 October 1980) 19:119.

9 See, for example: National Research Council, Office of International Affairs, *Food Aid: Projections for the Decade of the 1990s: Report of an Ad Hoc Panel Meeting, October 6 & 7, 1988* (Washington, DC: National Research Council 1988) and Raymond Hopkins, "Increasing food aid: Prospects for the 1990s," *Food Policy* (August 1990).

10 CIDA, Multilateral Programmes Branch, "Programme planning component review: Food aid" (Hull: mimeographed, May 1984), 5.

11 Stephen K. Commins, Michael F. Lofchie, and Rhys Payne, eds., *Africa's Agrarian Crisis: The Roots of Famine* (Boulder: Lynne Rienner 1986), 177.

12 D.A. Fitzgerald, *Operational and Administrative Problems of Food Aid*, World Food Program, Studies no. 4 (Rome: FAO 1965), 1.

13 Robert S. Walters, *American and Soviet Aid: A Comparative Analysis* (Pittsburgh: University of Pittsburgh Press 1970), 101.

14 Ibid., 103.

15 Andrzej Krassowski, *The Aid Relationship* (London: Overseas Development Institute 1968), 16.

16 George Cunningham, *The Management of Aid Agencies* (London: Croom Helm 1974), 4.

17 The following discussion draws on Walter, *American and Soviet Aid*, 103–19; Cunningham, *Management of Aid Agencies*, 2–6; and Krassowski, *The Aid Relationship*, 19–34. On the concept of "management structure" see William Newman, "Strategy and Management Structure," in John Veiga and John Yanouzas, eds., *The Dynamics of Organization Theory: Gaining a Macro Perspective*, 163–4 (New York: West Publishing Co. 1979).

18 For purposes of analysis I have adopted the distinction between activist and passive (or reactive) aid strategies as used by Cunningham, *Management of Aid Agencies*, 2–3 and Walters, *American and Soviet Aid*, 119. For a more complex classification of aid strategies on an active-passive continuum, see Krassowski, *The Aid Relationship*, 19ff. and Grant Reuber, "Canada's foreign aid policy: The strategy and tactics for allocating Canadian funds to foster economic development," CIDA Policy Review (Ottawa: mimeographed 1969), 31–3.

19 Walters, *American and Soviet Aid*, 119.

20 For a fairly comprehensive bibliography of this literature see Réal P. Lavergne, "Determinants of Canadian Aid Policy," in Olav Stokke, ed., *Western Middle Powers and Global Poverty: The Determinants of the Aid Policies of Canada, Denmark, the Netherlands, Norway and Sweden* (Sweden: Scandinavian Institute of African Studies 1989).

21 Kim Richard Nossal, "Mixed Motives Revisited: Canada's Interest in Development Assistance," *Canadian Journal of Political Science* 21, no. 1 (March 1988): 45.
22 Ibid., 35.
23 S.G. Triantis, "Canada's Interest in Foreign Aid," *World Politics* 24 (1971):1–18.
24 Theodore Cohn, " Canadian Food Policy and the Third World," *Current History* 79, no. 460 (November 1980): 146.
25 Cohn, *Canadian Food Aid*, 109.
26 Cranford Pratt, "Canadian Foreign Policy: Bias to Business," *International Perspectives* 3, no. 6 (November/December 1982): 3–6; Cranford Pratt, "Dominant Class Theory and Canadian Foreign Policy: The Case of the Counter-Consensus," *International Journal* 39, no. 1 (1984): 99–135; and Cranford Pratt, "Canadian Policy Towards the Third World: Basis for an Explanation," *Studies in Political Economy* 13 (1984): 27–56.
27 Carty and Smith, *Perpetuating Poverty*, 125–7.
28 Linda Freeman, "The Effects of the World Crisis on Canada's Involvement in Africa," *Studies in Political Economy* 17 (1985): 107–39.
29 Nossal, "Mixed Motives Revisited," 41.
30 Ibid., 55.
31 John White, *The Politics of Foreign Aid* (New York: St. Martin's Press 1974), 303.
32 Peter B. Evans, "Declining hegemony and assertive industrialization: us-Brazil conflicts in the computer industry," *International Organization* 43, no. 2 (Spring 1989): 235.
33 Ibid.
34 Ibid.
35 James G. March and Johan P. Olsen, "The New Institutionalism: Organizational Factors in Political Life," *American Political Science Review* 78, no. 3 (September 1984): 738.
36 Peter Hall, *Governing the Economy: The Politics of State Intervention in Britain and France* (New York: Oxford University Press 1986), 223.
37 Stephen Cohen, *The Making of United States International Economic Policy: Principles, Problems and Prospects for Reform* (New York: Praeger 1977), 31.

CHAPTER ONE

1 Jon McLin, "Surrogate International Organization and the Case of World Food Security, 1949–69," *International Organization* 33, no. 1 (Winter 1979): 52.
2 For a summary of the agricultural policies pursued by the two countries during this period see: T.W. Warley, *Agriculture in an Interde-*

pendent World: us and Canadian Perspectives (Montréal: Canadian-American Committee 1977).

3 A good summary of the history and evolution of the American food aid program can be found in Mitchell B. Wallerstein, *Food for War-Food for Peace: United States Food Aid in a Global Context*, (Cambridge, MA: MIT Press 1980).

4 Warley, *Agriculture in an Interdependent World,* 13.

5 J.C. Gilson, "A Canadian View of Conflicts and Consistencies in the Agricultural Policies of Canada and the United States," *American Journal of Agricultural Economics* 55, no. 5 (1973): 785–9.

6 McLin, "Surrogate International Organization," 49.

7 Canada, Parliament, *House of Commons Debates*, 4th Session, 21st Parliament, vol. 1 (21 February 1951), 538. On 1 February 1951, members of the Co-Operative Commonwealth Federation party (the predecessor to the New Democratic Party), had already suggested to the government that food be sent to India to deal with its shortages. Canada, Parliament, *House of Commons Debates*, 4th Session, 21st Parliament, vol. 1 (1 February 1951), 33.

8 K.J. Charles, "Foreign Aid–What's in it for Us?" *Canadian Dimension* 3 (March-April 1966): 43.

9 Quoted in Keith Spicer, *A Samaritan State? External Aid in Canada's Foreign Policy* (Toronto: University of Toronto Press 1966), 22–4.

10 Ibid., 23.

11 Canada, Parliament, *House of Commons Debates*, 6th Session, 21st Parliament, vol. 1 (2 April 1952), 1064.

12 Canada, Parliament, *House of Commons Debates*, 4th Session, 21st Parliament, vol. 3 (7 May 1951), 2792.

13 Canada, Parliament, *Report of the Auditor General to the House of Commons, 1953* (Ottawa: Queen's Printer 1953), 4.

14 Quoted in Spicer, *Samaritan State,* 179.

15 Ibid.

16 Unless indicated otherwise, data regarding food aid disbursements cited in this chapter have been taken from CIDA, FACE Centre, "Bilateral Food Aid Program as of 30 June 1978," and CIDA, *Annual Reports,* various years.

17 Canada, Parliament, *House of Commons Debates*, 1st Session, 23rd Parliament, vol. 1 (14 October 1951), 5–6.

18 Canada, Parliament, *House of Commons Debates*, 1st Session, 23rd Parliament, vol. 3 (8 January 1958), 2979.

19 Canada, Parliament, *House of Commons Debates*, 1st Session, 24th Parliament, vol. 1 (13 May 1958), 41.

20 Canada, Parliament, *House of Commons Debates*, 1st Session, 24th Parliament, vol. 3 (19 July 1958), 2429.

21 Canada, Department of Agriculture, *Canada and FAO* (Ottawa: Information Canada 1971), 14–5.

22 W.E. Hamilton and W.M. Drummond, *Wheat Surpluses and Their Impact on Canada/United States Relations* (Washington: Canada-American Committee 1959), 32–3.

23 McLin, "Surrogate International Organization," 50. The barter program involved the exchange of American wheat for minerals considered to be of importance to US security. UMR refers to "usual marketing requirements" which require recipients to buy a specified quantity of food through commercial channels in addition to the aid received. By using "tied UMR's", the US required that this additional amount be American wheat. For a detailed treatment of many of these issues, especially as they relate to Canadian-American relations, see Theodore H. Cohn, *The International Politics of Agricultural Trade: Canadian-American Relations in a Global Agricultural Context* (Vancouver: University of British Columbia Press 1990).

24 Keith Spicer, *A Samaritan State?* 188.

25 John Diefenbaker, *One Canada: The Years of Achievement, 1957–1962* (Toronto: MacMillan 1976), 140.

26 Canada, Parliament, *House of Commons Debates*, 5th Session, 24th Parliament, vol. 2 (20 February 1962), 1056.

27 FAO, *Ten Years of World Food Programme Development Aid, 1963–1972* (Rome: FAO 1973), 49.

28 Canadian Federation of Agriculture, *Presentation to the Prime Minister of Canada and Members of Parliament* (Ottawa, 26 February 1964), 9.

29 National Farmers Union, *Submission to the Government of Canada* (Ottawa: 6 April 1967), 23.

30 Spicer, *Samaritan State*, 183.

31 US Department of Agriculture, *Canada's Export Market Development for Agricultural Products*, Foreign Agricultural Economic Report 107 (Washington, DC, May 1975), 18.

32 Canada, Parliament, *House of Commons Debates*, 1st Session, 26th Parliament, vol. 3 (24 July 1963), 2559.

33 Ibid.

34 Canada, Parliament, *House of Commons Debates*, 1st Session, 26th Parliament, vol. 4 (4 October 1963), 3206.

35 See Robert Matthews, "Canada and Anglophone Africa," and Louis Sabourin, "Canada and Francophone Africa," in Peyton V. Lyon and Tareq Y. Ismael, eds., *Canada and the Third World* (Toronto: Macmillan 1976).

36 Peter C. Dobell, *Canada's Search for New Roles* (London: Oxford University Press 1972), 136.

37 For a review of CIDA's growth see, Sabourin, "Analyse des politiques de coopération internationale du Canada," in Paul Painchaud, ed., *Le*

Canada et le Québec sur la scène internationale (Québec: Centre Québecois de relations internationales 1978), 227–32.

38 Canada, Department of External Affairs, *Foreign Policy for Canadians: International Development* (Ottawa: Queen's Printer 1970).

39 Ibid., 16.

40 Ibid.

41 Wallerstein, *Food for War-Food for Peace*, 13–14.

42 Statistics Canada, *The Wheat Review* (Ottawa: Supply and Services August 1975): 11.

43 R.K. Sahi and W.J. Craddock, "Estimating the Effects of Operation Lift on 1970 Prairie Land Utilization." *Canadian Farm Economic*, 6, no. 5 (December 1971): 2–6.

44 Canada, Wheat Board, *The Report of the Canadian Grain Marketing Committee* (Winnipeg: 21 January 1971), 13, and *International Canada* 1, no. 7–8 (July-August 1970): 166. According to FAO criteria, these sales are classified as food aid transactions, similar to the Title 1 category of the American PL 480 program. However, in Canada, these sales were not categorised as aid and were not calculated as part of CIDA's food aid budget.

45 The Soviet purchases which were made in secret became the subject of great controversy in the US. For one account of this episode see James Trage, *The Great Grain Robbery* (New York: Ballantine Books 1975).

46 See Theodore Cohn, *Canadian Food Aid: Domestic and Foreign Policy Implications* (Denver: University of Denver, Graduate School of International Studies 1979), 24.

47 See Table 38 in Agriculture Canada, *Canada's Trade in Agriculture Products, 1978, 1979 and 1980* (Ottawa: Supply and Services 1980), 79.

48 R.M. Sorge, "Tons of Food Lost Yearly," *The Gazette*, 21 May 1975.

49 James Rusk, "Hungriest Get Food Last in Bangladesh," *Globe and Mail*, December 1974; Richard Peiper, "Corruption Saps Aid to Bangladesh, Missionary Says," *Toronto Star* (3 December 1974); and Marcel Pepin, "Il y a eu gaspillage de blé au Bangladesh," *La Presse*, (25 avril 1975).

50 Christopher Cobb, "MP Complains That Food Aid Sold by Authorities," *Ottawa Journal* (17 May 1975).

51 Paul Gérin-Lajoie, Report to the secretary of state for external affairs on the mission to Bangladesh, March 19–21, 1975 (Ottawa: mimeographed 1975).

52 See for example: C. Cobb and R. McKeown, "CIDA in a Rush to Spend Millions," *Ottawa Journal* (23 January 1975); and Charles Lynch, "CIDA Needs Watchdog," *The Citizen* (30 April 1975).

53 Canada, Parliament, House of Commons, *Report of the Auditor General of Canada to the House of Commons for the Fiscal Year Ended March 31, 1976* (Ottawa: Supply and Services 1976), 103.

54 CIDA, Task Force on Food Aid and Renewable Rource Policies for CIDA, Report to the President's Committee (Ottawa: mimeographed April 1975), 1.

55 CIDA, *Strategy for International Development 1975–1980* (Ottawa: Information Canada 1975).

56 Canada, Treasury Board Secretariat and CIDA, Evaluation of the Canadian food aid programme, (Ottawa: mimeographed May 1977), 11.

57 Ibid.

58 Ibid.

59 Ibid., 15.

60 Ibid., 16.

61 Ibid.

62 Ibid., 49

63 Ibid., 50.

64 Interdepartmental Working Group on Food Aid Policy, *Food aid policy recommendations* (Ottawa: mimeographed 26 June 1978), 24.

65 Ibid.

66 These decisions will be treated more fully in chapter 4.

67 CIDA, *Annual Aid Review: 1978 Memorandum to the OECD*, (Ottawa: Public Affairs Branch, CIDA 1978), 30.

68 Ibid.

69 CIDA, *Canada and Development Cooperation: Annual Report, 1979–80* (Ottawa: Supply and Services, 1980), 60.

70 Science Council of Canada, *Collaboration for Self-Reliance: Canada's Scientific and Technological Contribution to the Food Supply of Developing Countries* (Ottawa: Supply and Services Canada 1981), 11.

71 Canadian Council on International Cooperation, "Background Discussion Paper," Appendix 'RNSR-9' in Canada, Parliament, House of Commons, *Minutes of Proceedings and Evidence of the Special Committee on North-South Relations*, 1st Session, 32nd Parliament, Issue no. 10 (1 October 1980) 10A:31.

72 Robert Carty and Virginia Smith, *Perpetuating Poverty: The Political Economy of Canadian Foreign Aid* (Toronto: Between the Lines 1981), 114.

73 Paul Fromm and James Hull, *Down the Drain? A Critical Re-Examination of Canadian Foreign Aid* (Toronto: Griffin House 1981), 155.

74 Douglas Williams and Roger Young, *Taking Stock: World Food Security in the Eighties* (Ottawa: North-South Institute 1981).

75 Cohn, *Canadian Food Aid*, 109.

76 Canada, Parliament, House of Commons, *Minutes of Proceedings and Evidence of the Special Committee on North-South Relations*, 1st Session, 32nd Parliament, Issue no. 19 (28 October 1980), 19:119.

77 Canada, Parliament, House of Commons, *Minutes of Proceedings and Evidence of the Special Committee on North-South Relations*,

1st Session, 32nd Parliament, Issue no. 11 (2 October 1980) 11:38–9.

78 Ibid., 11:47.

79 Canada, Parliament, House of Commons, Parliamentary Task Force on North-South Relations, *Report to the House of Commons on the Relations Between Developed and Developing Countries*, (Ottawa: Supply and Services 1980), 49.

80 Barbara Insell, "A World Awash in Grain," *Foreign Affairs* 63, no. 3 (Spring 1985): 905.

81 For further discussion of some of these issues see Cohn, *International Politics of Agricultural Trade*, and Ronald Libby, "The Agricultural Subsidy War Between the US and the EEC," Paper presented at the Annual Meeting of the International Studies Association, Washington, DC, April 1990.

82 CIDA, *Annual Report, 1985–86* (Hull: Supply and Services 1986), 102.

83 For an official summary of the Emergency Coordinator's activities see David MacDonald, *The African Famine and Canada's Response* (Hull: Canadian Emergency Coordinator/African Famine 1985), and David MacDonald, *Forum Africa: Canadian Working Together* (Hull: Canadian Emergency Coordinator/African Famine 1986) and David MacDonald, *No More Famine: A Decade for Africa* (Hull: Canadian Emergency Coordinator/African Famine 1986).

84 CIDA, *Annual Report, 1985–86*, 102.

85 For a good overview of Africa's food situation see the series of articles in Stephen K. Commins, Michael F. Lofchie, and Rhys Payne, eds., *Africa's Agrarian Crisis: The Roots of Famine* (Boulder: Lynne Rienner 1986).

86 Notes for remarks by Margaret Catley-Carlson, President, Canadian International Development Agency, to the 20th Session of the World Food Programme Committee on Food Aid Policies and Programmes, Rome, Italy, October 1985, 3 (emphasis added).

87 Ibid.

88 Ibid.

89 CIDA, Program Evaluation Division, Policy Branch, Summary report on the evaluation of Canada's food aid program (Hull: mimeographed n.d.); 72.

90 Ibid., 17.

91 Cf. CIDA, *Food Aid: Contributing to Agricultural Development and Food Security* (Hull: CIDA 1986), 5–6.

92 Notes for remarks by Margaret Catley-Carlson, October 1985, 3.

93 Canada, Parliament, House of Commons, *For Whose Benefit? Report of the Standing Committee on External Affairs on the Relations Between Devel-*

oped and Developing Countries (Ottawa: Supply and Services May 1987), 58.

94 See "Too Much Food Aid Can Be Disastrous," *London Free Press*, 10 September 1987, and Patricia Owen, "Why West's Surplus Can't Abolish Famine," *Toronto Star*, 19 September 1987.

95 Canada, CIDA, *Canadian International Development Assistance: To Benefit a Better World, Response of the Government of Canada to the Report by the Standing Committee on External Affairs and International Trade* (Ottawa: Supply and Services 1987), 70.

96 *Globe and Mail*, 28 April 1989, A13, and 29 April 1989, A8.

97 Christopher Stevens, *Food Aid and the Developing World* (New York: St Martin's Press 1979), 204.

98 As we will see in later chapters, some of the changes in volume can also in part be accounted for by a shift towards more processed and more expensive food commodities such as fish.

99 CIDA, *Sharing Our Future: Canadian International Development Assistance* (Hull: Supply and Services 1987), 55.

100 OECD, *Development Cooperation: 1974 Review* (Paris: OECD 1974), Table V-3.

101 See FAO, *Food Aid in Figures* (Rome: FAO, 1986), 4 (1986), Table 1.

102 CIDA, VADA – *Voluntary Agricultural Development Aid* (Ottawa: July 1977), 3.

103 Hans Singer, et al., *Food Aid: The Challenge and the Opportunity* (Oxford: Clarendon Press 1987), 33.

104 This loan took the form of a fifty year credit with no interest and a ten year grace period before repayment begins. FAO, *Food Aid Bulletin*, 2 (April 1981): 34.

105 FAO, *Food Aid Bulletin*, 1 (January 1986), Table 13.

106 These figures should be treated with some caution, since not all transactions, particularly in emergency situations, are reported to the FAO's Committee on Surplus Disposal. The Canadian government does not publish its own figures regarding the type of food aid transactions it undertakes.

107 Interview, CIDA, Multilateral Branch, June 1979.

108 CIDA, Food Aid Centre, "1990/91 Food aid program annual report" (Hull: mimeographed, 30 July 1991).

109 In the 1980s, CIDA classified recipients according to three principal categories. Category I countries were high-priority countries in which comprehensive long-term programming of a full range of development assistance programs took place. Category II countries were countries in which Canada maintained a significant presence but did not engage in multiyear programming. Category III countries were those in which

Canadian development assistance played a minimal role, involving primarily emergency food assistance, non-governmental organizations and small amounts of mission administered funds. This system was abolished following the report of the Winegard Committee in 1987.

CHAPTER TWO

1 Canada, Agriculture Canada, *Orientation of Canadian Agriculture: A Task Force Report, vol. 2* (Ottawa: Supply and Services 1977), 27.
2 Canada, CIDA, *Annual Aid Review 1978* (Ottawa: Public Affairs Branch, CIDA 1978), 24.
3 Canada, Parliament, *House of Commons Debates*, 1st Session, 30th Parliament, vol. 12 (13 April 1976), 12779.
4 See, for example, "Seed Crushing More Competitive," *Toronto Globe and Mail* 12 November 1977.
5 Canada, Treasury Board and CIDA, *Evaluation of the Canadian food aid program* (Ottawa: mimeographed 1977), 27.
6 Ibid.
7 Canada, Wheat Board, *The Report of the Canadian Grain Marketing Committee* (Winnipeg: 21 January 1971), 13.
8 Quoted in *International Canada* 1, nos. 7–8 (July-August 1970): 166.
9 Canada, Industry, Trade and Commerce, *Annual Report, 1969–1970* (Ottawa: Queen's Printer 1970), 34. It should be noted that, although these credit sales qualified as food aid under FAO regulations, and were reported to the FAO Committee on Surplus Disposal as such, they were not included in CIDA's food aid budget.
10 D. Hutton, "Food Aid and Agricultural Trade," in Agriculture Canada, *Proceedings: Canadian Agricultural Outlook Conference-December 1985* (Ottawa: Agriculture Canada 1985), 123.
11 Ibid.
12 The controversial issues involved in the use of fish aid and the bureaucratic struggle to expand the fish aid program are discussed further in chapter 4.
13 Hutton, "Food Aid and Agricultural Trade," 124.
14 Canadian Wheat Board, *Annual Report, 1986/87* (Ottawa: Supply and Services 1987), 14.
15 Quoted in *International Canada* 2, no. 12 (December 1971): 249.
16 *International Canada* 8, no. 6 (June 1977): 191.
17 Keith Spicer, *A Samaritan State? External Aid in Canada's Foreign Policy* (Toronto: University of Toronto Press 1966), 12.
18 Interviews, CIDA, Bilateral Branch, May 1979, and External Affairs, Commodity and Energy Division, June 1979.

19 Interviews, CIDA, Bilateral Branch, May 1979, and Multilateral Branch, June 1979.
20 CIDA, *Annual Report, 1983–84* (Hull: Supply and Services 1984), 71.
21 CIDA, *News Release* no. 89/03 (17 January 1989).
22 See for example, the testimony of the director of CIDA's Food Aid Evaluation and Coordination Centre before a parliamentary committee in Canada, Parliament, House of Commons, *Minutes of Proceedings and Evidence of the Special Committee on North-South Relations,* 1st Session, 32nd Parliament, Issue no. 11 (2 October 1980), 11:38–39.
23 CIDA, "Food aid and food policies in Bangladesh" (Hull: mimeographed *ca.* 1980), 3.
24 CIDA, *Annual Report, 1986–1987* (Hull: Supply and Services 1987), 126.
25 Interview, CIDA, Multilateral Branch, June 1979.
26 On these two cases, as well as the Indian example mentioned below, see: Theodore Cohn, "The Politics of Food Aid: A Comparison of American and Canadian Policies," *McGill Studies in International Development 36* (Montreal: McGill University, Centre for Developing Area Studies January 1985).
27 Canada had halted bilateral food aid to Pakistan in 1978 after the Treasury Board evaluation had found that it had negative developmental consequences.
28 Canada, Parliament, *House of Commons Debates,* 1st Session, 30th Parliament, vol. 3 (22 January 1975), 2497.
29 Interdepartmental Food Aid Working Group, "Food aid policy recommendations" (Ottawa: mimeographed 26 June 1978), 20.
30 Interview, External Affairs, Commodity and Energy Policy Division, June 1979.
31 Canada, Parliament, House of Commons, *Minutes of Proceedings and Evidence of the Special Committee of North-South Relations,* 1st Session, 32nd Parliament, Issue No. 11 (2 October 1980), 11:34.
32 Interdepartmental Working Group, *Food Aid Policy Recommendations* 19.
33 CIDA, *Food Aid: Fact Sheet on CIDA's Involvement* (Ottawa: CIDA n.d.).
34 CIDA, *Canada and Development Cooperation, CIDA Annual Report, 1975–76* (Ottawa: Supply and Services 1976), 88.
35 Interdepartmental Working Group, *Food Aid Policy Recommendations* 24.
36 "Humanitarian Assistance: Wheat for Portugal," *Development Directions* 2, no. 1 (January-February 1979): 4.
37 FAO, *Food Aid Bulletin* 1 (Rome: FAO January 1975), Table 10.
38 Canada, Parliament, House of Commons, *For Whose Benefit? Report of the Standing Committee on External Affairs on the Relations Between Developed and Developing Countries* (Ottawa: Supply and Services May 1987), 58.

39 CIDA, *Annual Report, 1986–1987* (Ottawa: Supply and Services 1987), 73.

40 CIDA, Food Aid Centre, *1990/91 Food Aid Program Annual Report* (Hull: Food Aid Centre July 30, 1991).

41 CIDA, *Annual Report, 1975–76*, 88.

42 CIDA, Food aid and food policies in Bangladesh, 24.

43 CIDA, *Task Force on Food Aid*, Appendix IV, 28.

44 Ibid.

45 Interviews, CIDA, Multilateral Branch, April 1979, Policy Branch, April 1979, and Bilateral Branch, May 1979 and June 1979.

46 Interview, CIDA, Multilateral Branch, April 1979.

47 CIDA, Multilateral Branch, "Programme planning component review: Food aid," (Hull: mimeographed 1984), 4.

48 Canada, Parliament, House of Commons, *Minutes of Proceedings and Evidence of the Standing Committee on External Affairs and National Defence*, 1st Session, 30th Parliament, Issue no. 19 (2 May 1975), 19:9.

49 External Aid Office, *Annual Review, 1966–67* (Ottawa: Queen's Printer 1967), 16.

50 CIDA, "Food aid and food policies in Bangladesh," 2.

51 Interviews, CIDA, Bilateral Branch, May and June 1979, and Treasury Board, Program Branch, June 1979.

52 CIDA, *Canada and the Developing World: CIDA Annual Report, 1970–71* (Ottawa: Queen's Printer 1971), 24.

53 Canada, External Affairs, *Foreign Policy for Canadians: International Development* (Ottawa: Queen's Printer 1971), 17.

54 CIDA, "Programme planning component review: Food aid," (Ottawa: mimeographed 1984), 2. Emphasis in the original.

55 Ibid., 3.

56 CIDA, *Annual Report 1986–1987*, 73.

CHAPTER THREE

1 For a discussion of the evolution of the Food Aid Convention see, J. H. Parotte, "The Food Aid Convention: Its History and Scope," *IDS Bulletin* 14, no. 2 (1983): 10–5.

2 Ibid., 12.

3 Ibid.

4 Interdepartmental Working Group on Food Aid Policy, Food aid policy recommendations (Hull: mimeographed 1978), 9.

5 CIDA, *Annual Reports*, various years.

6 Historically the Grains Marketing Office was a part of the Department of Industry, Trade and Commerce (IT&C). However, with the reorgani-

sation of IT&C in 1982, this bureau was moved to the Department of External Affairs.

7 The formal Cabinet requirement of 25 per cent non-cereals was only for a period of three years. Nevertheless, the requirement still functions as an informal rule of thumb.

8 Interdepartmental Working Group, Food aid policy recommendations 28.

9 See for example: Desmond McNeil, *The Contradictions of Foreign Aid* (London: Croom Helm 1981), 88–90; David Wall, *The Charity of Nations: The Political Economy of Foreign Aid* (New York: Basic Books 1973), chapter 6; and E.K. Hawkins, *The Principles of Development Aid* (London: Penguin 1970), chapter 6.

10 CIDA, Task Force on Food Aid and Renewable Resources Policies for CIDA, Report to the President's Committee (Ottawa: mimeographed April 1975), Appendix 4, 28.

11 For a detailed discussion of the Bangladesh distribution system see, Roger Ehrhardt, *Canadian Development Assistance to Bangladesh* (Ottawa: North-South Institute 1983), 80–95.

12 Canada, Parliament, House of Commons, *Minutes of Proceedings and Evidence of the Standing Committee on External Affairs and National Defence,* 4th Session, 30th Parliament, Issue no. 7 (20 March 1979) 7A:6.

13 Ibid.

14 Minister of State for CIDA and the Secretary of State for External Affairs, "Canada in a Changing World – Part 2: Canadian Aid Policy," in Canada, Parliament, House of Commons, *Minutes of Proceedings and Evidence of the Standing Committee on External Affairs and National Defence,* 1st Session, 2nd Parliament, Issue no. 3 (10 June 1980) 3A:164.

15 CIDA, Report to the President's Committee, Appendix 4, 12.

16 D .A. Fitzgerald, *Operational and Administrative Problems of Food Aid,* World Food Program Studies no. 4 (Rome: FAO 1965), 4–5.

17 CIDA, Report to the President's Committee, Appendix 4, 25.

18 Ibid., 29.

19 The CFA has emerged as the logical forum for these discussions since it is composed of both donor and recipient countries, and involves virtually every country involved in the global food aid system. In contrast, the Food Aid Committee of the International Wheat Council, which oversees the Food Aid Convention, involves only donor countries and deals only with aid in cereals.

20 Canada, Parliament, House of Commons, Parliamentary Task Force on North-South Relations, *Report to the House of Commons on the Relations Between Developed and Developing Countries,* (Ottawa: Supply and Services 1980), 50.

21 Canada, Parliament, House of Commons, *For Whose Benefit? Report of the Standing Committee on External Affairs and International Trade on Canada's Official Development Assistance Policies and Programs* (Hull: Supply and Services May 1987), 58.

22 Ibid.

23 CIDA, Report to the President's Committee, Appendix 4, 24.

24 CIDA, FACE Centre, "Multilateral food aid program, 1979/80" (Ottawa: mimeographed 1980), 1–3.

25 Calculated from CIDA, FACE Centre, mimeographed, "Food Aid program by commodity, 1978–79," 1–2; "Food aid program by commodity, 1979–80," 1–2; and "Food aid program by commodity, 1980–81," 1–2.

26 Fisheries and Oceans, International Directorate, "Fish component of Food Aid Programme, 1980–81 to 1984–85" (Ottawa: mimeographed 1985).

27 Fitzgerald, *Operational and Administrative Problems* 5.

28 CIDA, Food Aid Centre, "Canadian food aid: Allocation between bilateral and multilateral channels" (Hull: mimeographed n.d.), 3.

29 CIDA, "Strategic plan: Food aid" (Hull: mimeographed 1985), 5.

30 Panos Konandreas, "Assessing the Components of Prospective Food Aid Requirements," *Food Policy* 11, no. 1 (February 1986): 23–5.

31 CIDA, Food Aid Centre, "Notes on project and programme food aid," (Hull: mimeographed n.d.), 1.

32 Ibid., 2–3.

33 For a recent description of the operations of the WFP, see: Ross Talbot, "The Organization of Power in the World Food Program and Its Policy Implications, ' Paper presented at the Midwest Conference of Political Scientists, Chicago, 10–12 April 1986.

34 Interviews, Agriculture Canada, International Directorate, April 1986.

35 The whole issue of FAO-WFP relations is discussed at some length in Mark Charlton, "Innovation and Interorganizational Politics: The Case of the World Food Programme," *International Journal*, forthcoming.

36 Ibid. In 1984, the CFA did give its authorisation to the use of a limited amount of WFP cash resources for non-food expenses that are considered essential to the implementation of food aid projects.

37 Interviews, WFP headquarters, Rome, February 1989.

38 CIDA, Task Force on Food Aid and Renewable Resource Policies for CIDA, Report to the President's Committee (Ottawa: mimeographed April 1975), appendix 4, 27.

39 Ibid.

40 Canada, Parliament, House of Commons, *Minutes of Proceedings and Evidence of the Special Committee on North-South Relations*, 1st Session, 32nd Parliament, Issue No. 20 (29 October 1980) 20:32.

41 North-South Institute, *Handle with Care: Skim Milk Aid to Developing Countries* (Ottawa: North-South Institute 1979), 9–10.

42 Ibid., 42.

43 CIDA, *Annual Report, 1985–86* (Hull: Supply and Services 1986), 102.

44 See Canadian Council for International Cooperation, " A Framework for Canada's Development Assistance," in Appendix "RNSR-2" in Canada, Parliament, House of Commons, *Minutes of Proceedings and Evidence of the Special Committee on North-South Relations,* 1st Session, 32nd Parliament, Issue no. 4 (17 July 1980), 4A:1–4.

45 Quoted in Robert Kreider and Rachel Waltner Gooseen, *Hungry, Thirsty, a Stranger: The MCC Experience* (Kitchener: Herald Press 1988), 378.

46 Ibid., 379.

47 Wilma Derksen, "New food aid policy points the way through the maze of aid decisions," *Mennonite Reporter* 17, no. 5 (2 March 1987): 1.

48 See Mennonite Central Committee (Canada), Commission on Peace and Social Concerns, "Mennonite Central Committee and government funding: To take or not to take more" (Winnipeg: mimeographed n.d.), 1–4.

49 CIDA, Report to the President's Committee 10.

50 CIDA, *Strategy for International Development Co-operation 1975–1980* (Ottawa: Information Canada 1975), 36.

51 Canada, Parliament, House of Commons, *Minutes of Proceedings and Evidence of the Standing Committee on External Affairs and National Defence,* 4th Session, 30th Parliament, Issue no. 7 (20 March 1979) 7A:6.

52 Ibid.

53 Ibid.

54 Ibid.

55 John Loxley, *Debt and Disorder: External Financing for Development* (Boulder: Westview Press 1986), 172.

56 CIDA, Policy Branch, Program Evaluation Division, Summary report of the evaluation of Canada's food aid program (Hull: mimeographed 1984), 22.

57 Canada, Parliament, House of Commons, *Minutes of the Proceedings and Evidence of the Special Committee on North-South Relations,* 1st Session, 32nd Parliament, Issue no. 2 (10 July 1980), 2:22.

58 CIDA, Report to the President's Committee, Appendix 4, 29.

59 CIDA, Summary report of the evaluation of Canada's food aid program, 21.

CHAPTER FOUR

1 These products include: wheat, flour, semolina, canola, canola oil, skim milk powder, beans, peas, feed wheat, rolled oats, canned fish,

dried fish, canned beef, egg powder, canned turkey, butter, corn, barley, and dehydrated potatoes.

2 CIDA, *Annual Aid Review 1978-Memorandum of Canada to the Development Assistance Committee of the OECD* (Hull: CIDA 1980), 24.

3 See for example, Canadian Federation of Agriculture, *1964* Presentation to the prime minister and members of Parliament (Ottawa: mimeographed 1964), 9, and National Farmers Union, Submission to the government of Canada, (Ottawa: mimeographed February 1963), 9. Similar statements can be found in subsequent presentations by these organisations to the government.

4 Canada, Parliament, House of Commons, *Minutes of Proceedings and Evidence of the Standing Committee on Agriculture,* 2nd Session, 28th Parliament, Issue no. 8 (5 February 1970) 8:9.

5 Canada, Parliament, House of Commons, *Minutes of Proceedings and Evidence of the Standing Committee on Agriculture,* 3rd Session, 28th Parliament, Issue no. 31 (11 March 1971) 31:101.

6 Canada, Parliament, House of Commons, *Minutes of Proceedings and Evidence of the Standing Committee on Agriculture,* 2nd Session, 28th Parliament, Issue no. 8 (5 February 1970) 8:9 and 8:23.

7 CIDA, Task Force on Food Aid and Renewable Resource Policies for CIDA, Report to the President's Committee (Ottawa: mimeographed 1975), Appendix 4, 31.

8 Ibid., 17.

9 Interview, Industry, Trade and Commerce, Grains Marketing Office, March 1979.

10 Don Mitchell, *The Politics of Food* (Toronto: Lorimer 1975), 157.

11 Grace Skogstad, "The Farm Products Marketing Agencies Act and the Food Policy Debate: Case Studies of Agricultural Policy," Paper presented to the Canadian Political Science Meeting Annual Meeting (London: mimeographed May 1978), 27–30.

12 *International Canada* 5, nos. 7–8 (July-August 1974): 142.

13 Canada, Parliament, House of Commons, *Minutes of Proceedings and Evidence of the Standing Committee on External Affairs and National Defence,* 1st Session, 30th Parliament, Issue no. 19 (2 May 1975), 19:16.

14 Mitchell, *Politics of Food,* 83.

15 Canada, Parliament, *House of Commons Debates,* 1st Session, 30th Parliament, vol. 2 (15 November 1974), 1357.

16 Quoted in Canada, Parliament, House of Commons, *Minutes of Proceedings and Evidence of the Standing Committee on External Affairs and National Defence,* 1st Session, 30th Parliament, Issue no. 19 (2 May 1975) 19:17.

17 "Eat More Hamburgers, Whelan Asks Canada in New Beef Program," *Globe and Mail,* 14 December 1974, and *International Canada* 5, no. 12 (December 1974): 245.

18 Canada, Parliament, House of Commons, *Minutes of Proceedings and Evidence of the Standing Committee on Agriculture*, 1st Session, 30th Parliament, Issue no. 26 (8 April 1975) 26:35.

19 On the background to this situation see, Mitchell, *Politics of Food*, chapter 6.

20 Diary Farmers of Canada, "Proposal for a large and long-term Canadian commitment of skim milk powder to the World Food Program" (Ottawa: mimeographed March 1976).

21 Canadian Federation of Agriculture, Presentation to the prime minister and members of Parliament, 1976 (Ottawa: mimeographed, 1976), 22

22 Canada, Parliament, *House of Commons Debates*, 1st Session, 30th Parliament, vol. 2 (19 March 1976), 11979.

23 Canada, Parliament, House of Commons, *Minutes of Proceedings and Evidence of the Standing Committee on Agriculture*, 1st Session, 30th Parliament, Issue no. 72 (17 March 1976) 72:10.

24 Ibid.

25 Interviews, CIDA, Resources Branch and Special Programs Branch, September 1979.

26 Canada, Parliament, *House of Commons Debates*, 1st Session, 30th Parliament, vol. 12 (April 1976), 12774.

27 CIDA, "Statement of foodstuffs supplied by Canada to the UN/FAO World Food Program during the fiscal years 1963/64 to June 1978," (Ottawa: mimeographed).

28 Interview, CIDA, Bilateral Branch, May 1979.

29 Bilateral skim milk powder increased from $2.1 million allocated to three countries in 1975–76 to $3.7 million divided among eight countries in 1976–77.

30 Interview, CIDA, Bilateral Branch, May 1979.

31 Interview, CIDA, Special Programs Branch, June 1979.

32 Interview, Agriculture Canada, International Liaison Service, March 1979.

33 Interviews, Finance, International Programs Division, June 1979, and Treasury Board, Program Branch, April 1979.

34 See Thomas C. Bruneau, Jan J. Jorgensen, and J.O. Ramsay, *CIDA: The Organization of Canadian Overseas Development Assistance*, Working Paper no. 24, (Montreal: McGill University Centre for Developing Area Studies October 1978), 37.

35 See, for example, the testimony of the Canadian Council on International Co-operation in: Canada, Parliament, House of Commons, *Minutes of Proceedings and Evidence of the Special Committee on North-South Relations*, 1st Session, 32nd Parliament, Issue no. 10, (1 October 1980).

36 See, for example, the criticisms of Canada of Canadian shipments of skim milk powder to Guatemala as cited in *International Canada* 7, no. 2 (February 1976): 44.

37 CIDA, *Strategy for International Development Cooperation: 1975–1980* (Ottawa: Information Canada 1975), 27.

38 CIDA, "Bilateral Food Aid Program as of 30 June 1978," 7–10.

39 CIDA, *Strategy for International Development* 27.

40 Ibid.

41 Interviews, CIDA, Bilateral Branch, May and June 1979, and Multilateral Branch, April 1979, and CIDA, Report to the President's Committee, Appendix 4, 18.

42 Canada, Treasury Board Secretariat and CIDA, Evaluation of the Canadian food aid programme (Ottawa: mimeographed May 1977), 33.

43 CIDA, Report to the President's Committee, Appendix 4, 18.

44 Canada, Parliament, House of Commons, *Minutes of Proceedings and Evidence of the Standing Committee on External Affairs and National Defence,* 1st Session, 30th Parliament, Issue no. 22, (16 May 1975), 22:25.

45 Interview, CIDA, Resources Branch, September 1978.

46 Interview, CIDA, Special Programs Branch, September 1978.

47 *International Canada* 7, no. 2 (February 1976): 44. On the dangers of skim milk powder, see: North-South Institute, *Handle With Care: Skim Milk Aid to Developing Countries* (Ottawa: North-South Institute 1979), 30–2.

48 CIDA, Report to the President's Committee, Appendix 4, 26.

49 Canada, CIDA, *Strategy for International Development Cooperation, 1975–1980* (Ottawa: Information Canada September 1975), 37.

50 *International Canada* 9, no. 3 (March 1978): 70.

51 "Jamaica Given $11 million for Food," *Development Directions* (May 1978): 3.

52 Interview, Treasury Board, Planning Branch, April 1979.

53 Canada, Parliament, House of Commons, Parliamentary Task Force on North-South Relations, *Report to the House of Commons on the Relations Between Developed and Developing Countries* (Ottawa: Supply and Services Canada 1980), 49.

54 Treasury Board, "Terms and Conditions of Country-to Country Food Aid," TB 793024, (29 March 1984), 2.

55 CIDA, Food Aid Centre, Food aid: A programming manual (Hull: mimeographed March 1986), B:10.

56 Ibid.

57 Canada, Parliament, House of Commons, *For Whose Benefit? Report of the Standing Committee on External Affairs and International Trade on Canada's Official Development Assistance Policies and Programs* (Ottawa: Supply and Services May 1987), 39.

58 Cf. CIDA, *Canada International Development Assistance: To Benefit a Better World* (Hull: Supply and Services September 1987), 58.

59 CIDA, Report to the President's Committee, Appendix 4, 13.
60 Interviews, Agriculture Canada, International Liaison Service, October 1978.
61 Interviews, Treasury Board, Program Branch, April 1979.
62 CIDA, Report to the President's Committee, Appendix 4, 13.
63 CIDA, *Strategy for International Development Co-operation* 36.
64 Canada, Parliament, House of Commons, *Minutes of Proceedings and Evidence of the Standing Committee on External Affairs and National Defence*, 1st Session, 30th Parliament, Issue no. 29, (20 November 1975), 29:19.
65 Sheldon Gordon, "What's in it for us?" *International Perspectives* (May/June 1976): 25.
66 Interview, Treasury Board, Program Branch, April 1979.
67 CIDA, President's Office, Michel Dupuy, Directions for the agency from now until the 1980s (Ottawa: Mimeographed 7 December 1978), 2.
68 Interdepartmental Working Group on Food Aid Policy, Food aid policy recommendations (Ottawa: mimeographed 26 June 1978), 35.
69 Interview, CIDA, Multilateral Branch, April 1979.
70 See in particular CIDA, Food aid: A programming manual, D10-D11.
71 Ibid.
72 Interview, CIDA, Multilateral Branch, March 1990.
73 Interview, Fisheries and Oceans, International Directorate, May 1985.
74 Interview, CIDA, Multilateral Branch, May 1985.
75 Fisheries and Oceans, International Directorate, Fish component of food aid programme, (Ottawa: mimeographed April 1985).
76 CIDA, Program Evaluation Division, Policy Branch, Summary report on the evaluation of Canada's food aid program (Hull: mimeographed 1983), 45–7.
77 Ibid.
78 Canada, Parliament, *Report of the Auditor General to the House of Commons, 1984* (Ottawa: Supply and Services 1984), 9–15.
79 "Canadian Milling Firms Charged with Rigging Prices on Wheat for Famine Aid," *Globe and Mail*, 6 March 1990, 1; and "Milling Companies Accused of Routinely Rigging Bids," *London Free Press* 10 March 1990 B13; and "Mills Fined for Rigging CIDA Bids," *Globe and Mail*, 8 December 1990, A1.
80 Theodore Cohn, *Canadian Food Aid: Domestic and Foreign Policy Implications* (Denver: University of Denver, Graduate School of International Studies, Monograph Series in World Affairs 1979), 109.
81 Ibid.
82 Ibid.

CHAPTER FIVE

1 One exception is Theodore Cohn, who provides a general discussion in his *Canadian Food Aid: Domestic and Foreign Implications* (Denver: University of Denver, Graduate School of International Studies, 1979), 10–15.

2 See Graham Allison and Peter Szanton, *Remaking Foreign Policy: The Organizational Connection* (New York: Basic Books 1976), and Stephen Cohen, *The Making of United States International Economic Policy: Principles, Problems and Proposals for Reform* (New York: Praeger 1977).

3 See Grant Reuber, "Canada's foreign aid policy: The strategy and tactics for allocating Canadian aid funds to foster economic development," CIDA Policy Review (Ottawa: mimeographed 1969), 29–33, and George Cuningham, *The Management of Aid Agencies* (London: Croom Helm 1974), 2–4.

4 Interview, Agriculture Canada, International Affairs Directorate, May 1985.

5 Suteera Thomson, *Food for the Poor: The Role of CIDA in Agriculture, Fisheries, and Rural Development* (Ottawa: Science Council of Canada 1980), 52.

6 For further discussion of this problem in relation to one specific recipient see Roger Ehrhardt, *Canadian Development Assistance to Bangladesh* (Ottawa: North-South Institute l983), 116–7.

7 See North-South Institute, *North-South Encounter: The Third World and Canadian Performance* (Ottawa: North-South Institute 1977), 122.

8 Desmond McNeill, *The Contradictions of Foreign Aid* (London: Croom Helm 1981), 12.

9 Judith Tendler, *Inside Foreign Aid* (Baltimore: John Hopkins University Press 1975) 88.

10 Ibid., 54–72.

11 Thomas Bruneau, Jan J. Jorgenson, and J.O. Ramsay, *CIDA: The Organization of Canadian Overseas Assistance* (Montreal: McGill University Centre for Developing-Area Studies, Working Paper 24, October 1978), 30. See also Thomson, *Food for the Poor,* 52, and Ehrhardt, *Canadian Development Assistance to Bangladesh,* 111–13.

12 CIDA, Task Force on Food Aid and Renewable Rource Policies for CIDA, Report to the President's Committee (Ottawa: mimeographed April 1975), Appendix 3, 29.

13 Ibid.

14 Ibid. Canada also committed itself to providing at least 20 per cent of its food aid through the World Food Program. As it turned out, improved grain production in some recipient countries following 1975 limited the extent to which the bilateral channel could be expanded.

As a result, about 40 per cent of the food grains were channelled through the World Food Program.

15 Ibid.

16 CIDA, *Canada and Development Cooperation: Annual Report 1979–80* (Hull: Supply and Services Canada 1980), 60.

17 Interview, CIDA, Bilateral Programs Branch, May 1979.

18 John White, *The Politics of Foreign Aid* (New York: St Martin's Press 1974), 290.

19 In principle, any country deemed eligible by the Canadian federal cabinet to receive Canadian development assistance is automatically eligible to receive Canadian food aid.

20 Interview, Treasury Board, Program Branch, June 1979.

21 Interview, External Affairs, Commodity and Energy Policy Division, June 1979.

22 Interview, CIDA, Bilateral Branch, May and June 1979.

23 Canada, Parliament, *House of Commons Debates*, 1st Session, 30th Parliament, vol. 3 (22 January 1975), 2497.

24 Interview, CIDA, Bilateral Programs Branch, June 1979.

25 See Charles Taylor, "Will Ottawa See Urgency of Aid Plan for Indochina?" *Globe and Mail*, 12 June 1975.

26 Canada, Parliament, *Report of the Auditor-General of Canada to the House of Commons for the Fiscal Year Ended March 31, 1976* (Ottawa: Supply and Services 1976), 103.

27 CIDA, Report to the President's Committee, Appendix 4, 17.

28 Canada, Treasury Board Secretariat and CIDA, Evaluation of the Canadian food aid programme (Ottawa: mimeographed May 1977), 12.

29 Canada, Parliament, *Report of the Auditor-General of Canada to the House of Commons for the Fiscal Year Ended March 31, 1976* (Ottawa: Supply and Services 1976), 103

30 CIDA, Report to the President's Committee 16–17, and Appendix 4, 17.

31 Canada, Parliament, House of Commons, *Minutes of Proceedings and Evidence of the Standing Committee on External Affairs and National Defence*, 3rd Session, 30th Parliament, Issue no. 18 (5 May 1978), 18:10.

32 CIDA, *Annual Aid Review: 1978 Memorandum to the OECD* (Ottawa: CIDA 1978), 30. Two factors appear to have influenced the selection of the Multilateral Branch. By 1978, more than half of Canada's food aid was being sent through multilateral channels, particularly the World Food Program. Moreover, the Multilateral Branch was smaller than the Bilateral Branch, containing only two divisions compared to the seven of the Bilateral Branch. Cf. Canada, House of Commons, *Minutes of Proceedings and Evidence of the Standing Committee on External Affairs and National Defence*, 3rd Session, 30th Parliament, Issue no. 18 (5 May 1978), 10.

33 Ibid.

34 Under the system of food aid programming, established in the early 1970s, all food aid allocations were submitted to the Treasury Board for assessment and approval. However, in 1985 CIDA was given new signing authority for food aid transactions. As a result, an omnibus submission to Treasury Board is no longer necessary. Instead, new signing authority of up to and including $3 million has been given to the president and vice-presidents of CIDA and up to $15 million at the level of the minister responsible for CIDA. Since most food aid transactions are above $3 million, most proposals are thus now approved by the minister.

35 Cf. CIDA, "Guidelines for the preparation of bilateral requests of nonemergency food aid," (Hull: mimeographed, n.d.).

36 Cf. CIDA, Food Aid Centre, Food aid: A programming manual (Hull: mimeographed March 1986).

37 James Austin and Mitchel Wallerstein, "Reformulating US Food Aid Policy for Development" World Development 7 (1979): 642–43.

38 CIDA, Report to the President's Committee, Appendix 4, 30.

39 Interview, Finance, International Programs Division, June 1979.

40 CIDA, Sharing Our Future: Canadian Development Assistance (Ottawa: Supply and Services 1987), 54.

41 Interview, Treasury Board, Planning Branch, June 1979.

42 Interviews, CIDA, Special Programs Branch, September 1978 and Agriculture Canada, International Liaison Service, October 1978.

CHAPTER SIX

1 See for example, the comments of David Hopper, a former president of the International Development Research Centre and now a vice-president of the World Bank in Canada, Parliament, House of Commons, Minutes of Proceedings and Evidence of the Special Committee on North-South Relations, 32nd Parl., 1st Session, no. 19, (28 October 1980), 19.

2 Cf. Gerald K. Helleiner, "Aid and Dependence in Africa: Issues for Recipients," in T. Shaw and K. Heard, eds., The Politics of Africa: Dependence and Development (New York: Africana Publishing Comp. 1979), 233–4.

3 Jeffrey L. Pressman, Federal Programs and City Politics: The Dynamics of the Aid Process in Oakland (Berkeley: University of California Press 1975), 107–9.

4 Ibid., 133.

5 Harmut Schneider, Food Aid for Development (Paris: Development Centre of the OECD 1978), 20–1.

6 CIDA, Task Force on Food Aid and Renewable Resources Policies for CIDA, Report to the President's Committee (Hull: mimeographed April 1975), Appendix 4, 28.

7 Ibid.

8 Interviews, CIDA, Multilateral and Bilateral Branches, June 1979.

9 CIDA, Report to the President's Committee, Appendix 10, 130.

10 The recipient most dependent on food aid to make this system operate is Bangladesh where food aid accounts for 80–90% of the total PDS supplies. On the Bangladesh system, see Ehrhardt, *Canadian Development Assistance to Bangladesh,* 80–95.

11 Interview, CIDA, Bilateral Branch, June 1979.

12 CIDA, "Food aid and food policies in Bangladesh" (Hull: CIDA, mimeographed n.d.), 3.

13 FAO, FAO *Principles of Surplus Disposal and Consultative Obligation of Member Nations* (Rome: 1972), 14–15.

14 Cf. FAO, *Food Aid Bulletin,* 4 (October 1973): 26; FAO, *Food Aid Bulletin* 3 (July 1976): 25; and FAO, *Food Aid Bulletin* 1 (January 1977): 33.

15 *Canadian Objection to Practice of "Tied Sales" in Food Aid Transaction,* Committee on Commodity Problems, Consultative Sub-Committee on Surplus Disposal, CCP/CSD/73/54, 10 April 1973, 1–2. For more on the issue of UMR's, particularly as they related to US-Canadian trade issues, see Theodore Cohn, *The International Politics of Agricultural Trade: Canadian-American Relations in a Global Agricultural Context* (Vancouver: University of British Columbia Press 1990).

16 See Keith Spicer, *A Samaritan State? External Aid in Canada's Foreign Policy* (Toronto: University of Toronto Press 1966), 188.

17 Ibid., 189.

18 Ibid.

19 Canada, Department of External Affairs, *Foreign Policy for Canadians: International Development,* (Ottawa: Information Canada 1970), 19. However, the use of counterpart funds has been largely removed from public scrutiny. Beginning in 1966, statistics regarding the generation and allocation of counterpart funds were no longer recorded in the annual reviews. By making them a matter of internal senior management in CIDA, there has been little subsequent reporting on their use.

20 CIDA, *CIDA Manual: Handbook 8 – Bilateral Programmes* (Hull: CIDA 1981), Ch. 20, Art. 008.

21 Interviews, CIDA, Bilateral Branch, May 1979.

22 CIDA, *Handbook for CIDA Officers Transferred Abroad* (Hull: CIDA 1973), 15.

23 CIDA, *CIDA Manual,* ch. 20, Art. 008.

24 Canada, Parliament, House of Commons, *Minutes of Proceedings and Evidence of the Special Committee on North-South Relations,* 1st Session, 32nd Parliament, Issue no. 11 (2 October 1980), 11:39.

25 CIDA, Report to the President's Committee, Appendix 4, 17.

26 Ibid.

27 The number of times when Canada has withheld food aid for foreign policy reasons is quite rare. See Theodore Cohn, "The Politics of Food Aid: A Comparison of American and Canadian Policies," *McGill Studies in International Development 36* (Montreal: McGill University Centre for Developing-Area Studies January 1985).

28 James Rusk, "Hungriest Get Food Last in Bangladesh," *Globe and Mail,* December 1974; Richard Piper, "Corruption Saps Aid to Bangladesh, Missionary Says," *Toronto Star,* 3 December 1974; and Marcel Pépin, "Il y a eu gaspillage au Bangladesh," *La Presse,* 25 April 1975.

29 Christopher Cobb, "MP Complains Food Aid Sold by Authorities," *Ottawa Journal,* 17 May 1975.

30 See for example, C. Cobb and R. McKeown, "CIDA Is in a Rush to Spend Millions," *Ottawa Journal,* 23 January 1975, and Charles Lynch, "CIDA Needs Watchdog," *The Citizen,* 30 April 1975.

31 CIDA, "Report to the secretary of state for External Affairs by Mr. Paul Gérin-Lajoie, President, CIDA, on the mission to Bangladesh," (Hull: mimeographed 10 April 1975).

32 CIDA-Treasury Board, "Evaluation of the Canadian food aid programme, May 1977," (Hull: mimeographed 1977), 15.

33 See particularly, Francis Moore Lappé, J. Collins, and D. Kinley, *Aid As Obstacle: Twenty Questions about Our Foreign Aid and the Hungry* (San Fransisco: Institute for Food and Development Policy 1980).

34 Cf. Paul Fromm and James Hull, *Down the Drain? A Critical Re-examination of Canadian Foreign Aid* (Toronto: Griffin House 1981), 155.

35 Canada, Parliament, House of Commons, *Report of the Auditor General of Canada to the House of Commons for the Fiscal Year Ended March 31, 1984* (Ottawa: Supply and Services 1984), 9–12.

36 Canadian Council on International Cooperation, "Background Discussion Paper," Appendix "RNSR-9," in Canada, Parliament, House of Commons, *Minutes of Proceedings and Evidence of the Special Committee on North-South Relations,* 1st Session, 32nd Parliament, Issue no. 10 (1 October 1980).

37 Stephen Commins, Michael Lofchie, and Rhys Payne, *Africa's Agrarian Crisis: The Roots of Famine* (Boulder, Colorado: Lynne Rienner Publishers, Inc. 1986), 177.

38 Notes for remarks by Margaret Catley-Carlson, President, Canadian International Development Agency, to the 20th Session of the World Food Programme Committee on Food Aid Policies and Programmes, Rome, Italy, October 1985, 3.

39 Ibid, 3.

40 Ibid.

41 World Bank, *Accelerated Development in Sub-Saharan Africa: An Agenda for Action,* (Washington: IBRD 1981).

42 CIDA, *Elements of Canada's Official Development Strategy, 1984* (Hull: CIDA 1984), 18.

43 Ibid., 7.

44 Cf. CIDA, *Food Aid: Contributing to Agricultural Development and Food Security* (Hull: CIDA 1986), 5–6. For a more recent elabloration of these points see, CIDA, Food Aid Centre, *Issues to be Addressed when Using Food Aid in Support of Structural Adjustment Programs* (Hull: Food Aid Centre February 1991).

45 On this point see particularly, C. Peter Timmer and Matthew Guerreiro, "Food Aid and Development Policy," in G.O. Nelson, et al., *Food Aid and Development* (New York: Agricultural Development Council 1981), 13–30; W.P. Falcon, "Recent Food Policy Lessons from Developing Countries," *American Journal of Agrarian Economies,* 66 (May 1984): 180–5; and Raymond Hopkins, "The Evolution of Food Aid: Towards A Development First Regime," *Food Policy* 9, no. 4 (November 1984): 345–62.

46 Notes for remarks by Margaret Catley-Carlson, 7.

47 See CIDA, *Annual Aid Review, 1982* (Hull: CIDA 1982), 38; CIDA, *Elements of Canada's Official Development Strategy, 1984* (Hull: CIDA 1984), 18; and notes for remarks by Margaret Catley-Carlson.

48 CIDA, *Annual Aid Review, 1982,* 38.

49 Ibid.

50 CIDA, *Report of the President's Committee,* Appendix 3, 6.

51 Benjamin Higgins, "Counterpart Funds: Background Material," in CIDA, *Handbook for CIDA Officers,* 16.

52 Ibid., 20.

53 Ehrhardt, *Bangladesh,* 105, 117.

54 Two notable exceptions to this are Senegal and Ghana, where in 1990 Canada provided 32% and 43% repspectively of these countries cereal aid. See World Food Programme, *1991 Food Aid Review* (Rome: World Food Programme 1991), Table 10.

55 OECD, *Development Co-operation-1984 Review,* (Paris: OECD, Development Assistance Committee 1983), 128–9.

56 Interviews, CIDA, Bilateral Branch, June 1979.

57 Unless otherwise indicated, the following discussion is based on information gathered from a series of interviews conducted in CIDA's Multilateral and Bilateral Branches in June 1985 and April 1986.

58 Cf. Hopkins, "The Evolution of Food Aid," 357.

59 CIDA, *Report to the President's Committee,* Appendix 4, 30.

60 Interview, Treasury Board, Program Branch, April 1979.

61 Interview, CIDA, Multilateral Branch, October 1991. A multi-year agreement was also negotiated with Egypt, but has not been implemented for what has been described as administrative reasons.

62 Interview, CIDA, Bilateral Branch, June 1981.

63 CIDA, *Annual Aid Review: 1982* (Hull: CIDA 1982), 39.

64 CIDA, FACE Centre, "Bilateral Food Aid Program, 1980/81," 1–5.

65 Interview, CIDA, May 1987.

66 Raymond F. Hopkins, "Food Aid: solution, palliative, or danger for Africa's food crisis?," in Commins, Lofchie, and Paynes, eds., *Africa's Agrarian Crisis*, 203.

67 "Review of selected national experience with food aid: the Canadian experience," World Food Programme Committee on Food Aid Policies and Programmes, 20th Session, 11 October 1985, 10.

68 It should be noted that the Parliamentary review of the Canadian aid program recommended that this system of country categories be abolished. In September 1987, the government agreed to develop a new eligibility system. Cf. Canadian International Development Agency, *Canadian International Development Assistance: To Benefit a Better World*, (Ottawa: September 1987), 75.

69 Notes for remarks by Margaret Catley-Carlson, 10.

70 CIDA, Food Aid Centre, Food aid: A programming manual (Hull: mimeographed March 1986), B10.

71 Roger Young, *Canadian Development Assistance to Tanzania* (Ottawa: North-South Institute 1983), 71.

72 Interviews, CIDA, June 1986.

73 Ehrhardt, *Bangladesh*, 105.

74 See also Just Faaland, ed., *Aid and Influence: The Case of Bangladesh*, (Bergen: Chr. Michelsen Institute 1981), and Rehman Sobhan, *The Crisis of External Dependence: The Political Economy of Foreign Aid to Bangladesh* (Dhaka: University Press 1982).

75 CIDA, Food aid: A programming manual, 11.

76 Cf. Terry Ross, "Canadian Foreign Aid to the Eastern Caribbean: A Model of North-South Relations." Paper presented at the Annual Meeting of the Canadian Political Science Association, June 1986, Winnipeg, Manitoba and the North-South Institute's studies on Haiti, Bangladesh, and Tanzania.

77 CIDA, Food aid 6.

78 World Bank, *Toward Sustained Development in Sub-Saharan Africa: A Joint Program of Action* (Washington: World Bank 1984).

79 CIDA, Food Aid Centre, "Issues to be addressed when using food aid in support of structural adjustment programs (Hull: mimeographed 1991), 9.

80 Ibid.

81 Ibid., 8.

82 Interview, Multilateral Branch, October 1991.

83 Economic Intelligence Unit, *Quarterly Economic Review of Guinea, Mali, Mauritania*, 4 (1985): 18–19.

84 Notes for remarks by Margaret Catley-Carlson, 7.

85 CIDA, *Elements of Canada's Official Development Strategy, 1984* (Hull: CIDA 1984), 19.

86 Faaland, *Aid and Influence*, 22.

87 Quoted in Canada, Parliament, House of Commons, *For Whose Benefit? Report of the Standing Committee on External Affairs and International Trade on Canada's Official Development Assistance Policies and Programs* (Ottawa: May 1987), 83.

88 Cranford Pratt, "Canadian Policy Towards the International Monetary Fund: An Attempt to Define a Position," *Canadian Journal of Development Studies* 6, no.1 (1985): 17.

89 Canada, *For Whose Benefit?*, 84.

90 For a study of these two cases see, "Bread Riots in North Africa: economic policy and social unrest in Tunisia and Morocco," in Peter Lawrence, ed.,*World Recession and the Food Crisis in Africa* (Boulder: Westview 1986).

91 Interview, Treasury Board, Planning Branch, June 1979.

92 Interviews, CIDA, Bilateral Branch, June 1985.

93 See CIDA, *Food Crisis in Africa* (Hull: CIDA 1985).

94 "Fraud, mismanagement targets of CIDA sawmill probe," *Windsor Star*, 11 March 1987, A16.

95 Canada, Parliament, House of Commons, *Minutes of Proceedings and Evidence of the Standing Committee on External Affairs and National Defence*, 1st Session, 32nd Parliament, Issue no. 6 (15 March 1985), 6:11–3.

96 Ibid. See also the importance given to this issue in the Second Report of David MacDonald in Canada, Parliament, House of Commons, *Minutes of Proceedings and Evidence of the Standing Committee on External Affairs and National Defence*, 1st Session, 33rd Parliament, Issue no. 14 (April 18, 1985).

97 James Rusk, "Hungriest Get Food Last in Bangladesh," *Globe and Mail*, 20 December 1974; "Corruption Saps Aid to Bangladesh Missionary Says," *Toronto Star*, 3 December 1974: and Jack Cahill, "In Asia 7 Million Starved and Rulers Turned Tough," *Toronto Star*, 27 December 1974.

98 See press reports in *International Canada*, 5, (12 December 1974): 244.

99 Paul Gérin-Lajoie, "Report to the secretary of state for External Affairs on the mission to Bangladesh, 19–21 March 1975," (Ottawa: mimeographed 1975).

100 "Michel Gratton rencontre Paul Gérin-Lajoie," *Le Droit*, 25 August 1975.

101 See especially the exchange between Brian Ross, director of the Food Aid Coordination and Evaluation Centre and MP Douglas Roche in Canada, Parliament, House of Commons, *Minutes of Proceedings and Evidence of the Special Committee on North-South Relations*, 1st Session, 32nd Parliament, Issue no. 11 (2 October 1980) 11:38–9.

102 Ibid., 11:33.

103 For an official summary of the Canadian response, see David Mac-Donald, *The African Famine and Canada's Response* (Hull: Canadian Emergency Coordinator/African Famine 1985)

104 Ibid, 56.

105 Interview, staff of the Office of Emergency Coordinator/African Famine, May 1986.

106 Interview, David MacDonald, Canadian emergency coordinator, April 1986.

107 See for example, "Fact-finding Mission to Ethiopia Finds Canadian Aid Gets Through," *Globe and Mail*, 19 December 1984, A5; "Reports of Abuse in Ethiopia 'False' Canadians Say," *Toronto Star*, 19 March 1986, A24; "Ethiopian Death Figure Rejected," *Globe and Mail*, 19 March 1986, A11; and "Le Canada veut vérifier la situation en Éthiopie avant d'accroître son aide," *La Journal de Montréal*, 16 March 1986, 4.

108 See, Office of the Canadian Emergency Coordinator, "Use of Canadian public cash contributions for shipment of relief and recovery supplies to Sudan." mimeographed, n.d.

109 Interview, Oxfam Canada, Ottawa, May 1986.

110 Interview, staff of the Office of Emergency Coordinator/African Famine, May 1986.

111 Cf. Canada, Parliament, House of Commons, *Minutes of Proceedings and Evidence of the Standing Committee on External Affairs and International Trade*, 2nd Session, 33rd Parliament, Issue no. 73 (28 April 1988) 73:18.

112 *Canadians and Africa: What Was Said*, A report of the Canadian Emergency Coordinator/African Famine of a nation-wide survey by Decima Research Ltd, conducted in February 1986 (Ottawa: 1986), 14–15.

113 Interview, Oxfam Canada, Ottawa, February 1990.

114 Canada, Parliament, House of Commons, *Minutes of Proceedings and Evidence of the Standing Committee on External Affairs and International Trade*, 2nd Session, 33rd Parliament, Issue no. 73 (28 April 1988), 73:15.

115 Unfortunately, space does not permit a detailed discussion of the Ethiopian case. For more discussion of the human rights dimensions of supplying food aid to Ethiopian the series of articles in Bruce Nichols and Gil Loescher, *The Moral Nation: Humanitarian and US Foreign Policy Today* (Notre Dame: University of Notre Dame Press 1989)

116 For a critique of the wfp's role in emergency feeding situations see, Rachel Garst and Tom Barry, *Feeding the Crisis: u.s. Food Aid and Farm Policy in Central America* (Lincoln: University of Nebraska Press 1990), chapter 5.

117 Canada, Parliament, House of Commons, *Minutes of Proceedings and Evidence of the Standing Committee on External Affairs and International Trade,* 2nd Session, 33rd Parliament, Issue no. 73 (28 April 1988) 73:19.

118 Canada, Parliament, House of Commons, *Minutes of Proceedings and Evidence of the Special Committee on North-South Relations,* 1st Session, 32nd Parliament, Issue no. 19 (28 October 1980) 19:19.

CONCLUSIONS

1 CIDA, "Food Aid: Fact Sheet on CIDA's Involvement," (Ottawa: n.d.), 1.

2 Canada, Parliament, House of Commons, *Minutes of Proceedings and Evidence of the Special Committee on North-South Relations,* 1st Session, 32nd Parliament, Issue no. 11, (2 October 1980) 11:47.

3 James Eayrs, "Canada's Emergence as a Foremost Power," *International Perspectives* (May-June 1975): 15–21.

4 On the concept of a "limited control" aid strategy, see Andrzej Krassowski, *The Aid Relationship* (London: Overseas Development Institute 1968), 19.

5 On the concept of a developmental food aid regime see Raymond F. Hopkins, "The Evolution of Food Aid: Toward a Development-First Regime," in J. Price Gittinger et al., eds., *Food Policy* (Baltimore: John Hopkins University 1978).

6 See for example, Theodore Cohn, *Canadian Food Aid: Domestic and Foreign Policy Implications* (Denver: University of Denver, Graduate School of International Studies 1979), Douglas Williams and Roger Young, *Taking Stock: World Food Security in the Eighties* (Ottawa: North-South Institute 1981), and North-South Institute, *World Food and the Canadian "Breadbasket"* (Ottawa: North-South Institute 1978).

7 Cf. Cranford Pratt, "Canadian Policy Towards the Third World: Basis for an Explanation," *Studies in Political Economy* 13 (Spring 1984): 27–55.

8 Margaret A. Biggs, *The Challenge: Adjust or Protect?* (Ottawa: North-South Institute 1980) and David R. Protheroe, *Imports and Politics: Trade Decision-making in Canada, 1968–1979* (Montreal: Institute for Research on Public Policy 1980).

9 On the concept of negotiated environment, see Jeffrey Pfeffer and Gerald Salanick, *The External Control of Organizations: A Resource Dependent Perspective* (New York: Harper and Row 1978), 143 ff.

10 On boundary-spanning, see Philippe Le Prestre, *The World Bank and the Environmental Challenge* (Selinsgrove: Susquehanna University Press 1989), 120–1.

11 On regionalism as a factor in federal spending decisions, see Donald Savoie, *The Politics of Public Spending in Canada* (Toronto: University of Toronto Press 1990).

12 This distinction is drawn from National Research Council, *Food Aid Projections for the Decade of the 1990s* (Washington, DC: National Academy Press 1989), 2.

13 Interdepartmental Working Group on Food Aid Policy, Food aid policy recommendations (Hull: mimeographed 1978), 24.

14 CIDA, Programme planning component review: Food aid (Hull: mimeographed 1984), 4.

15 Olav Stokke, ed., *Western Middle Power and Global Poverty: The Determinants of the Aid Policies of Canada, Denmark, the Netherlands, Norway and Sweden* (Uppsala: Scandinavian Institute of African Studies 1989), 309.

16 Cranford Pratt, "Canada: An Eroding and Limited Internationalism," in Cranford Pratt, ed., *Internationalism Under Strain: The North-South Policies of Canada, the Netherlands, Norway, and Sweden* (Toronto: University of Toronto Press, 1989), 49.

17 Ibid.

18 Ibid. Cf. Ronald Manzer, *Public Policies and Political Development in Canada* (Toronto: University of Toronto Press 1985).

19 Cited in Real Lavergne, "Determinants of Canadian Aid Policy," in Stokke, *Western Middle Power and Global Poverty* , 37.

20 Decima Research Limited, *The Canadian Public and Foreign Policy Issues* (Toronto: Decima August 1985), 62.

21 David MacDonald, *Canadians and Africa: What Was Said* (Hull: Canadian Emergency Coordinator/African Famine 1986), 28.

22 Decima, *The Canadian Public and Foreign Policy Issues*, 62.

23 Peyton V. Lyon and Brian W. Tomlin, *Canada as an International Actor* (Toronto: Macmillan 1979), 158–9.

24 CIDA, Policy Branch, Program Evaluation Division, Summary report of the evaluation of Canada's food aid program (Hull: mimeographed 1983), 16.

25 Ibid., 17.

26 Cf. Marcel Massé, "Testimony before the Standing Committee on External Affairs and International Trade," House of Commons, Ottawa, 31 October 1989.

27 John White, *The Politics of Foreign Aid* (New York: St Martin's Press 1974), 303.

28 Kim Richard Nossal, "Mixed Motives Revisited: Canada's Interest in Development Assistance," *Canadian Journal of Political Science* 21, no. 1 (March 1988): 52.

29 Ibid., 52.

30 Ibid., 52–3.

31 Ibid., 53.

32 Ibid.

33 For a review of this literature see, Savoie, *Politics of Public Spending.*

34 Interestingly, the comparative study of western middle power donors also found that concerns about administrative feasibility and convenience was a recurring explanation for specific choices in aid strategy. See the conclusions in Stokke, ed., *Western Middle Power and Global Poverty.*

35 Savoie, *Politics of Public Spending.*

36 Jeffrey L. Pressman, *Federal Programs and City Politics: The Dynamics of the Aid Process in Oakland* (Berkeley: University of California Press 1975) and Judith Tendler, *Inside Foreign Aid* (Baltimore: Johns Hopkins University Press 1975).

37 The following discussion draws on Tendler, *Inside Foreign Aid,* chapter 8.

38 Paul Mosley, "The Political Economy of Foreign Aid: A Model of the Market for a Public Good," *Economic Development and Cultural Change* 33 (1985): 377–8.

39 Nossal, "Mixed Motives Revisited," 50.

40 Ibid., 51.

41 Stephen Kranser, "Structural Causes and Regime Consequences: Regimes as Intervening Variables," in Stephen Kranser, ed., *International Regimes* (Ithaca, NY: Cornell University Press 1982), 1.

42 Robert Keohane, *After Hegemony: Cooperation and Discord in the World Political Economy* (Princeton: Princeton University Press 1984), chapter 6.

43 Margaret Karns and Karen Mingst, "The United States and Multilateral Institutions: A Framework for Analysis," in Margaret Karns and Karen Mingst, eds., *The United States and Multilateral Institutions: Patterns of Changing Instrumentality and Influence* (Boston: Unwin Hyman 1990), 4.

44 Ibid.

45 Ibid.

46 See Theodore H. Cohn, *The International Politics of Agricultural Trade: Canadian-American Relations in a Global Agricultural Context* (Vancouver: University of British Columbia Press 1990), chapter 5.

47 Cf. *Guidelines and Criteria for Food Aid.* WFA/CFA 7/6-A, Rome, Italy, 1979.

48 Diane Spearman, a FACE director, wrote the introduction for Hans Singer, et al., *Food Aid: The Challenge and the Opportunity* (Oxford: Clarendon Press 1987).

49 Peter Hass has defined "epistemic community" as "knowledge based groups of experts and specialists who share common beliefs about cause and effect relationships in the world and some political values concerning the ends to which policies should be addressed." Cf. Peter Haas, *Saving The Mediterranean: The Politics of International Environmental Cooperation* (New York: Columbia University Press 1990), xviii.

50 Nossal, "Mixed Motives Revisited," 50.

51 CIDA, Multilateral Programmes Branch, "Programme planning component review: Food aid," (Hull: mimeographed 1984), 2.

52 Canada, Parliament, House of Commons, *For Whose Benefit? Report of the Standing Committee on External Affairs and International Trade on Canada's Official Development Assistance Policies and Programs* (Ottawa: Supply and Services May 1987), 58.

53 National Research Council, Office of International Affairs, *Food Aid: Projections for the Decade of the 1990s: Report of an Ad Hoc Panel Meeting October 6 & 7 1988* (Washington, DC National Research Council 1988).

54 Raymond Hopkins, "Increasing Food Aid: Prospects for the 1990s," *Food Policy* 15, no. 4 (August 1990).

55 Olav Stokke, "The Determinants of Aid Policies: Some Propositions Emerging from a Comparative Analysis," in Stokke, *Western Middle Powers*, 306.

56 An alternative would be to relax the commercial restriction which prohibits the re-exporting of food aid. Additional assistance could be provided to some countries if the rules were relaxed to permit them to food in order to obtain foreign exchange. Cf. Frances Stewart, "Adjustment with a Human Face: The Role of Food Aid," *Food Policy* 13, no. 1 (February 1988): 22.

57 On the concept of "adjustment with a human face," the various ways that food aid can be linked to structural adjustment programmes in a more positive way, see the special theme issue of *Food Policy* in February 1988.

58 Edward Clay and Charlotte Benson, "Aid for Food: Acquisition of Commodities in Developing Countries for Food Aid in the 1980s," *Food Policy* 15, no. 1 (February 1990): 37.

Index